PENGUIN BOOKS

HELLO BOYS

Jacky Fleming was born in London to German–Jewish refugees. She went to school, but never quite got the hang of it. She studied Fine Art at Chelsea, and Leeds University, and once wrote a thesis on the *commedia dell'arte*. She has also written to the Home Secretary, but he didn't reply. She now lives in Yorkshire, has never been married to an eminent art historian and has no children. At all. Not even a little one. Her cooking is unusually bad.

Also published by Penguin:

Be a Bloody Train Driver
Never Give Up
Falling in Love
Dear Katie

JACKY FLEMING

HELLO BOYS

PENGUIN BOOKS

PENGUIN BOOKS

Published by the Penguin Group
Penguin Books Ltd, 27 Wrights Lane, London W8 5TZ, England
Penguin Books USA Inc., 375 Hudson Street, New York, New York 10014, USA
Penguin Books Australia Ltd, Ringwood, Victoria, Australia
Penguin Books Canada Ltd, 10 Alcorn Avenue, Toronto, Ontario, Canada M4V 3B2
Penguin Books (NZ) Ltd, 182–190 Wairau Road, Auckland 10, New Zealand

Penguin Books Ltd, Registered Offices: Harmondsworth, Middlesex, England

First published 1996
10 9 8 7 6 5 4 3 2 1

Printed in England by Clays International Ltd, St Ives plc

Professor, is it true that thanks to new computerised technology there is now remarkable new evidence that there ARE minute but significant differences between the brains of men and women?

Indeed it is, John. It would appear that men are statistically at a slight advantage when it comes to fly fishing, as women's brains are still preoccupied with not leaving the children entirely alone all day. Of course we're still in the early stages of this research, but the evidence is reasonably conclusive so far, and new evidence is coming in all the time

Professor, I believe one of your more controversial discoveries is that the male brain has no cognitive area for remembering to buy birthday cards, and a significantly dense cortex layer for responding to lingerie

Indeed, John. We also discovered that despite the greater neural densities in the cortex layers relating to the ability to secure highly paid executive posts, there seems to be no brain area relating to the location of household utensils thus demonstrating a natural disadvantage in relation to carrying out the more banal domestic chores

Professor, it also appears from the data gathered during your research that you have located an area of the male brain which is preoccupied with mobile telephones, and which, according to your report, is 'non-existent in the female'

That does indeed appear to be the case, John. We found no sign of an equivalent neural region in the female brain, which again suggests that the male is better suited to activities away from home, such as a highly paid executive post which involves travel and staying overnight.

Finally, Professor, if, as your report claims, girls do have the advantage in choosing fabrics and preparing picnics, the implications are very serious indeed, if not potentially explosive

That's right, John. Even though these minute differences are barely discernible even with the help of the most sophisticated computer technology, we are clearly sitting on a very hot potato

Thank you,
Professor

my pleasure

Men like us to watch their unforgettable accomplishments . . .

see me run

see me jump

see me drink

count my pressups

I'M JUST TAKING THE RUBBISH OUT

thank-you
no really
it's nothing

thank-you

dirty laundry goes on the floor... and eventually reappears clean in the cupboard...

INCREDIBLE

It's the long shiny things that live at the bottom of the sink, sometimes for several years. . . .

dirty laundry goes
on the floor
and reappears
clean in the
cupboard . . .

. . AGAIN

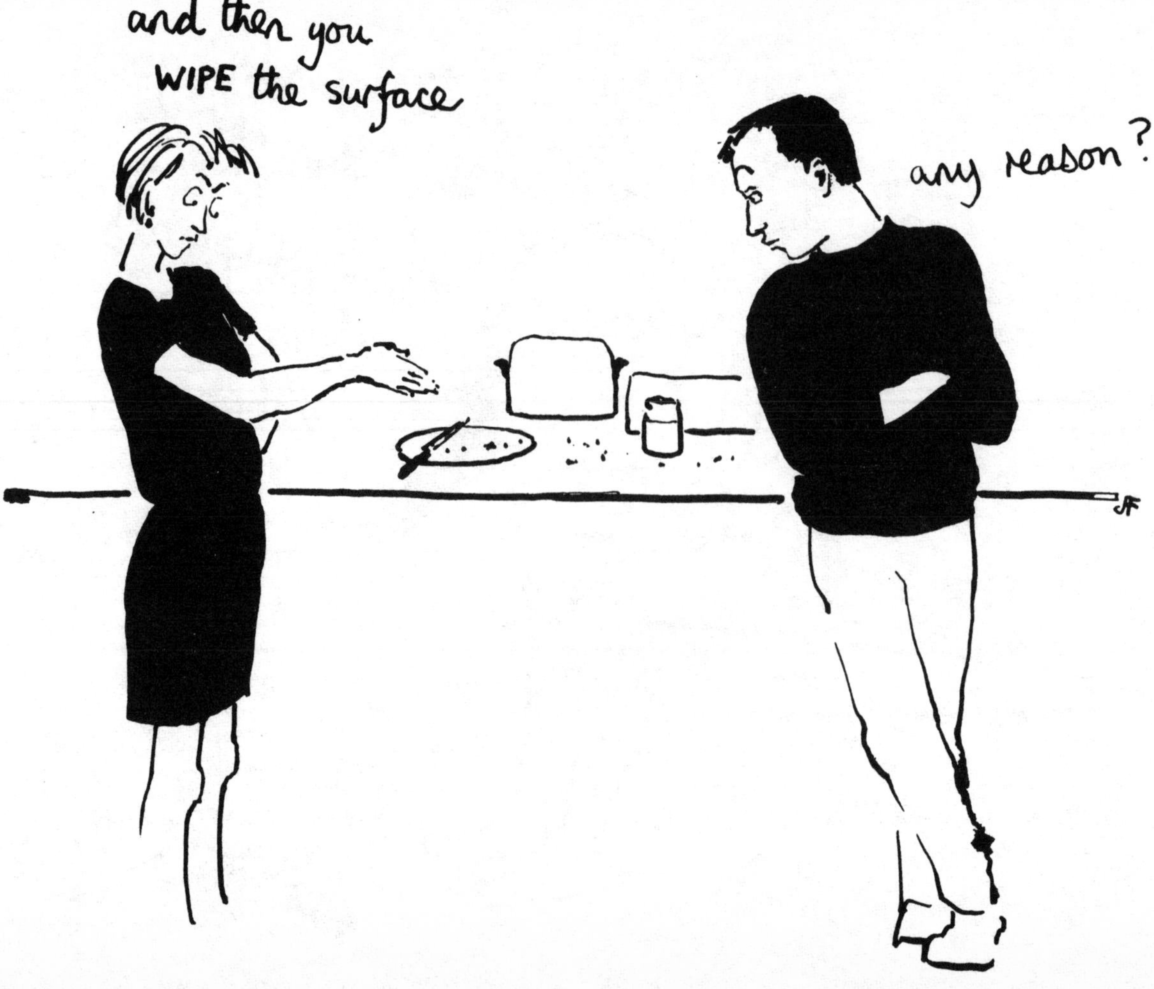
and then you
WIPE the surface
any reason?
JF

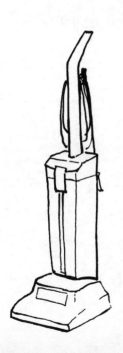

...and stops reappearing in the cupboard

Don't wait up for me — I've got a couple of parachute jumps to do with the boys. It's risky — but we need the fresh air

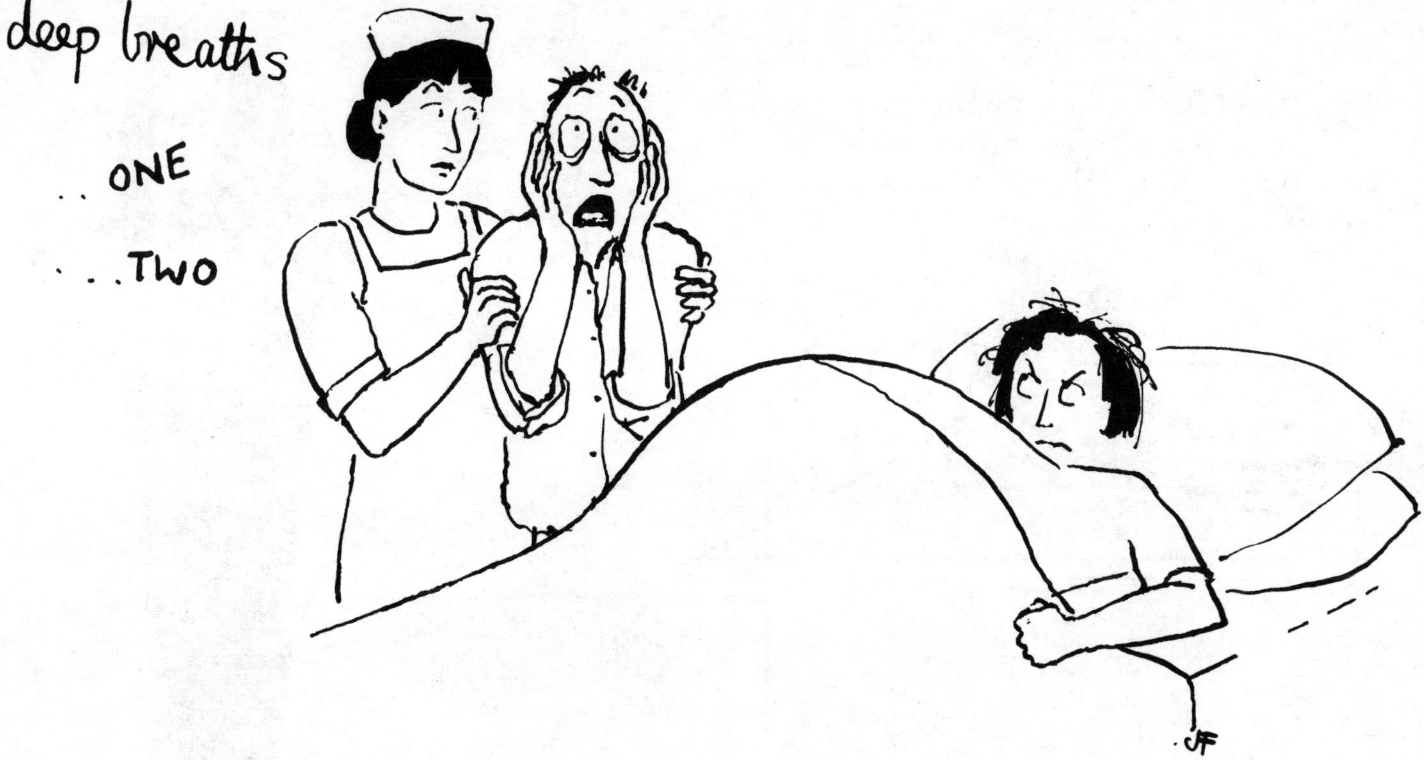
deep breaths
. . ONE
. . . TWO
JF

yes darling, in a saucepan, then heat it gently and don't forget to turn the gas off again

Who looks after my children? A fantastic woman ... gets on really well with them .... I'm married to her funnily enough ... er, my wife, in fact

Yes I can honestly say that losing my job was the best thing that ever happened to me because it's given me the opportunity to spend all day with my children

Delighted to meet you - your face is certainly familiar. Do help yourself to a drink
I live here Dad
VF

you're SO EMOTIONAL
an obvious shortcoming in a human being I suppose
JF

The Multi Million Turnover Perpetually Shifting Female Erogenous Zone

then there was Julie who I have to say
was a really sexy woman, not quite
as good as Helen when it came to..er..
although she did have a terrific body
and stunning legs..

it all used to be so simple
— the BLUE dungarees
or the GREEN ones...

HELLO
GIRLS.

THE ONE AND ONLY
Wonderpouch

You are the person I LOVE — the person who gets to know my darkest secrets — the person from whom I will hide NOTHING

At what point do depictions of sexual violence towards women fall OUTSIDE the category of entertainment for men?

Would these images be offensive to REASONABLE people?

What is the difference between EROTICISM and sexualized violence?

I know this one

Questions not asked by great men in the great pornography debate

this image
is illegal

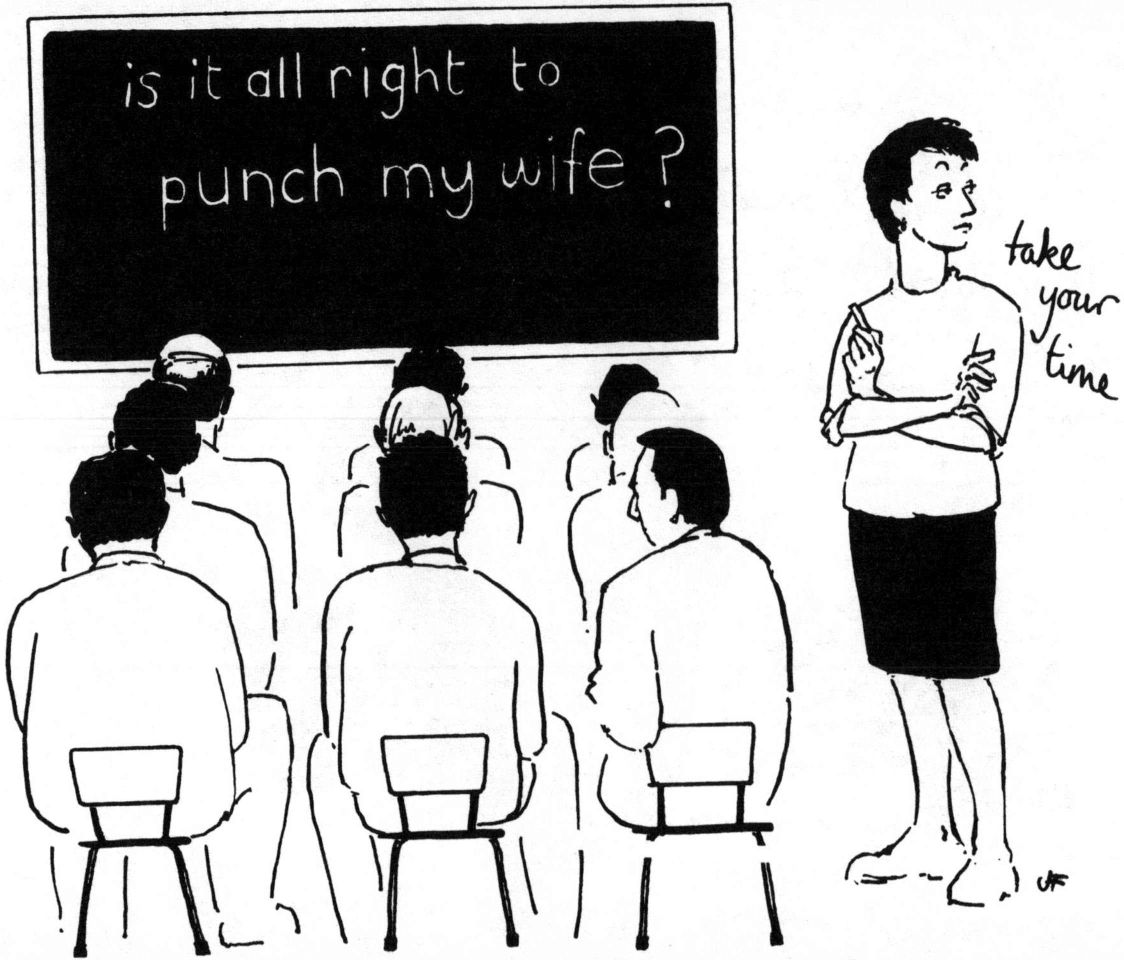
is it all right to
punch my wife ?
take your time
JF

women are forever changing their minds —
ONE minute they agree to a cup of coffee,
and the NEXT minute they object to a bit of
rough and tumble
at knifepoint

I genuinely believed she'd consented to rape, your Honour
the HUSSY
JF

Since when has ANY woman
accused a man of 'date-rape' just
because she regrets having sex with him.
You can't spend your whole LIFE
in and out
of court . . .

OR ARE YOU JUST PLEASED TO SEE MY TITS?

and, of course, we do have the latest model over here, very fashionable at the moment, sir, fully guaranteed for twelve months. I highly recommend this design, sir, in fact, I've got one myself

JF

as a last resort sir, you can of course ADAPT your wife with the help of this garment

so what you're really asking is -
if I met someone EXACTLY like you
AND with bigger breasts, would I leave you for her?

yes

in other words, you think I regard you
as I might.. a car, and if a newer model
became available WITH a built in cigarette
lighter, I'd HAVE to have it ?

yes

and do you believe many men
regard women in that way?

yes

but that must be intolerable -
to be seen as an exchangeable
sex-toy, perpetually at risk of obsolescence
on the puerile whim of someone
whose values you
can't respect

are you from this planet?
You can tell me -
I'm your friend

PESTOSTERONE

IT WAS AN ORDINARY SPRING DAY.
A SMALL BIPLANE WAS SPRAYING
CROPS WITH PESTICIDE. ONLY A
HANDFUL OF PEOPLE WERE EVER
TO KNOW WHAT HAD REALLY
BEEN UNLEASHED INTO THE
FOOD CHAIN.....

Potential DISASTER, Mike.
Needs hushing up. Vast
quantity of PESTOSTERONE
used by mistake. We
need to talk, NOW.

These are the likely symptoms..?
Looks like it's men who
are at risk

Afraid
so

what's wrong with finding women sexy, anyway?
an IMPLANT should not be confused with a WOMAN, Russell
JF

FIRST there was Adam...

THEN there was Eve

second time lucky, then

The Princess and the Frog

Once upon a time there was a princess who was niftily dribbling a football round the palace garden when she heard a pitiful croak

CROAK

coming from a large bulbous frog

What is it you want?

asked the princess, keeping the ball in the air with remarkable dexterity and control

CROAK

The frog explained that really he was
a handsome prince and if the
princess would just ...

The frog admitted he'd just got
a bit carried away

after which they became good friends

and he never did turn into a prince.

I'm having a SERIOUS relationship
I'm so sorry, that must be horrible
JF

There's something I
have to tell you —
I'm having
an affair

You'd really
like her

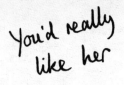

maybe not

I just finished a MARVELLOUS book on the menopause...

I was COUNTING on him leaving me for a younger woman
oh well
JF

Mum said we can come and live with you and your new girlfriend

Come on Alan, you're not trying. There MUST be ways in which women have kept us down

PANODRAMA

ominous dramatic music

more ominous dramatic music

You seem to have hit on the right formula for a new men's magazine in the 90s. What's the secret of your success?
lads
Well, I just had a HUNCH that pictures of women with no clothes on would capture the imagination of men today. It was a risk but it seems to have paid off
JF

HELLO
BOYS

Don't Forget Us!

I · COME · FROM

BOSNIA

Anita Ganeri

A Watts Book

LONDON · NEW YORK · SYDNEY

© Aladdin Books Ltd 1993
Designed and produced by
Aladdin Books Ltd
28 Percy Street
London W1P 9FF

First published in
Great Britain in 1993 by
Watts Books
96 Leonard Street
London EC2A 4RH

Editor: Sally Matthews
Designers: Peter Bennett
           Tessa Barwick
Illustrator: David Burroughs
Consultant: Dr John Channon
Photo Research: Emma Krikler

Printed in Belgium
A CIP catalogue record for this
book is available from the
British Library.

ISBN 0 7496 1361 0

CONTENTS

INTRODUCTION

Hello! My name is Samira and I am a Muslim from Bosnia. I came here just a few months ago with my family to escape from the war which is destroying my country.

Before the war, our way of life in Bosnia was similar to life over here. We, as Muslims, were used to living peacefully with Serb and Croat neighbours. But now that has all changed. Neighbour is fighting neighbour and our towns and villages are being ruined, in what seems like a never-ending civil war.

Come with me and I'll tell you about Bosnia – how it was before the war and what it's like now.

Since Bosnia declared independence from the former Yugoslavia in 1992, the Serbs, Croats and Muslims living there have all been fighting to seize as much territory as possible. Before the war Bosnia had a population of 4.5 million people. Three-quarters of these people have lost their homes, about 140,000 are dead or missing and over 2 million refugees have fled to safety.

BOSNIA TODAY

There are three main groups of people in Bosnia – the Serbs, the Croats and the Muslims. Each group has its own customs, religion and culture. There have always been traditional rivalries between these groups, but most people used to live and work together in peace. But now these differences have led to the bitter civil war in Bosnia today.

Many different languages are spoken in Bosnia. Everyone speaks Serbo-Croat, the official language. But many Muslims also speak Turkish or Albanian. Serbo-Croat is written in two different alphabets. The Serbs write it in the Cyrillic alphabet, which is also used to write Russian. The Croats and Muslims write it in the Roman alphabet, which is used to write French, Spanish and English.

zdravo
здраво

The words on the left both mean Hello in Serbo-Croat. The top word is written in the Roman alphabet and the bottom word is written in the Cyrillic alphabet.

4

COUNTRY AND LANDSCAPE

Bosnia is made up of two regions – Bosnia in the north and Hercegovina in the south. But it is usually just called Bosnia, for short. It is located in a region called the Balkan Peninsula in south-eastern Europe. Bosnia is a very small country, only about one-tenth of the size of France. But from 1918-1992, it was part of a larger country called Yugoslavia. At that time Bosnia and Yugoslavia shared the same flag (right).

Bosnia's neighbours are Croatia, Serbia and Montenegro, which along with Slovenia and Macedonia made up the old country of Yugoslavia. Bosnia's capital city is Sarajevo.

Bosnia is a mountainous country with very little coastline. As well as the high mountains of the Dinaric Alps, there are flat plains, large areas of forest and many lakes and rivers.

The Turkish bridge at Mostar (right) was one of Bosnia's most famous landmarks. It was built in the 16th century across the River Neretva. Sadly, this beautiful and historic bridge has been destoyed, becoming yet another casualty of the war in Bosnia.

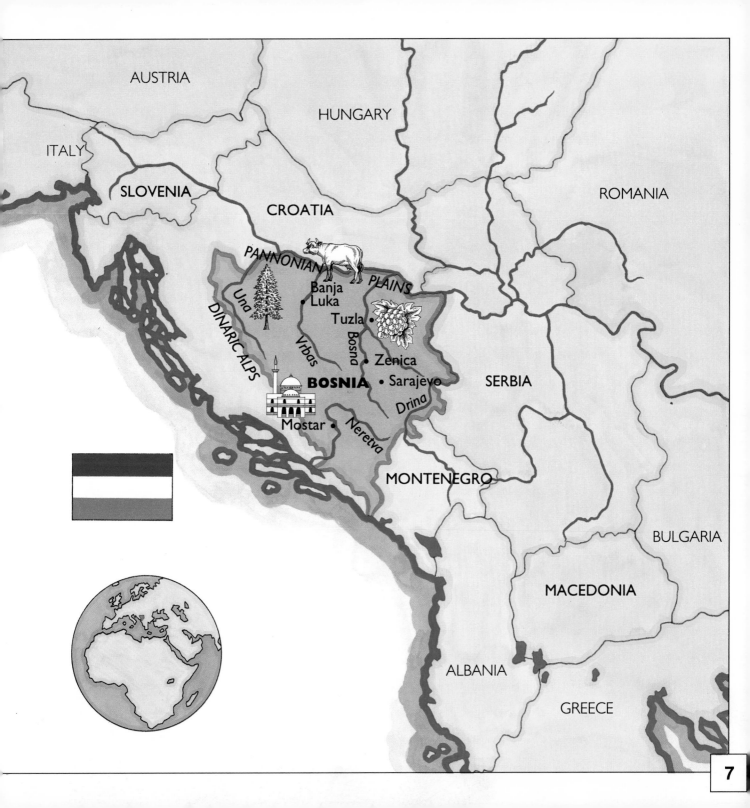

AUSTRIA

ITALY

SLOVENIA

HUNGARY

CROATIA

ROMANIA

PANNONIAN PLAINS

Una

DINARIC ALPS

Banja Luka

Tuzla

Vrbas

Bosna

Zenica

BOSNIA

Sarajevo

SERBIA

Drina

Mostar

Neretva

MONTENEGRO

BULGARIA

MACEDONIA

ALBANIA

GREECE

7

CLIMATE

Bosnia has a range of different types of weather, vegetation and wildlife.

The winters are very cold and snowy in the mountains and on the northern plains, and milder in the south. The summers are warm and rainy in the mountains but dry, sunny and very hot in the rest of the country.

Strong winds are common in Bosnia. The wind called the *Jugo* brings rain, the *Maestral* brings relief from the summer heat, and the *Bura* is a bitterly cold wind from the north-east.

The area is also frequently struck by earthquakes. In 1979, a huge earthquake damaged many of Bosnia's towns and villages.

Fir trees cover the mountain slopes (far left). The ancient Pančić Spruce is a type of tree which has been on the Earth for millions of years – longer than human beings. Many wild animals live in the mountains and forests, such as wild boar, lynxes, bears and wolves (left).

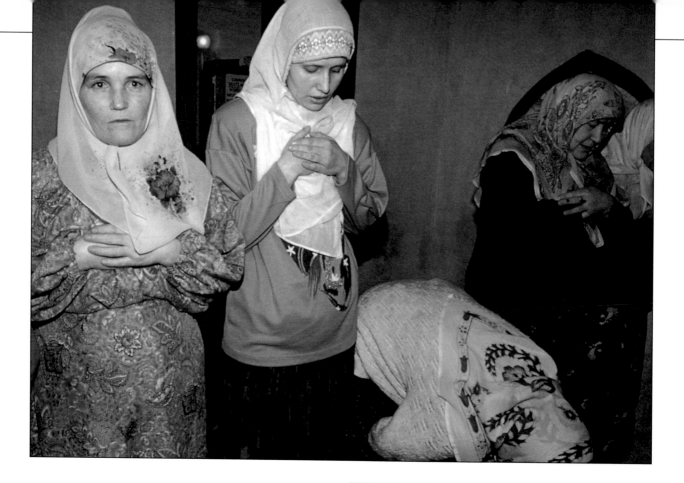

There are Muslims living all over the world. Bosnia and the rest of the former Yugoslavia is home to the biggest Muslim group in Europe (above). Most of the people who live in the Middle-East, North Africa, Pakistan and Bangladesh are Muslims. There are also large groups of Muslims in Malaysia and Indonesia. The largest group of Muslims in the world lives in India (right).

THE MUSLIMS

The first Muslims were the Arabs. In the 7th century, they began to build a huge empire which stretched across many countries. At the beginning of the 14th century, a group of Turkish Muslims called the Ottomans conquered Bosnia. Many Bosnians became Muslims at this time. Today, about 40 per cent of the people in Bosnia are Muslims, like my family.

Muslim and Turkish influences can be seen all over the country. There are many beautiful mosques where the Muslims worship. In the cities there are exotic Turkish bazaars where you can see men wearing fez hats, snake charmers and children eating Turkish Delight.

Some Muslim communities are very strict about how people dress. The women have to cover themselves up completely whenever they go out. This is to prevent strangers from looking at them. They wear long robes and veils or masks, called Yashmaks, like this woman from Oman (left). Most Muslim women in Bosnia have more freedom in the way they dress, but they usually cover their heads with scarves.

THE SERBS AND CROATS

About half of the people in Bosnia are either Serbs or Croats. Their ancestors came to the area from Poland and Russia in the 6th and 7th centuries.

The Serbs and the Croats were the two largest groups in the former Yugoslavia. Many of them lived in their own states of Serbia and Croatia. But many Serbs and Croats also lived in other former Yugoslavian states, such as Bosnia.

In 1991, Croatia declared itself a separate country. This was because the Croat majority thought that the Serbs had too much power in the central Yugoslavian government. This led to a civil war between the Croats and the Serbs living in Croatia. Soon after this war ended, in early 1992, the Serbs and Croats living in Bosnia started fighting over power and territory. The war Bosnia is still going on to this day.

The Serbs and Croats each have their own customs and traditions. Croatian folk dancers can be seen in villages all around Bosnia (right). Traditional clothes, like the Croatian national dress (left), are often worn for weddings and other special occasions.

BELIEFS

In the streets of Bosnia you can hear the unusual combination of church bells chiming and the chant of the Mussiens (priests) calling Muslims to prayer. This reflects the mixture of different religions.

Muslims, like me, believe in Allah (God) and the teachings of his prophet, Muhammed. He was born in the 6th century in Mecca, Saudi Arabia. We always have to turn to face the direction of Mecca when we pray (right). The buildings where we worship are called mosques.

Most Serbs and Croats are Christians. There are many different forms of Christianity. Many Serbs follow the Eastern Orthodox Church and most of the Croats are Roman Catholics. Like other Christians, they worship in churches and cathedrals.

Different religions have different holy books. The Christians follow the teachings in the Bible. The holy book of the Muslims is the Koran (left), which contains the words that Allah passed down to Muhammed.

OUR WAY OF LIFE

Our way of life in Bosnia was very similar to that in many other developed countries. Most people had a fairly high standard of living – higher than in most other Eastern European countries. Like many other Bosnian families, my family lived in a modern flat (right), just like flats over here. We also had a car and a television. My parents both had full-time jobs. While they were at work, I went to school. My younger sister and brother were looked after at a day centre run by the government.

However, life in Bosnia has changed since the war began. Families have been broken up and many homes have been damaged or destroyed in the fighting.

Traditional Bosnian dishes include kebabs, spicy meat balls and goulash stew. We also eat lots of sweet, sticky Turkish pastries, like baclava (right).

LIVING IN THE CITY

The capital city of Bosnia is Sarajevo (left). It is the political, economic and cultural centre of the country. The other major cities are Banja Luka, Zenica, Tuzla and Mostar.

When my family and I lived in Sarajevo, it was a busy, exciting city – a mixture of old and new, east and west. Skyscrapers, supermarkets and modern offices stood alongside mosques, open markets and Turkish bazaars.

Today, Sarajevo is a very different place. Almost every day there is fighting and many buildings have been destroyed. Many people in the city have no electricity and very little food. They have to risk being hit by gunfire in the streets just to get the water they need to live (below right).

The currency of Bosnia is the dinar (top left). But the Bosnian economy has collapsed due to the war. Today, American dollars (middle left) and German marks (bottom left) are more valuable than dinars in Bosnia.

In some places, the way of farming
hasn't changed for hundreds of years.
People still use old-fashioned ploughs
pulled by oxen or horses to farm their
fields (above). They take their goods
to market in wooden carts (right). But
there are also many farmers who use
modern machinery and up-to-date
methods of farming.

VILLAGE LIFE

The countryside in Bosnia is scattered with villages. Many village people work as farmers. They grow a variety of crops including barley, oats, oranges and lemons, grapes, plums, potatoes and other vegetables. Many farmers also raise livestock such as cattle, pigs and sheep.

In the villages most people live in small houses built of stone or wood. About three-quarters of village homes have electricity and nearly all the houses have running water.

Over the past 50 years the number of farmers in Bosnia has steadily declined. Before the war, many farmers left their villages to look for better-paid jobs in the cities. More recently, many people have been forced to leave because their villages have been destroyed in the fighting.

Bosnia has many vineyards where wine grapes are grown. Wine is a popular drink and has been made there for hundreds of years. Some Bosnian wines are exported to other countries. Two popular brands of wine are Blatina, which is a red wine, and Zilavka, which is a white wine (right).

WORK AND SCHOOL

Before World War II, three-quarters of the people in the former Yugoslavia were farmers. After the war, the communist government worked to change the country from an agricultural nation to an industrial nation. By the 1980s, only a quarter of the people worked in agriculture and the rest worked in mining, manufacturing, construction and service industries.

In Bosnia about 40 per cent of the people work in industry. Bosnia's industries include making clothes and textiles, food processing, mining coal and iron ore, manufacturing cars and making steel.

Bosnia also has many businessmen, teachers, lawyers and doctors. The busiest people today are the doctors and nurses looking after people wounded in the war (far right).

Bosnia also has many skilled craftsmen. Mostar and Sarajevo are famous for their exotic rugs and carpets. They come in a wide range of intricate designs (right) woven from brightly-coloured wools.

About 85 per cent of people in Bosnia can read and write. Education is free and all children from the age of 7 to 14 go to school. When I lived in Sarajevo, I went to a special Muslim school (below). Unlike my school over here, the boys and girls were separated into different classes. Like here, we studied many different subjects. But we also had to spend time every day learning about Islam and reading the Koran.

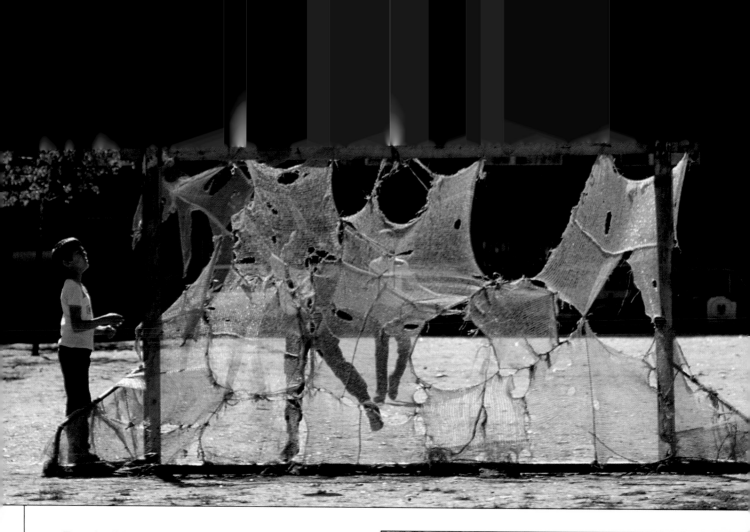

Football is very popular in Bosnia. The former Yugoslavia had a world-class football team (right) which reached the quarter finals of the World Cup in 1990. Children also love to play football. It doesn't matter if there is no proper football pitch, they can always make their own goal out of old plastic bags, netting and string (above).

SPORT AND LEISURE

Just like children in other countries, we like to watch television, listen to pop music, read comics, play games and go to the cinema after we get home from school.

The mountains provide a whole range of sporting activities as well. Hunting and hiking are both popular, and there are challenging peaks for people who enjoy mountain climbing. In the winter many people go skiing. In the summer they enjoy swimming and fishing in the lakes.

In the evening, many people take part in an old custom called korzo – they stroll along the main street of their town and stop to chat to the friends they meet. They may also pop into one of the many coffee houses which are called kafanas.

Bosnia is proud of its world-class ski slopes. Many people believe that the snow on Mount Bjelasnica, near Sarajevo, is the deepest and best in Europe. In 1984, Sarajevo hosted the 14th Winter Olympic Games. The Olympic mascot was a fox called Vucko (left). Vucko could be seen everywhere in the city – on posters, in the shops and on the television. His face became known all over of the world.

WHY I'M HERE

Since Bosnia declared itself independent in 1992, it has become a battlefield for a bitter civil war between the Serbs, Croats and Muslims.

The rival groups are fighting each other over territory, and thousands of people on all sides are being wounded and killed. One of the terrible aspects of this war is 'ethnic cleansing'. This is when one group of people tries to force all other ethnic groups out of a certain area, driving them from homes where their families have lived for generations (right).

Despite peace talks, the war continues. This is why my family came to this country. It was just too dangerous for us to stay in Bosnia any longer.

From 1953-1980, the Communist leader Josip Broz Tito (right) united the different states and ethnic groups of Yugoslavia. But after his death in 1980, traditional conflicts re-emerged, the Communist Party lost control and Yugoslavia was split into separate states.

THE FUTURE

I don't know what will happen to my country. So many places have been destroyed and many people have lost their homes. It will take a long time for the thousands of refugees to return to Bosnia and get back to normal life. Whatever happens, it will never be the same again. The country may be split up between the Serbs, Croats and Muslims. At the moment, the only thing people have to look forward to are the food and clothes brought by the United Nations trucks (left). Sometimes, even these are stopped by the soldiers.

I have only been in this country for a few months now and it still feels very strange. But I have started going to school and am learning to speak the language. Over here I can live peacefully with friends and neighbours of all different races and religions. I still have nightmares about the gunfire in Sarajevo, but I know that I am one of the lucky ones, safe in my new home.

FACT FILE

Official name: Republic of Bosnia and Hercegovina

Main language: Serbo-Croat

Other languages: Turkish, Albanian

Population: 4.5 million (pre-war population)

Currency: Dinar

Capital city: Sarajevo

Other major cities: Banja Luka, Zenica, Tuzla, Mostar

Main religions: Muslim, Roman Catholic, Eastern Orthodox

Ethnic groups: Bosnian Muslim (40%), Serb (32%), Croat (18%)

Climate: Continental in the north, mediterranean in the south

Major rivers: Neretva, Bosna, Drina, Una, Vrbas

Highest mountain: Maglic (2,386 metres above sea-level)

Crops: Maize, barley, oats, wheat, potatoes, plums, grapes, citrus fruits

Mineral resources: Iron ore, brown coal, lignite, bauxite, rocksalt, asbestos

Industries: Iron and steel works, chemicals, car and machinery manufacture, metal and timber products, mining, food processing, clothing and textiles

Major exports: Machinery, high quality clothing and footwear, chemicals

Major imports: Raw materials, petroleum and mineral fuels, consumer goods

Form of government: Multi-party Republic

Head of state: President

Literacy rate: 85.5%

Eligibility to vote: Universal

INDEX

Photocredits
Front cover: Panos Pictures; Front cover inset, 3, 29: Roger Vlitos; Title page, 10
bottom, 11, 15, 17, 18, 23 both, 24 both, 25, 27, 28: Frank Spooner Pictures; 4, 6, 9,
12, 13, 19, 20 both: Eye Ubiquitous; 10 top: Spectrum Colour Library.

Race Leys Junior School
Boston Road, Bedworth
Warwickshire CV12 8HG

flavours of the world

paul gayler

flavours
of the world

photography georgia glynn smith

kyle cathie limited

First published in Great Britain in 2002 by
Kyle Cathie Limited, 122 Arlington Road, London NW1 7HP
general.enquiries@kyle-cathie.com, www.kylecathie.com

ISBN 1 85626 441 6

Project Editor: Sheila Davies
Editors: Jane Middleton and Morag Lyall
Editorial Assistant: Sarah Epton
Designer: Paul Welti
Photographer: Georgia Glynn Smith
Production: Lorraine Baird and Sha Huxtable

A CIP catalogue record for this book is available from the British
Library.

Printed and bound in Singapore by Tien-Wah Press

Acknowledgements
To my wife Anita and family, without whose support of my endless ambitions
   and culinary journeys, I might have never have travelled this road.
To Georgia Glynn Smith and Linda Tubby, photographer and food stylist, a
   talented and formidable team, who were a great delight to work with. To
   Penny Markham, for sourcing superb props.
To Jane Middleton and Morag Lyall who, between them, skillfully shaped this
   book into what it is. To Paul Welti for his inspired design.
To Lara Mand-King, her endless hours of typing and re-typing of the recipes
   made the foundation of this book possible.
To my Sous-Chefs and all my team at The Lanesborough, for always
   enthusiastically endorsing our kitchens on a daily basis.
To Mr Geoffrey Gelardi, for his support at all times.
To Fiona and Linda, my agents at Limelight, there for me as always.
A special tribute: to Kyle, Sheila and all at Kyle Cathie who, once again, have
   guided me in producing another book. I deeply value their support,
   enthusiasm and, more importantly, their friendship. Without them, I could
   not have begun to bring this entire project together. A big thank you.

Contents

introduction

Flavourings are not the mainstay of our diet, yet imagine how dull food would be without their bright accents. Pungent or delicate, fiery or cooling, they stimulate the appetite, transforming what we eat from mere fodder to something that delights all the senses.

Flavour has been defined as 'the blend of taste and smell sensation experienced when food and drink are placed in the mouth' (*International Dictionary of Food and Cooking* by Charles Sinclair). Where flavourings are concerned, this link between taste and aroma is the key to their allure. It is often their smell that draws you to them in the first place, and then makes the food appetising. Think of ginger, a gnarled and knobbly root whose unglamorous appearance provides no clue to its power. Yet crush it roughly and you are instantly hit by a waft of warm spice, giving you a foretaste of its flavour and offering a world of opportunity, from spicy Indian dals and Chinese stir-fries to rich, sticky gingerbreads.

Over the last twenty years, our love of flavours has become global in its scope, so it's no surprise to see Lemongrass listed next to Mint in this book, or Tamarind next to Salt. Several stints working in the Far East have given me a real passion for flavourings such as lemongrass, ginger, holy basil, cumin, coriander and chilli. These tastes define their native cuisines but I believe they also have a role to play in Western cooking – for example, adding lemongrass to an Italian panna cotta (see page 113). Purists may disapprove, but spices have been imported from the East for centuries, and using them to give vibrancy and excitement to our cooking can be seen as following an honourable tradition.

Herbs and spices are not the only flavourings, of course. When deciding what to include in this book, I couldn't possibly leave out chocolate, coffee, honey, olives and that overwhelmingly popular condiment, balsamic vinegar. The latter stopped being an exclusively Italian flavouring years ago, and it seems our love affair with it is not over yet. It has undoubtedly been overused but I still think it is one of the great flavours of the world. Like many flavourings, part of the appeal of balsamic vinegar is its versatility: it is just as successful in ice-cream or sprinkled over strawberries as used in a salad dressing or with meat or fish.

New flavours come into vogue all the time, and two recent ones that spring to mind are lavender and coffee. Lavender has been used in French cuisine for centuries, in both savoury and sweet dishes, but it is now being taken up by chefs in the UK and elsewhere. I have always been intrigued by the culinary telepathy that seems to operate between chefs, which means that associated ideas and flavours will suddenly start to crop up in unconnected places. Just recently I have been experimenting with coffee in savoury dishes, resulting in my Veal Fillet with Mocha Porcini Sauce (see page 55), among others. On a short break in Paris, I went to the Crillon for lunch, where I was astonished to see that the chef, Dominique Bouchet, had included chicken cooked in coffee butter on the menu.

Now that almost all foods are available all year round, flavourings can act as a gentle reminder of the seasons. Cooling mint and basil add freshness to summer dishes, while cumin and coriander, mustard and cinnamon give a warm glow on winter days. Others have year-round appeal. Rosemary, for example, is wonderful tossed on a summer barbecue to flavour grilled meats or fish, and also makes a superb addition to a hearty

cold-weather dish such as Baked Onions (see page 157).

Using flavourings that are appropriate to the season is reminiscent of the time when they played an important role in peasant cuisine. Fresh herbs and dried spices were an economical way of livening up humble staples such as pasta (for example, chilli in the Italian dish, Pasta Arrabbiatta) and lentils (black pepper in the Indian soup, Rasam – see page 146). Some herbs, spices and flavourings are associated with luxury – think of saffron, vanilla and balsamic vinegar – but even these need not be expensive, as just a small quantity will leave its unique stamp on a dish.

Each flavouring in this book really deserves an entire book to itself, and there simply hasn't been space for all the recipes I would have liked to include. But for every flavouring I have given a list of complementary flavours, which I hope will inspire you to come up with your own ideas for using them. Remember that flavourings should enhance food rather than overpower it, and try not to mix too many together, otherwise it confuses the palate. If in any doubt, think about the country the flavouring comes from and combine it with ones from the same area.

I hope you will enjoy the recipes in this book and be inspired to create your own world of flavours. One final tip: herbs, spices and other flavourings should be as fresh as possible, otherwise they lose their potency and their magical ability to transform a dish. Use fresh herbs, respect the sell-by dates on ingredients such as mustards and vinegars, and buy dried spices in small quantities as you need them.

ALL RECIPES SERVE 4 UNLESS OTHERWISE STATED.

balsamic vinegar

Food is like fashion: styles come and go from month to month, year to year. Every so often a new ingredient hits the shops and takes off. Balsamic vinegar, or *aceto balsamico*, is one such ingredient, finding instant appeal with chefs, cooks and food lovers alike. Its presence can now be seen on menus from London to New York to Sydney. However, this vinegar is not new to the world: it has been a staple in Italy for many centuries.

This thick, radiant, dark brown essence with its extraordinarily complex fragrance has nothing in common with other vinegars we know. It has a unique character, with sweet and sour overtones, and an almost velvet-like consistency.

At this point I should explain that I am talking about the authentic and fabulously expensive balsamic vinegar, which bears the words *tradizionale* or *naturelle*, and not the cheap imitations available in some supermarkets.

DESCRIPTION

Balsamic vinegar is made in the area around Modena and Reggio nell' Emilia in Italy. Unlike other vinegars, it is made from wine marc (a liquid produced from the grape skins, pips and stalks that remain after pressing) and not wine itself. This marc comes from the Trebbiano grape, an Itialian variety, which ripens on the slopes nearby.

Its manufacture is a lengthy process, which begins with crushing the must (freshly harvested grape berries and juice). This produces 70 litres (15 gallons) of marc per 100kg (220lb) of fruit, which is first heated to 82°C (180°F) and then simmered until almost 50 per cent has evaporated to concentrate the natural sugars.

Once cooled, it is poured into casks called *demijohns* (generally made of ash, cherry or chestnut), and blended with some balsamic vinegar from an earlier vintage. It is then aged in rows in airy attics called *acetaia*. Here, over a period of years – even decades – it is exposed to changes in the weather and seasons: warmth and cold, dryness and dampness, all of which enhance and develop the vinegar, according to connoisseurs.

Through gradual fermentation, the liquid is transformed into a deep, rich, brown syrupy vinegar to which no flavourants or additives are added. About 10 per cent of the liquid evaporates each year. Generally the older the vinegar, the better the flavour, the thicker the intensity, and, of course, the more expensive it is to buy.

The name Aceto Balsamico Tradizionale has been legally protected since 1983 for vinegar from Modena, and since 1987 for that from Reggio nell' Emilia, both of which have a minimum age of twelve years.

BUYING

The quality of industrially produced balsamic vinegar varies greatly. I generally use a moderately priced eight-year-old, which generally has all the qualities I need, but as a rule always buy the best you can afford.

CULINARY USES

Although Italian chefs have long admired the qualities of this wonderful vinegar and used it to flavour many traditional dishes (such as Coniglio con Aceto Balsamico), today chefs are using it to create exciting new tastes. Balsamic vinegar's distinctive flavour goes well with fish, meat and vegetables, in salad dressings and on carpaccio.

complementary flavours

MUSTARD

VEGETABLES (ESPECIALLY
RED CABBAGE, RED ONIONS
AND TOMATOES)

FRUIT (ESPECIALLY
STRAWBERRIES,
RASPBERRIES, AND
APRICOTS)

OYSTERS

It can even be used in ice-cream (try my Balsamic Butter Ice-Cream on page 13 — you won't be disappointed!) and marries particularly well with strawberries and apricots.

If you get your hands on a bottle of balsamic vinegar that has been aged for more than twenty-five years (these are prized in Italy and treated with the respect of old wine vintages), be aware that you should use it sparingly as it will have a complex and very intense taste.

A recent introduction to the market is white balsamic vinegar. Although not technically an actual vinegar, it is a clear liquid with a sweet, delicate flavour, similar to cider vinegar. The only advantage I can see with it is that its clear colour mixes well with other ingredients as, for example, in salad dressings. Watch out for its progress in the near future.

A few sips of balsamic vinegar were traditionally taken to improve digestion.

duck with balsamic cherries
and shiitake mushrooms
Duck served with sweet cherries has long been a classic of French cuisine, the sauce made from a sugar and vinegar base. Here balsamic vinegar and dried sour cherries do a wonderful job. The shiitake mushrooms give an interesting twist and, more importantly, a good, meaty-flavoured sauce. Serve on a bed of Swiss chard, bok choy or spinach.

2 tablespoons demerara sugar

4 tablespoons balsamic vinegar (preferably aged)

75g (3oz) dried sour cherries

150ml (¹/4 pint) red wine

1 tablespoon five-spice powder

3 tablespoons honey

4 x 175g (6oz) duck breasts, skin on

3 tablespoons olive oil

12 shiitake mushrooms, thickly sliced

100ml (3¹/2fl oz) well-flavoured duck stock (or chicken stock)

25g (1oz) unsalted butter, diced

Salt and freshly ground black pepper

Preheat the oven to 200°C/400°F/gas mark 6. Put the sugar in a heavy-based saucepan and melt over a low heat. Raise the heat and cook, stirring frequently, until it becomes a light amber colour. Add the balsamic vinegar, dried cherries and red wine and simmer over a low heat for 6–8 minutes, until reduced and syrupy. Set aside.

Mix together the five-spice powder, honey and a little cracked black pepper (see page 142) and spread this mixture liberally over the skin side of the duck breasts. Heat the olive oil in a large ovenproof frying pan until very hot. Add the duck breasts, skin side down, and cook on a medium heat for 2–3 minutes, until golden; take care or the honey will caramelise too quickly and burn. Turn the duck breasts over, then transfer to the oven and cook to your liking – about 4–5 minutes for rare, longer if you prefer them more cooked. Remove from the pan and keep warm.

Drain off most of the fat from the pan, leaving about 2 tablespoons. Add the shiitake mushrooms and place in the oven for about 5 minutes to brown. Remove the pan from the oven, place on the hob and add the duck or chicken stock. Bring to the boil and simmer for 4–5 minutes. Add the balsamic cherries, mix well and cook for 5 minutes longer, stirring to scrape up the caramelised residue from the base of the pan. Swirl in the butter to enrich the sauce, then adjust the seasoning.

Carve the duck breasts and arrange on serving plates. Pour over the cherry and shiitake sauce and serve.

balsamic braised red cabbage
with cranberries

650g (1lb 7oz) red cabbage, cored and finely
shredded
400ml (14fl oz) red wine
5 tablespoons balsamic vinegar
1 tablespoon brown sugar
125g (4^1/$_2$ oz) fresh or frozen cranberries
2 tablespoons cranberry jelly (or redcurrant jelly)
Salt and freshly ground black pepper

Preheat the oven to 200°C/400°F/gas mark 6. Place the
shredded cabbage in a large casserole, pour over the red
wine and balsamic vinegar and place over a medium heat for
5 minutes. Sprinkle over the sugar and season lightly. Pour in
600ml (1 pint) of water and bring to the boil, then add the
cranberries. Cover with a tight-fitting lid and transfer to the
oven. Braise for 1 hour or until the cabbage is very tender. If
any liquid remains, place the casserole on the hob and cook,
uncovered, until it evaporates. Stir in the cranberry jelly,
adjust the seasoning and serve immediately.

grilled pork with balsamic
onions and beetroot
A light dish with
sweet and sour flavours, simple to prepare.

12 baby beetroot
25g (1oz) unsalted butter
4 tablespoons virgin olive oil
4 pieces of pork fillet, about 175–200g (6–7oz) each
1 teaspoon ground coriander
1 tablespoon chopped fresh coriander
Salt and freshly ground black pepper

FOR THE BALSAMIC ONIONS:
50g (2oz) unsalted butter
3 red onions, thinly sliced
3 tablespoons demerara sugar
100ml (3^1/$_2$ fl oz) balsamic vinegar
4 tablespoons red wine

For the balsamic onions, heat the butter in a saucepan, add
the onions and cook gently until soft but not coloured. Add
the sugar, vinegar and red wine, raise the heat and cook for
25–30 minutes, until the mixture is thick and syrupy. Season
to taste and keep warm.

Cook the baby beetroot in boiling salted water until
tender, then drain well and peel. Heat the butter in a pan, add
the beetroot and toss to glaze with the butter. Season to
taste and keep warm.

Heat a ridged grill pan or heavy-based frying pan until
very hot and brush with half the olive oil. Season the pork
with the ground coriander and some salt and pepper and
cook for 7–8 minutes, turning regularly until golden, cooked
through and slightly charred. Remove from the heat and
keep warm.

Mix the remaining olive oil with the chopped coriander
and some seasoning. Quickly reheat the beetroot if
necessary. Arrange a bed of balsamic onions on each serving
plate, slice each pork fillet into 5 and place on top.
Arrange the glazed beetroot on the pork, pour
over a little of the coriander oil and serve.

butternut squash and porcini risotto with balsamic caramel

25g (1oz) dried porcini mushrooms

4 tablespoons olive oil

1 small butternut squash, peeled, deseeded and cut into 2cm ($^3/_4$in) cubes

100g ($3^1/_2$ oz) unsalted butter

3 garlic cloves, cut into slices 3mm ($^1/_8$ in) thick

1 sprig of thyme

500ml (18fl oz) well-flavoured vegetable stock (or chicken stock)

2 shallots, finely chopped

225g (8oz) *vialone nano* risotto rice

85ml (3fl oz) dry white wine

Salt and freshly ground black pepper

FOR THE BALSAMIC CARAMEL:

4 tablespoons caster sugar

125ml (4fl oz) balsamic vinegar

Soak the dried porcini in 125ml (4fl oz) hot water for 30 minutes. Meanwhile, heat 2 tablespoons of the oil in a large sauté pan, add the butternut squash and fry until golden all over. Add 25g (1oz) of the butter, then the garlic and thyme, and fry over a moderate heat for 5 minutes. Season with salt and pepper, then remove from the pan and set aside.

Drain the mushrooms, reserving the soaking water, and chop them coarsely. Put the soaking water and stock in a saucepan and bring to the boil. Keep at simmering point while you make the risotto.

Wipe out the sauté pan, add the remaining oil and 25g (1oz) of the remaining butter, then add the shallots and chopped porcini and cook for 2 minutes. Add the rice and stir well to coat the grains with the butter. Increase the heat, then stir in the wine and boil for 1 minute. Then start adding the hot stock, a ladleful at a time, waiting until it has been absorbed before adding more. Keep the risotto simmering as you add the stock and stir constantly until the rice is tender but still retains bite; this will take 20–25 minutes. Add the cooked butternut squash, season to taste and stir in the remaining butter.

For the balsamic caramel, put the sugar in a small, heavy-based pan and heat gently until melted. Raise the heat and cook, without stirring, until it becomes a golden amber colour. Add the balsamic vinegar (stand well back, as it will splutter) and boil for 3 minutes. Divide the risotto between 4 plates, drizzle over the balsamic caramel and serve.

balsamic butter ice-cream
with citrus salad and passionfruit jelly

SERVES 8

165g (5^1/$_2$ oz) caster sugar
600ml (1 pint) full-fat milk, hot
75g (3oz) unsalted butter
6 egg yolks
1 teaspoon cornflour
4 tablespoons balsamic vinegar
12 tiny mint leaves

FOR THE CITRUS SALAD AND PASSIONFRUIT JELLY:

2 blood oranges
2 pink grapefruit
2 oranges
200ml (7fl oz) passionfruit pulp (you will need about 10 fruits)
25g (1oz) caster sugar
3 gelatine leaves
85ml (3fl oz) stock syrup (see Tip below)
2 tablespoons Cointreau

Put 150g (5oz) of the sugar in a small, heavy-based pan and heat gently until melted. Raise the heat and cook, without stirring, until it becomes a golden amber colour. Pour on the hot milk (stand well back, as it will splutter), stir well and boil for 1 minute, then remove from the heat and set aside. In a

separate pan, heat the butter until it foams up and gives off a nutty fragrance. Quickly strain it through a sieve into a bowl, then cover and set aside.

In a separate bowl, whisk together the egg yolks and remaining sugar until pale and creamy. Whisk in the cornflour. Gradually pour in the caramelised milk and whisk until smooth. Finally, whisk in the melted butter and balsamic vinegar and leave to cool. Place in an ice-cream machine and freeze according to the manufacturer's instructions. Transfer to a container and freeze overnight to allow the flavours to strengthen.

For the citrus salad and jelly, cut off all the peel and pith from the citrus fruits, then cut out the segments from between the membranes – do this over a bowl to catch the juice, squeezing out the membrane from each fruit after you have taken out all the segments. Set aside the juice and the segments.

Place the passionfruit pulp in a saucepan with the sugar and 4 tablespoons of water. Crush the shells with your hands and add them too (they give a wonderful pink colour). Bring to the boil and simmer for 3–4 minutes. Meanwhile, cover the gelatine leaves with cold water for 5 minutes Strain the passionfruit mixture into a bowl and stir in 125ml (4fl oz) of the reserved citrus juice, the stock syrup and Cointreau. Squeeze out excess water from the gelatine and add to the passionfruit mixture, stirring until dissolved. Strain into 8 shallow bowls and leave in the fridge overnight.

To serve, top the jelly with the citrus fruit segments, place a scoop of balsamic ice-cream on top, then decorate with the mint leaves.

PG TIP To make stock syrup, put 225g (8oz) caster sugar in a saucepan with 300ml (^{1}/$_2$ pint) of water and bring slowly to the boil, stirring until the sugar has dissolved. Boil rapidly for 2 minutes to form a light syrup. Leave to cool, then store in a cool place. Use for sweet sauces, ice-creams, sorbets etc.

basil

For me, basil conjures up the real essence and flavour of summer. And who would believe that basil, a herb I love to use at any opportunity, would have such a long and interesting history? Basil is native to India, Asia and the Mediterranean, and Hindus used to wash their dead in basil water and place a leaf of holy basil on the deceased's chest before burial to ward off evil spirits. So highly do Hindus still regard basil that they regularly grow the plant beside their temples.

recipes

In Italy, basil holds many connotations too; for instance a pot of fresh basil placed on a woman's windowsill to this day extends an invitation to visit her. Perhaps it has a lot to answer for in establishing the country's romantic image!

DESCRIPTION

There are believed to be over 100 varieties of basil, ranging from the ornamental to the fragrant varieties that we love to use in cooking.

Most basils are annuals and grow into bushy plants up to 30cm (1ft) high. The most commonly used variety for cooking is sweet basil (*Ocimum basilicum*) which has oval, shiny green, buttery soft leaves. Other commonly used varieties include anise basil, lemon basil, the gingery flavoured purple or opal basil, lettuce leaf basil and Thai basil (otherwise known as holy basil). Less common varieties include a Mexican one called cinnamon basil, which is unfortunately not available in this country, but is great used in marinades and spicy dishes. Thai basil (*O. sanctum*), which must be cooked in order to release its flavour, has a stronger and more intense flavour than sweet basil and is good in Asian-style curries, and delicious added to spicy soups and stir-fries.

When people are asked to describe the taste of basil, opinions differ: some claim overtones of sweet liquorice, others cloves; some say spicy, others sweet. You may be surprised to know that in fact basil is a member of the mint family.

GROWING/BUYING, STORING AND PREPARATION

As hardy as basil looks, it can be difficult to grow. I personally have not had much success in my own herb patch. It likes sunshine and shade, plenty of water but not too much, and, more importantly, temperatures above 15°C (60°F). Luckily we now have access to basil throughout the year, sourced from all over the world.

When purchasing basil, always look for stumpy, shiny, bright green leaves and not those that are limp or blackened in appearance. Only buy it when required (it doesn't keep very well unless you buy a rooted plant), and pick as needed. I find the best way to keep it is to wrap the leaves in a damp cloth and store in the fridge.

Great care is needed when using sweet basil, as the leaves are fragile and bruise easily. When using it in dishes, crush in a mortar and pestle or simply chop the leaves. For salads I prefer to tear the leaves into small pieces.

CULINARY USES

Basil is one of the most popular herbs worldwide, typically playing a supporting role in dishes, such as a pesto stirred into a light vegetable soup (Soupe au Pistou, see page 16), or added to sauces, eggs, fish and meat dishes. Where, for example, would the Italians be without the fragrance of basil in many of their staple sauces and pasta dishes, or the Thais without holy basil in their curries and noodle dishes?

can spoil its flavour. For a fresher taste, I find it is better to add more towards the end of the cooking time.

IDEAS WITH BASIL
• Use plenty with olive oil to marinate goat's cheese or mozzarella.
• Basil butter (see below) is superb on grilled fish or vegetables.

Basil butter
8oz butter
4 tablespoons chopped basil
1 teaspoon lemon juice
Soften the butter with a wooden spoon. Add the basil and lemon juice. Shape into a bonbon or sausage in wax paper and refrigerate. Slice when required.

• Pesto or basil oil (see below), added to the same amount of basic vinaigrette makes a delicious dressing for salads.

Basil oil
100g (3¹/₂oz) basil leaves
200ml (7fl oz) virgin olive oil
Blanch the basil leaves in boiling water for 10 seconds, drain and refresh in iced water. Remove, squeeze dry and blitz in a blender with the olive oil until smooth. Leave to settle overnight. Strain through muslin, and use as required. Any left-over basil oil should be stored in the refrigerator.

• Use the larger leaves to wrap around prawns or asparagus, just before steaming.
• Add to sweet syrup to make a delicious poaching liquid for fruits such as peaches, strawberries and rhubarb.
• Dip basil leaves in melted chocolate to make an interesting and attractive decoration for desserts

Fresh basil leaves make a very effective and aromatic garnish, and are wonderful added to salads — try a mixture of sweet and purple basil. Basil, as the Italians show, marries particularly well with tomatoes, both cooked and raw.

Basil intensifies with cooking, so start with small amounts and remember that overcooking

complementary flavours

SOFT CHEESES (RICOTTA, FETA, MOZZARELLA AND GOAT'S CHEESE)

PARMESAN CHEESE

VEGETABLES (ESPECIALLY FENNEL, ROASTED PEPPERS AND TOMATOES)

GARLIC

OLIVE OIL

ORANGES AND LEMONS

MEAT (ESPECIALLY LAMB)

FISH AND SHELLFISH (ESPECIALLY SEA BASS, SALMON, MULLET, SCALLOPS AND MUSSELS)

COCONUT MILK AND GINGER (FOR THAI BASIL))

soupe au pistou

This simple, fragrant vegetable soup is synonymous with the South of France, but its distinctive flavour can only be achieved with good fresh tomatoes and lots of fresh pistou — a basil paste similar to pesto — added at the last moment. In France, the pistou would be made with a mortar and pestle but a blender or food processor is fine, too.

1 leek, white part only

1 potato

1 onion

1 celery stick

1 courgette

2 carrots

10 French beans

6 ripe plum tomatoes, skinned and deseeded

2 tablespoons olive oil

$^1/_4$ teaspoon thyme leaves

1 small bay leaf

1 litre (1$^3/_4$ pints) well-flavoured chicken stock (or vegetable stock)

Salt and freshly ground black pepper

FOR THE PISTOU:

100g (3$^1/_2$ oz) basil leaves

3 garlic cloves, roughly chopped

1 tablespoon pine kernels

2 tablespoons Parmesan cheese, freshly grated (optional)

About 100ml (3$^1/_2$ fl oz) virgin olive oil

Cut all the vegetables into 5mm ($^1/_4$ in) dice. Heat the olive oil in a large saucepan, add all the vegetables except the tomatoes, then add 3 tablespoons of water and cover with a lid. Leave to cook gently until the water has evaporated, but don't let the vegetables brown. Add the thyme and bay leaf and pour over the stock. Bring to the boil, reduce the heat to a simmer and cook for 20–25 minutes, until the vegetables are tender.

Meanwhile, prepare the pistou. Put all the ingredients except the oil in a food processor or blender and blitz to a paste. Slowly add the oil, while the motor is still running, until the pistou has a smooth, slightly runny texture. Season to taste.

Add the pistou to the soup, followed by the diced tomatoes, and stir thoroughly; do not let it boil again. Season and serve.

summer vegetable salad

A wonderful crisp summer salad. Be sure to use prime-quality vegetables and serve them warm, which really brings out the flavour.

300g (11oz) asparagus, trimmed

300g (11oz) baby carrots, trimmed

8 baby courgettes, trimmed

200g (7oz) sugarsnap peas, trimmed

200g (7oz) baby leeks, trimmed

3 tablespoons balsamic vinegar

4 tablespoons extra virgin olive oil

4 tablespoons chopped basil (a mixture of purple and green looks good)

2 tablespoons white wine vinegar

4 organic or free range eggs

2 tablespoons pine kernels, toasted

Salt and freshly ground black pepper

Bring a large pan of salted water to the boil, add the asparagus and simmer for 3–4 minutes, until tender. Remove with a slotted spoon and place in a large bowl of iced water (this helps preserve the colour). Drain immediately and set aside.

Return the water to the boil and cook the other vegetables in it until just tender, plunging them into iced water as well. When all the vegetables are cooked, mix them together in a large bowl and set aside.

For the dressing, put 3 tablespoons of the balsamic vinegar in a bowl, add some salt and pepper, then beat in the olive oil and basil. Set aside.

Bring a large pan of water to the boil, add the white wine vinegar, then reduce the heat and poach the eggs in it. Meanwhile, warm the vegetables in a little boiling water for 1 minute, or place in a microwave for 30 seconds.

Arrange the drained vegetables on 4 serving plates, spoon over the basil dressing and sprinkle over the pine kernels. Place a poached egg on the side of each salad and serve immediately.

goat's cheese and basil mousse
with basil and almond sauce

The recent popularity of goat's cheese is quite astonishing. In this recipe, puréeing it with basil and roasted garlic to make a mousse, then topping it with a basil and almond sauce makes a great dish. A tomato and olive salad and some toasted bread rubbed with garlic and olive oil goes well with it.

2 garlic cloves, unpeeled
1 tablespoon olive oil
12 large basil leaves
50ml (2fl oz) single cream
200g (7oz) soft goat's cheese
50ml (2fl oz) double cream
A little cayenne pepper
2 gelatine leaves
Salt and freshly ground black pepper

FOR THE BASIL AND ALMOND SAUCE:
25g (1oz) ground almonds
6 basil leaves
$^1/_2$ small garlic clove, crushed
100ml (3$^1/_2$ fl oz) virgin olive oil

Preheat the oven to 180°C/350°F/gas mark 4. Put the garlic cloves in a small dish, pour over the oil and roast for 20 minutes, until tender and brown. Leave to cool, then pop the garlic from its skin.

Blanch the basil leaves for the mousse in boiling water for 30 seconds, then drain and refresh in iced water. Drain again and dry well. Place in a food processor or blender with the garlic and single cream and blend until smooth. Pour into a bowl, add the goat's cheese and double cream and mix well. Season with cayenne, salt and pepper.

Cover the gelatine leaves with cold water and leave to soak for 5 minutes. Drain and squeeze out excess water, then place in a small saucepan with 2 tablespoons of water. Heat gently to dissolve, without letting the water boil. Stir the dissolved gelatine into the mousse mixture. Pour into 4 ramekins, or small coffee cups, and place in the fridge for about 4 hours, until set.

Meanwhile, make the sauce. Put the ground almonds, basil and garlic in a food processor or blender and gradually pour in the olive oil, blitzing it to a coarse purée, pesto style.

To serve, dip each ramekin into a little hot water, run a knife around the edge and turn out on to a serving plate. Top each mousse with a spoonful of the sauce.

spaghetti with lobster, basil
and tomatoes
Lobster is expensive, I know, but when you're looking for something light, tasty and simple yet special, this dish fits the bill. A taste of summer, if ever there was one. It is also good served cold as part of a barbecue buffet.

1 x 900g (2lb) lobster, cooked
100ml (3$^1/_2$ fl oz) lobster oil (see Tip below), made with the lobster shell
450g (1lb) firm plum tomatoes, skinned, deseeded and cut into 5mm ($^1/_4$in) dice
1 garlic clove, crushed
Juice of $^1/_2$ lemon
16 large basil leaves
450g (1lb) spaghetti
Salt and freshly ground black pepper
Freshly grated Parmesan cheese, to serve

Remove the lobster meat from the claws and body, cut it into chunks and set aside. Use the shell to make the lobster oil.

The following day, place the tomatoes, garlic, lemon juice and lobster oil in a bowl. Tear half the basil into small pieces and add to the bowl, then add the lobster chunks and season to taste. Leave to marinate at room temperature for up to 1 hour.

Cook the spaghetti in plenty of boiling salted water until al dente. Drain in a colander and return to the pan. Add the lobster and marinade and toss together. Place in a serving bowl and sprinkle over the Parmesan and the remaining torn basil leaves.

PG TIP To make lobster oil, crush the lobster shells into small pieces using a rolling pin and fry in 2 tablespoons oil for 10–15 minutes. Add a handful of a chopped garlic, onion, celery and carrot, mixture plus a bay leaf and a few tarragon stalks. Pour over 150ml ($^1/_4$ pint) dry white wine and simmer for 15 minutes. Reduce the heat, add 1 pint (600ml) vegetable oil and simmer for 30 minutes. Remove from the heat, cover and leave overnight (do not refrigerate). Strain through muslin or a filter and store in the fridge.

oven-glazed mozzarella cakes
with aubergine and basil
This colourful dish with its robust flavours makes a great first course or vegetarian dish.

150ml (¹/₄ pint) olive oil

2 garlic cloves, crushed

2 beefsteak tomatoes, peeled, deseeded and chopped

125ml (4fl oz) pistou (see page 16)

2 aubergines, cut into slices 1cm (¹/₂ in) thick

1 buffalo mozzarella cheese, cut into 8 slices

150ml (¹/₄ pint) double cream

1 egg yolk, beaten

2 tablespoons freshly grated Parmesan cheese

Salt and freshly ground black pepper

FOR THE MOZZARELLA CAKES:

500ml (18fl oz) full-fat milk

50g (2oz) unsalted butter, diced

250g (9oz) chickpea flour (gram flour)

1 buffalo mozzarella cheese, grated

1 teaspoon salt

1 teaspoon sugar

1 large egg yolk

3 tablespoons olive oil

First make the mozzarella cakes. Put the milk and butter in a pan and bring to the boil. Combine the flour with the grated mozzarella, salt and sugar and rain this mixture into the hot milk. Stir until well combined. Reduce the heat and cook for 4–5 minutes, until the mixture leaves the sides of the pan clean. Beat in the egg yolk thoroughly, then leave to cool. Roll the mixture into eight 5cm (2in) balls and flatten them slightly.

Preheat the oven to 180°C/350°F/gas mark 4. Heat the olive oil in a large frying pan, add the mozzarella cakes and fry for 5–6 minutes on each side, until golden. Keep warm.

Heat 50ml (2fl oz) of the olive oil in a pan and add the garlic, tomatoes and half the pistou. Reduce the heat and cook until the the mixture is concentrated. Season to taste.

Heat the remaining oil in a frying pan and fry the aubergine slices for 4–5 minutes on each side, until golden. Remove and drain on kitchen paper. Lay 8 slices in an oiled gratin dish and top each with a mozzarella cake, a slice of mozzarella, some tomato sauce, another slice of aubergine and more tomato sauce. Pour a little pistou over each stack. Mix the cream with the egg yolk, Parmesan and the remaining pistou and pour it over each stack. Bake for about 20 minutes, until golden and glazed.

red mullet with orange and basil stuffing
Red mullet is a firm-fleshed fish from the Mediterranean. The orange stuffing keeps it wonderfully moist during cooking. If the thought of boning the fish is daunting, ask your fishmonger to do it for you.

4 x 300g (11oz) red mullet, cleaned

4 tablespoons olive oil

Salt and freshly ground black pepper

FOR THE STUFFING:

75g (3oz) basil leaves

2 garlic cloves, crushed

4 tablespoons pine kernels

4 tablespoons freshly grated Parmesan cheese

Grated zest of 1 orange

100ml (3¹/₂ fl oz) virgin olive oil

125g (4¹/₂ oz) fresh white breadcrumbs

To make the stuffing, place the basil, garlic, pine kernels, Parmesan and orange zest in a blender or food processor and slowly add the oil, with the motor running, to give a smooth purée. Add the breadcrumbs and blitz for 10 seconds.

Preheat the oven to 200°C/400°F/gas mark 6. Using a sharp knife, cut each red mullet down the backbone, then snip the bone with scissors behind the head and the tail. Remove the bone, keeping the head and tail intact, and take out the pinbones. Open the vent and fill with the stuffing. Lightly tie the fish with string to secure the filling.

Butter 4 pieces of foil, approximately 38cm (15in) square. Place the red mullet on top, spoon over the olive oil and season. Lift up the sides of the foil and twist to seal. Bake for 15–20 minutes, depending on the size of the fish.

Serve at the table, opening the parcels in front of your guests to let the smell of basil pervade the room.

lamb noisettes with basil and parmesan crust

The beauty of this crust is that it can be made well in advance and used as needed. It has a fantastic flavour and is so versatile it could be used on most meats, especially chicken and beef, or as a topping for fish.

Grilled vegetables, such as aubergines, courgettes and peppers, make an ideal accompaniment to this summery dish.

4 tablespoons olive oil
8 lamb noisettes
Salt and freshly ground black pepper

FOR THE BASIL AND PARMESAN CRUST:
100g (3½ oz) basil leaves
100g (3½ oz) softened unsalted butter
150g (5oz) fresh white breadcrumbs
75g (3oz) Parmesan cheese, freshly grated
50g (2oz) Gruyère cheese, grated
1 garlic clove, crushed
25g (1oz) pine kernels, toasted

FOR THE SAUCE:
50g (2oz) unsalted butter
1 shallot, finely chopped
4 tomatoes, peeled, deseeded and cut into small dice
85ml (3fl oz) dry white wine
300ml (½ pint) lamb stock (or other meat stock)
10 basil leaves, chopped

For the basil and Parmesan crust, place the basil leaves in a food processor with the butter and a little seasoning and blitz until smooth. Add the remaining ingredients and process until smooth again. Transfer the mixture to a piece of foil and wrap into a bonbon shape. Place in the freezer until needed.

For the sauce, heat 10g (¼oz) of the butter in a pan, add the shallot and cook for a few minutes, until soft but not coloured. Add the tomatoes and cook for 5 minutes, then add the white wine and boil for 5 minutes. Pour in the stock and simmer until the sauce has reduced by half its volume. Stir in the basil. Dice the remaining butter, whisk it into the sauce, then season to taste and keep warm.

Heat the olive oil in a large, heavy-based frying pan until very hot, season the lamb noisettes and fry for 2–3 minutes on each side, until golden on the outside but still pink inside. Remove from the heat and keep warm.

Preheat the grill to its highest setting. Remove the crust from the freezer, cut it into fairly thick slices and place them between 2 sheets of clingfilm. Roll out to about 3mm (⅛in) thick. Cut out 8 rounds of crust and place one on top of each lamb noisette. Put the noisettes on a baking tray and place under the grill until golden and crisp. Serve with basil sauce.

monkfish curry with green mango and thai basil

With its firm-textured flesh, monkfish is the ideal choice for this fragrant Asian curry. If kaffir lime leaves are not available, replace them with a bay leaf and ½ teaspoon of grated lime zest.

2 tablespoons vegetable oil
2 tablespoons green curry paste
450g (1lb) monkfish fillet, cut into large dice
1 lemongrass stalk, hard outer layers removed,
   tender inner core chopped
300ml (½ pint) coconut milk
4 kaffir lime leaves
1 teaspoon ground turmeric
1 teaspoon ground coriander
1 aubergine, cut into large batons
2 tablespoons *nam pla* (Thai fish sauce)
3 green chillies, finely sliced
½ green, unripe mango, peeled, stoned, thinly sliced
10 Thai basil leaves, roughly chopped

Heat the oil in a large heavy-based frying pan, add the curry paste and fry until it bubbles and becomes fragrant. Add the monkfish and lemongrass and cook over a gentle heat for about 2 minutes. Stir in the coconut milk, kaffir lime leaves, turmeric and coriander and bring to the boil. Add the aubergine and fish sauce and cook over a gentle heat for about 5 minutes, until the fish is cooked. Finally stir in the green chillies and the mango. Serve immediately sprinkled with the basil.

cardamom

Cardamom is native to the East and grows in India (the largest producer), Sri Lanka, South America and the South Pacific. It is one of the most ancient spices in the world, as well as one of the most popular and highly valued, ranking as the third most expensive spice, behind saffron and vanilla. Sometimes called the Queen of Spices, its seeds were prized in India long before the birth of Christ.

DESCRIPTION

Cardamom (*Elettaria cardamomum*) is a member of the ginger family, a woody perennial that takes three years to produce seeds. The fruits pods are picked just before they ripen and left to dry on open platforms under the hot sun, or in special drying rooms.

The seed pods are white, green or black. The black (or brown) pods are larger than the green variety, the white ones have been bleached. The best green cardamom comes from Kerala, in India, and sets the standard for quality and price.

Cardamom is prized for its inner brown-black seeds (the tough outer pod is inedible and generally only used to flavour dishes such as rice, then discarded). In Western countries cardamom, with its delicate, camphor-like flavour, is still considered fairly exotic.

There are many 'false' cardamom varieties which, though related to 'true' cardamom, are inferior in terms of flavour and aroma, and are marketed as cheap substitutes. False varieties include Nepal, Chinese and Japanese cardamom.

BUYING AND STORING

I generally buy whole cardamom pods for optimum freshness and flavour. You are most likely to come across the green variety, which connoisseurs consider to be the best (the black variety tends to have a blunter, more camphorous flavour). The spice is generally available from supermarkets although I prefer to buy it from

Middle Eastern or Asian shops, which have a brisker turnover and where it is therefore more likely to be fresh. As with all spices, it is hard to know how long they have been sitting on the shelves, so I find it is best to buy small quantities and use them quickly. The pods should be plump, hard in texture, aromatic in smell and blemish-free.

PREPARATION

The easiest way to extract the seeds is to crush the cardamom with a rolling pin, or kitchen mallet, then pick the seeds from the pods (this can be quite a tedious task, so look out for packets of seeds already removed from their pods in Indian and Pakistani food shops). If I am preparing a stew or Asian-style curry, however, I add the whole pods for flavour, but remember to remove them before serving. You can purchase a ground form of cardamom but, like many spices, its flavour is inferior to freshly ground. When a recipes calls for ground cardamom, simply pulverise the seeds in a mortar or spice grinder.

CULINARY USES

Cardamom features in many curries (such as Indian and Persian), spice mixes (like the Iranian *advieh*, or the Moroccan *ras el hanout*) and in a fiery Yemeni paste, *zoug*, which is added to soups and stews or used as a dip for bread.

It is delicious added to garam masala and to rice pilaffs. Its flavour also works surprisingly well

complementary flavours

MILK PUDDINGS, CUSTARDS
AND ICE-CREAMS

GINGER

COFFEE

CHOCOLATE

CITRUS FRUITS

VANILLA

DATES

MEAT (ESPECIALLY LAMB
AND CHICKEN)

in sweet dishes and hot drinks. All over the Middle
East it is used to perfume Arabic coffees, either
alone or with other sweet spices. It adds an
exquisite flavour to milky desserts, such as rice
pudding and custards, and it is used to great
effect in Indian-style ice-cream, kulfi. It is good in
spicy biscuits and cakes, and is a great flavouring
for chocolate desserts. In Sweden cardamom is
regularly used in bread-making and baking.

OTHER USES

In India cardamom is used not only in cooking, but
as a breath freshener and digestive aid: when
crushed between the teeth, a powerful lemony
flavour is released, which has cleansing
properties. In the past cardamon was also used to
relieve flatulence and to treat stomach disorders.
It is still sometimes blended with water and used
as a gargle for sore throats.

cardamom spinach purée
Serve this as a interesting side dish. It's particularly good with Middle Eastern spicy leg of lamb and roast chicken.

750g (1lb 10oz) young spinach leaves
25g (1oz) unsalted butter
2 shallots, finely chopped
1 teaspoon freshly ground cardamom
$^1/_4$ teaspoon dried chilli flakes
100ml ($3^1/_2$ fl oz) double cream
Grated zest of $^1/_2$ lemon
3 tablespoons flaked almonds, toasted, to garnish
Salt and freshly ground black pepper

Blanch the spinach in boiling salted water for 30 seconds, then drain in a colander and refresh under cold running water. Squeeze out the water from the spinach with your hands until it is dry, then place the spinach in a blender or food processor and blitz to a coarse purée.

Heat the butter in a saucepan, add the shallots and cook for 1 minute, until softened Add the cardamom and chilli flakes and mix well. Stir in the spinach and cream and heat gently, until they are lightly bound together. Add the lemon zest, season with salt and pepper and serve, sprinkled with the toasted almonds.

lebanese lentil soup

4 tablespoons olive oil
1 onion, finely chopped
1 garlic clove, crushed
200g (7oz) red lentils
1 tablespoon freshly ground cardamom
$^1/_4$ teaspoon ground allspice
$^1/_2$ teaspoon grated lemon zest
1 litre ($1^3/_4$ pints) beef stock
25g (1oz) unsalted butter
3 slices of white bread, crusts removed, cut into
    5mm ($^1/_4$in) dice
2 tablespoons lemon juice
Salt and freshly ground black pepper
A few roughly crushed cardamom seeds, to garnish

Heat half the oil in a large pan, add the onion and garlic and cook for 2–3 minutes, until softened. Add the lentils and stir until coated in the oil. Add the cardamom, allspice and lemon zest, then pour in the stock and bring to the boil. Reduce the heat and simmer for about 30 minutes, until the lentils are very tender. Cool slightly, then blitz to a coarse-textured purée in a blender. Return to the pan, reheat gently and season to taste.

Heat the butter in a large frying pan and fry the diced bread in it until golden. Stir the lemon juice and the remaining oil into the soup, add the bread croûtons, then garnish with the crushed cardamom and serve immediately.

shoulder of lamb with yoghurt and cardamom

This is one of the great dishes of Middle Eastern cooking. It originates from Persia and is so tender that carving is not necessary; you can simply pull the meat apart with a spoon and fork. Serve with a minted onion and tomato salad and hot grilled pita bread.

SERVES 6—8

1.8kg (4lb) shoulder of lamb, boned and rolled
4 garlic cloves, cut into slivers
4 tablespoons cardamom pods
3 tablespoons olive oil
Juice and grated zest of 1 lemon
¹/₄ teaspoon saffron strands
150g (5oz) Greek yoghurt
2 tablespoons brown sugar
Salt and freshly ground black pepper

Season the lamb with salt and pepper and make some deep cuts in it with a small, sharp knife. Insert the garlic slivers into the cuts. Lightly crush the cardamom pods and remove the seeds, then sprinkle them over the lamb and rub them in. Leave at room temperature for at least 5 hours (or overnight in the fridge).

Preheat the oven to 200°C/400°F/gas mark 6. Heat the oil in a heavy-based roasting tin, add the lamb and brown on all sides. Transfer to the oven and roast for about 20—30 minutes, until well coloured. Remove from the oven and allow to cool slightly while you prepare the lemon yoghurt coating. Reduce the oven temperature to 170°C/325°F/gas mark 3.

Put the lemon juice and saffron in a small pan and heat gently. Leave to cool, then mix with the lemon zest, yoghurt and sugar. Pour half this mixture over the lamb. Return the lamb to the oven and cook, adding more lemon yoghurt every 30 minutes or so, for about 2¹/₂—3 hours, until the lamb is very tender and is topped with a golden yoghurt crust. Allow to cool slightly before serving.

rhubarb and cardamom flognarde

Flognarde is a classic batter pudding from the Auvergne. To all intents and purposes it is identical to the famous clafoutis, made in homes all over France.

250g (9oz) caster sugar
750g (1lb 10oz) rhubarb, cut into 2.5cm (1in) lengths
100ml (3¹/2 fl oz) full-fat milk
150ml (¹/4 pint) whipping cream
1 teaspoon freshly ground cardamom
¹/2 vanilla pod, slit open lengthways
4 eggs
20g (³/4 oz) cornflour
2 tablespoons kirsch
Icing sugar for dusting

Put half the sugar in a large saucepan, add 100ml (3¹/2 fl oz) water and heat gently until the sugar has dissolved. Bring to a gentle simmer, add the rhubarb, then raise the heat a little and cook for 3–4 minutes, until the rhubarb is just tender. Remove from the heat and drain, then spread the rhubarb out on a clean tea-towel to get rid of excess moisture.

Put the milk, cream, cardamom and vanilla pod in a pan and gently bring to the boil, then remove from the heat and leave to infuse for 5 minutes.

Preheat the oven to 180°C/350°F/gas mark 4. In a large bowl, whisk the eggs and the remaining sugar together until creamy. Add the cornflour and kirsch and whisk well. Strain in the hot milk mixture through a sieve and whisk again.

Butter 4 individual gratin dishes, about 250ml (9fl oz) in capacity, and divide the rhubarb between them. Pour over the cream mixture and bake for 15–20 minutes, until golden and slightly souffléed. Dust with icing sugar and serve, with soured cream or vanilla ice-cream.

PG TIP (Right) To test if your bread is cooked, turn it out of the tin and tap the base with your knuckles; it should sound hollow. Alternatively, insert a cocktail stick in the centre and check if it comes out clean.

green cardamom and apricot bread

This is a Swedish speciality, traditionally served on festive occasions. Here it is baked in loaf tins but it is more usually braided into plaits.

MAKES 2 LOAVES

25g (1oz) dried yeast
500ml (18fl oz) full-fat milk
150g (5oz) unsalted butter, diced
2 eggs
5 tablespoons honey
1 teaspoon freshly ground green cardamom
1.5kg (3lb 5oz) strong white flour
100g (3¹/2 oz) dried apricots, chopped
4 tablespoons flaked almonds

Put the yeast in a bowl, add 125ml (4fl oz) warm water and stir until the yeast has dissolved. Set aside. Bring the milk to the boil in a pan, add the butter and remove from the heat. Leave until the butter has melted. Put the eggs, honey and cardamom in a large bowl and beat until well combined. Add the milk and mix again. Gradually mix in 500g (1lb 2oz) of the flour, then leave to cool slightly. Add the dissolved yeast and enough of the remaining flour to make a workable, elastic dough. Turn out on to a floured surface and knead for about 10 minutes, until smooth and pliable, adding more flour if necessary. Place in a greased bowl, cover with a damp cloth and leave to rise in a warm place for 1 hour or until doubled in size.

Punch the dough down, turn out and knead again for 1 minute. Return to the bowl, cover and leave to rise again until doubled in size. Punch down one more time, then divide the dough in half and place in 2 greased 900g (2lb) loaf tins. Leave to rise again, for about 30 minutes this time. Meanwhile, preheat the oven to 190°C/375°F/gas mark 5.

Sprinkle the loaves liberally with the apricots and almonds and bake for 25–30 minutes, until golden brown. Turn out on to a wire rack to cool.

chillies

Following my book *Raising the Heat*, which expounds the virtues of chillies and other 'hot' ingredients, I still relish the opportunity to cook with chillies at any time, so you will see them regularly throughout these pages.

DESCRIPTION

All chillies and peppers belong to the Capsicum family. While most sweet peppers (along with a few of the hot varieties like the Carliston pepper) come from *Capsicum annum*, most of the small, pungent chilli varieties fall under the category *Capsicum frutescens*. There are hundreds of varieties of chilli grown widely throughout the world (in Mexico, China, Japan and Indonesia), of all different shapes, sizes and colours – not to mention pungencies. To the average cook, chillies are merely hot, very hot or mind-blowing, but to the true chilli lover each has a particular aroma and flavour. Unfortunately, however, relatively few varieties of chilli have yet beaten a path to the average British supermarket or food shops.

The most common chillies are listed below, but, as a general rule, the smaller the chilli, the hotter the beast! For example, the small red Thai chilli (or Birds Eye as it is known), is hot and mind-blowing. Scotch Bonnet or Habanero have extremely hot qualities that will probably only really be appreciated by chilli aficionados. Do not to be fooled by the colour: some small green chillies can also be extremely hot. And long chillies are generally hotter than round ones. When recipes in this book simply call for red chillies, use larger red or green chillies unless otherwise stated.

Small red chillies (or Birds Eye chillies): These are tiny, blisteringly hot, pointed chillies, usually not more than 2.5cm (1in) long. Traditionally used in Thai and Chinese cooking. Use with care.

Large red chillies (Lombok): These long, red chillies originate from Indonesia and are now commonly found in food shops simply labelled mild chillies. They provide a good starting-out variety for those taking the plunge with chillies for the first time.

Small green chillies (Jalepeños): A torpedo-shaped, bright green chilli from Mexico. It was originally a very hot chilli, although it now seems to vary and can be mild. The Jalepeño can also be sold ripe and red, when it is slightly sweeter and less hot. These chillies should be used with care as they vary from batch to batch. Cutting one open and running your fingers over the seeds will generally give an indication of the intensity of that particular lot: this test should merely cause a slight tingle.

Large green chillies: Again, the larger variety is less hot than the smaller green variety; use for general recipes throughout the book.

Dried chillies: Buying dried chillies can be as confusing as buying fresh ones, and specialist shops stock numerous varieties. They are generally used in Mexican cooking and vary tremendously in heat. In some of the recipes I have used dried chilli flakes, which are a safe bet for most dishes because the vein and seeds have been removed.

Chilli powder is also available, and although it takes a lot of the hard work out of preparation I do not recommend it except as a last resort.

BUYING AND STORING

When buying fresh chillies, select only those that are plump, firm, shiny and unwrinkled, especially close to the stem. Stored in the fridge, they will last for several weeks. Remove any that seem to be getting soft as they will quickly rot and spoil the rest. Buy dried chillies in small quantities and store in a cool dark place.

PREPARATION

Chillies have little aroma, but vary enormously in taste. Capsaicin, the pungent irritant constituent that gives chillies their ultimate kick, is present in the vein and seeds of the chilli (more so than the skin), depending on the species and the state of ripeness. To reduce the heat in a dish, I suggest removing both the vein and seeds before use. One

word of caution: when handling chillies, wash your hands well and avoid touching your eyes, or any sensitive areas or cuts.

CULINARY USES

Fresh chillies are generally associated with Asian and Mexican cooking, but they are also widely used across South America, the Caribbean and West Africa, where many regional recipes call for the more dramatic chillies (such as the Habanero and Scotch Bonnet). Mexican Tex Mex, chilli con carne and chilli rellenos (deep-fried whole stuffed chillies cooked in batter) have become firm favourites in the West too. Chillies are also, of course, used extensively in Chinese (particularly Sichuan), Thai and other South-east Asian cooking – from salads (like the particularly fiery *Som Tam*) to traditional sambals. The seeds are also often left in, for extra heat!

Many curry pastes (such as red, green and yellow Thai pastes) and sauces have a chilli base. In Morocco, couscous is traditionally served with a fiendishly hot chilli sauce called harissa. Chillies also form the base of many commercial products such as chilli sauce and Tabasco, and seasonings such as paprika and cayenne pepper.

HOW TO SOFTEN THE BLOW

Beware of over indulgence – chillies can burn and cause considerable discomfort. Another word of warning: never drink water to dull the pain after eating very hot chilli – it only heightens the heat. Instead, eat some bread or yoghurt, or drink some milk, to neutralise the effect.

OTHER USES

Chillies have antiseptic properties and are apparently a constituent of sticking plasters. They are said to stimulate digestion and awaken appetite. They also have a very high vitamin C content. Chillies are used in meat preservation and, in some cultures, were used as a means of torture!

complementary flavours

GARLIC

NAM PLA (THAI FISH SAUCE)

SHALLOTS

LIMES

BLACK BEANS

COCONUT MILK

LEMONGRASS

YOGHURT

GINGER

nuoc cham mackerel salad

Nuoc cham (or sometimes *nuoc mam*) is a condiment based on the fish sauce of the same name. Used as freely as salt and pepper, it is popular all over Vietnam, although it does vary slightly in character from place to place.

In Asia, fresh mackerel is a popular fish because it is cheap and widely available. Here I have substituted smoked mackerel, which gives the dish an unusual smoky flavour that permeates the dressing.

1/2 cucumber

1cm (1/2in) piece of fresh root ginger, peeled and finely chopped

400g (14oz) smoked mackerel fillet, skinned and flaked

4 spring onions, shredded

200g (7oz) beansprouts

1 teaspoon black sesame seeds

FOR THE NUOC CHAM:

3 tablespoons palm sugar (or demerara sugar)

4 garlic cloves, crushed

2 red chillies (or 1 Thai chilli), finely sliced

Juice of 2 limes

2 tablespoons *nuoc mam* (Vietnamese fish sauce) or *nam pla* (Thai fish sauce)

3 shallots, thinly sliced

Put all the ingredients for the *nuoc cham* in a bowl and mix until the sugar has dissolved. Leave for 2 hours for the flavours to meld.

Cut the cucumber in half lengthways and scrape out the seeds with a teaspoon. Thinly slice the cucumber into long strips lengthways, using a vegetable peeler. Place in a bowl, add the ginger, flaked mackerel, spring onions and beansprouts and pour over the *nuoc cham* dressing. Toss lightly together. Place on a serving plate, sprinkle over the sesame seeds and serve.

spice-grilled pumpkin salad

1 garlic clove, crushed

1 teaspoon ground cumin

2 red chillies, finely chopped

4 tablespoons rice wine vinegar

1 tablespoon soft brown sugar

2 tablespoons *ketjap manis* (Indonesian soy sauce)

3 tablespoons olive oil

1 tablespoon dark sesame oil

1 small pumpkin (or butternut squash), deseeded and cut into wedges

2 tablespoons chopped coriander (optional)

Place the garlic, cumin, chillies, vinegar and sugar in a saucepan, bring to the boil, then reduce the heat and simmer until the mixture has reduced to a light syrup. Transfer to a large bowl and add the *ketjap manis*, olive oil and sesame oil.

Cook the pumpkin wedges in boiling salted water for 10 minutes, then drain well and place in the chilli oil. Leave to marinate for 1 hour.

Heat a ridged grill pan, place the pumpkin pieces on it and cook for 10–12 minutes, until caramelised, turning regularly. Serve warm, sprinkled with the coriander, if liked.

crisp chilli-coconut sea bream

750g (1lb 10oz) sea bream fillets, skinned
2 red chillies, deseeded and finely chopped
4 tablespoons light soy sauce
1 tablespoon finely chopped coriander
Juice of 2 limes
100ml (3$^{1}/_{2}$ fl oz) *nam pla* (Thai fish sauce)
4 tablespoons beer
1 tablespoon olive oil
40g (1$^{1}/_{2}$oz) plain flour
65g (2$^{1}/_{2}$oz) cornflour
Vegetable oil for deep-frying
3 tablespoons unsweetened dried coconut

TO SERVE:
Steamed jasmine rice (or basmati rice)
150ml ($^{1}/_{4}$ pint) *nam jim* (see page 102)
Coriander leaves
2 limes or lemons, cut into wedges

Cut the bream fillets into thumb-sized strips. Place in a bowl, add half the chilli, plus the soy sauce, coriander, lime juice and half the fish sauce. Cover and leave to marinate at room temperature for 30 minutes.

In a blender, blitz the remaining chilli with the remaining fish sauce, plus the beer, olive oil, flour and cornflour. Add enough water to form a light batter and then leave to stand for 10 minutes.

Heat the vegetable oil in a deep-fat fryer or large, deep saucepan to 180°C/350°F (or until a cube of day-old bread browns in 30 seconds). Remove the pieces of fish from the marinade and dip them into the batter so they are lightly coated, then into the coconut. Fry in the hot oil for 2–3 minutes, until golden and crisp (do this in batches, if necessary). Serve with rice and lots of *nam jim* dressing, garnished with coriander leaves and lime or lemon wedges.

asian-style dirty rice

Dirty rice is a Cajun dish, usually made with chicken livers and lots of pepper and served with chicken. This is my own, Asian-inspired, style of dirty rice, using the cooking liquid from black beans to give the rice a dark grey colour.

Black beans, available in tins from Chinese food shops, are small soy beans that have been preserved with salt and spices and cooked. I cook them for a further 30 minutes to create a wonderful, fragrant stock in which to cook the rice.

400g (14oz) cooked salted black beans, roughly chopped
50g (2oz) unsalted butter
300g (11oz) long grain rice
1 green chilli, deseeded and sliced
1 red chilli, deseeded and sliced
500g (1lb 2oz) raw tiger prawns, shelled, de-veined (see Tip below) and finely chopped
1 teaspoon ground cumin
2 tablespoons chopped coriander
6 spring onions, chopped
2 tablespoons *nam pla* (Thai fish sauce)
2 tablespoons light soy sauce

Put the black beans in a saucepan, cover with 750ml (1¹/₄ pints) of water, then bring to the boil and simmer for 30 minutes. Drain well, reserving the cooking liquid.

Gently heat the butter in large, wide saucepan, add the rice and cook for 1 minute. Add the chillies, prawns and cumin and cook for a minute longer. Add the cooking liquid from the beans and bring to the boil. Reduce the heat, cover and cook for 20 minutes, until the rice is tender. Add the cooked black beans, coriander and spring onions. Mix well, season with the fish sauce and light soy sauce and serve.

PG TIP To de-vein prawns, remove the shells, then run the tip of a sharp knife down the back of the prawn and lift out the thin black thread (intestinal vein).

chilli-crab noodle omelette

150g (5oz) fresh rice noodles
8 organic or free range eggs
2 teaspoons *nam pla* (Thai fish sauce)
1 red chilli, deseeded and finely chopped
1 tablespoon chopped coriander
Oil for frying
4 spring onions, shredded on the diagonal
150g (5oz) fresh crabmeat
Salt and freshly ground black pepper

Cook the rice noodles in a large pan of boiling water for about 5 minutes, until tender, then drain well and dry. Set aside.

Beat the eggs in a bowl with the fish sauce, chilli, half the coriander and some salt and pepper.

Heat 2 tablespoons of oil in a frying pan, add the spring onions and cook for 1 minute. Add the crab and warm through, then season to taste. Keep warm.

Heat a little oil in an omelette pan, add a quarter of the noodles and toss for 30 seconds to reheat them. Pour in a quarter of the beaten egg mixture and cook, drawing in the egg mixture from the sides of the pan, until set underneath. Spoon a quarter of the crab mixture down the centre of the omelette, fold in half and turn out on to a warm plate and keep warm while you cook the remaining 3 omelettes in the same way. Serve immediately, sprinkled with a little of the remaining coriander.

chocolate

Understandably, chocolate finds favour almost everywhere and it can be prepared and served in all manner of ways, from luscious desserts to surprisingly interesting fish, meat and vegetable dishes. Some may reject chocolate on health grounds: it has been associated with allergic reactions, depression, migraines, ulcers, and is said to heighten hyper-activity in children. Others believe it has aphrodisiac qualities. However, many of these contra-indications are yet to be proven – which is just as well as, let's face it, chocolate is for many (myself included) simply irresistible.

recipes

Sometimes called 'the food of the gods', chocolate has a long history. The Mayans were the first to establish cacao plantations (in Yucatán, in Mexico), around AD 600. Around the same time, the Aztecs made a bitter drink called Xocolat from roasted crushed cocoa beans whisked into boiling water and flavoured with honey and chilli. Cocoa was as precious as gold in Aztec towns, where 100 beans could buy a slave and ten could buy the favours of a woman – even taxis were paid in cocoa beans.

Europe was first introduced to cacao in 1502 by Columbus who, having encountered it in Nicaragua, presented it to the Spanish court of King Ferdinand and Queen Isabella. A little later, Hernando Cortés, a conquistador, tasted Xocolat at the court of King Montezuma, and on his return it soon became the preferred beverage of the Spanish aristocracy, sweetened with a little sugar. Much later, this became the hot chocolate beverage we all know and serve to this day as a warming, comforting drink.

It was not until late the eighteenth century, however, that the first eating chocolate was produced, flavoured with vanilla to cater for European tastes.

DESCRIPTION

Chocolate is made from the beans of the evergreen cacao tree (*Theobroma cacao*), which is mainly indigenous to the rainforests of South America, all within 20° latitude of the equator.

The oval pods are harvested by hand twice a year, in late spring/early summer and again in winter. As the pods ripen, they turn from light green to vibrant reds and golden yellow, and are then cut from the trees. The harvested fruit is collected, the pods are hooked open to reveal the beans and they are assessed for ripeness. The beans themselves are covered in a thick, pulpy, white substance, naturally high in sugar but with a tart taste.

The beans are then dried in the sun, and must be continually shuffled to ensure even drying. Next they are shelled, to expose the nibs or kernels, then roasted and ground to produce a thick, dark brown viscous matter known as cocoa mass or liquor. This is then refined, and the fat content or cocoa butter is extracted to leave a solid cake, which is then ground into what we know as cocoa powder.

Chocolate-making begins when sugar and natural vanilla are added to the cocoa liquor, which after various processes is cooled and shaped. It is a highly processed commodity which explains why the better qualities are expensive. The better the chocolate, the higher the price. Chocolate is produced plain (dark), milk (semi-sweet), white, or as cocoa powder. Plain (dark) chocolate gives the best flavour, milk is sweeter and softer, and white is mainly all cocoa butter.

Plain (Dark): Also known as bitter or unsweetened chocolate, this variety must contain a minimum of 34 per cent cocoa solids (mass or butter). The

higher the percentage of solids the better the quality; look out for 50–70 per cent varieties. Usually the higher the percentage, the darker and less sweet the chocolate will be. There are many excellent concentrated varieties available; for me Valrhona is the best with 72 + per cent cocoa solids, although it is difficult to find except through specialist kitchen shops or chocolate shops.

Milk (Semi-sweet): This is made in a similar way, but contains less cocoa mass. In its place, milk powder is added, making it sweeter and milder in flavour. It is generally used as an eating chocolate. I sometimes use it in mousses, when dark is not readily available.

White: This does not contain any cocoa mass, and is in fact a mixture of cocoa butter and sugar with flavourings and milk powder added. It has nowhere near the depth of flavour of dark chocolate and is more usually eaten in chocolate bar form. The best varieties are always creamy in colour, never really white. The Lindt brand is particularly acceptable, I find.

Cocoa powder: The mass that remains when the extraction of the cocoa butter and liquor is completed is ground to form cocoa powder, which is used in cooking or to make a drink.

CULINARY USES

When using chocolate in cooking, I generally break it into bite-size pieces, which makes it easier to melt. Place the chocolate pieces in a bowl over a pan of simmering water and allow to melt, stirring occasionally. When smooth and silky, remove from the heat. If I'm in a hurry, I sometimes melt chocolate in the microwave on a medium heat. Take care not to overheat as it makes the chocolate grainy. In certain dishes, particularly sauces, I find it best to grate the chocolate before adding.

In Italy, a little chocolate is added to a sweet and sour vegetable dish called Caponata. The Europeans, especially the Germans, have long used it in rich sauces served with venison, hare and game birds. In Mexico, the birthplace of chocolate, the beans are roasted very dark and are mixed with cinnamon or almonds (not just vanilla) and added to molés or sauces to give them a smooth, interesting flavour.

Chocolate adds a mellow silkiness to savoury dishes and rounds out flavour – especially when combined with chillies, as in Mole Poblano (Turkey in Chocolate Sauce – see page 37).

Of course, chocolate is also used to flavour a huge number of desserts, gateaux, mousses, biscuits and drinks.

CHOCOLATE TIPS

To prepare a simple decoration for chocolate desserts, pull a potato peeler evenly across the surface of a chocolate bar at room temperature to produce chocolate shavings.

Or, dip the underside of fresh dry leaves with raised veins (such as bay leaves or rose leaves) in melted chocolate. Leave to set hard, then carefully peel away the leaf to reveal the chocolate replica. Basil leaves can similarly be dipped, for a completely edible decoration.

complementary flavours

NUTS

CARAMEL

COFFEE AND TEA
(ESPECIALLY EARL GREY)

DRIED FRUIT (ESPECIALLY
DRIED APRICOTS AND PEARS)

FRESH FRUIT (ESPECIALLY
RASPBERRIES AND PEARS)

ALCOHOL (ESPECIALLY RUM,
CRÈME DE CACAO, COGNAC
AND VODKA)

HERBS (ROSEMARY, MINT,
LAVENDER AND BASIL)

SPICES (CINNAMON, GINGER,
VANILLA, SAFFRON AND
STAR ANISE)

CHILLIES

braised monkfish with chocolate sauce

An interesting dish of braised fish in a smooth red wine and chocolate sauce with a hint of spice. Curiously enough, the chocolate gives the sauce a wonderfully silky texture but does not taste too sweet.

1kg (2¹/₄lb) monkfish fillet, cut in 2.5cm (1in) dice
4 tablespoons olive oil
150ml (¹/₄ pint) fish stock
150ml (¹/₄ pint) veal stock (or chicken stock)
16 button onions, peeled
125g (4¹/₂ oz) streaky bacon, cut into lardons
   (little strips)
12 button mushrooms
25g (1oz) best-quality dark chocolate (at least
   70% cocoa solids), grated
25g (1oz) chilled unsalted butter, cut into small
   pieces
1 tablespoon chopped parsley
Salt and freshly ground black pepper

FOR THE MARINADE:
400ml (14fl oz) red wine
600ml (1 pint) orange juice
1 bay leaf
1 red chilli, deseeded and finely chopped
1 garlic clove, crushed
1 carrot, finely chopped
1 celery stick, finely chopped
1 onion, finely chopped

Put the diced monkfish in a bowl and pour over the red wine and orange juice. Add all the remaining marinade ingredients, then cover and leave to marinate for 1 hour.

Strain the monkfish and vegetables, reserving the marinade. Heat the oil in a casserole, add the monkfish and season with salt and pepper. Fry for 2 minutes, then add the vegetables from the marinade and cook for 1 minute. Pour over the marinade and stock, cover with a lid and simmer for 6–8 minutes, until the monkfish is cooked. Remove the fish and keep warm. Return the sauce to the boil, add the button onions, then reduce the heat and simmer until the onions are tender and the sauce has thickened enough to coat the back of a spoon.

Heat a frying pan without any oil, add the bacon lardons and fry for 2–3 minutes, until crisp and golden. Add the mushrooms and fry until golden, then add to the sauce. Remove the sauce from the heat and stir in the grated chocolate, then whisk in the butter until smooth. Return the monkfish to the sauce, sprinkle with the parsley and serve.

mole poblano (turkey in chocolate sauce) Turkey in chocolate sauce?

It might sound outrageous but it is a treasured national dish of Mexico, dating from the seventeenth century, when it was prepared with over a hundred ingredients. Even today, it remains a favourite for weddings, baptisms and other festive occasions. My version, by the way, is far less complicated but still wonderfully tasty. I like to serve it with white rice and freshly toasted tortillas. You could substitute chicken for the turkey, if you prefer.

SERVES 8—10

1 small turkey, about 4kg (9lb), jointed into small
    serving pieces
4 garlic cloves
2 onions, roughly chopped
100ml (3^1/$_2$ fl oz) vegetable oil
1 cinnamon stick
^{1}/$_4$ teaspoon ground aniseed
75g (3oz) almonds
75g (3oz) peanuts
150g (5oz) ancho chillies, cut lengthways in half and
    deseeded
75g (3oz) pasilla chillies, cut lengthways in half and
    deseeded
50g (2oz) chipotle chillies, cut lengthways in half
    and deseeded
2 corn tortillas
400g (14oz) can of chopped tomatoes
50g (2oz) best-quality dark chocolate (at least 70%
    cocoa solids), grated
1 tablespoon sugar

2 tablespoons sesame seeds, toasted, to garnish
Salt and freshly ground black pepper

Place the turkey pieces in a large pan with 1 clove of garlic, cut into slices, and half the chopped onions. Cover with water and bring to the boil. Poach for up to 1 hour, until the turkey is just tender, then remove from the heat, drain and reserve the stock, and set aside.

For the sauce, heat 2 tablespoons of the oil in a large frying pan, add the turkey pieces and fry until golden. Remove from the pan and set aside. Crush the remaining garlic and add to the pan with the remaining onions. Cook for 5–6 minutes, until softened, then add the cinnamon, aniseed and nuts and sauté for a further 2–3 minutes.

In a separate pan, heat another tablespoon of the oil and fry the dried chillies over a low heat for 2 minutes, ensuring they do not burn or they will taste bitter. Place in a bowl, cover with hot water and leave to soak for 30 minutes. Drain in a colander.

Now place the sweated onions, garlic and nuts in a blender, add the corn tortillas, tomatoes and soaked chillies and blitz to a fine purée. Heat the remaining oil in a large pan, add the purée and bring to the boil. Reduce the heat and simmer for 5 minutes, then add 600ml (1 pint) of the turkey stock and the chocolate. Stir in the sugar and some salt and pepper. Return the turkey pieces to the sauce and reheat gently for 20 minutes. If the sauce is too thick, add a little more stock.

Transfer to a serving bowl, sprinkle with the toasted sesame seeds and serve.

PG TIP If you can't get hold of the dried chillies, replace with one teaspoon dried chilli ppwder

chocolate rosemary custards

150ml (¹/₄ pint) sweet white wine
150ml (¹/₄ pint) full-fat milk
300ml (¹/₂ pint) double cream
2 teaspoons chopped rosemary
6 egg yolks
50g (2oz) caster sugar
150g (5oz) good-quality milk chocolate, coarsely
  chopped

Put the wine, milk, cream and rosemary in a saucepan and bring slowly to the boil. Set side and leave to infuse for 10 minutes. In a bowl, whisk together the egg yolks and sugar until creamy. Strain the milk mixture on to the egg and sugar mixture, whisking constantly. Return to the pan and cook, stirring, over a low heat until the mixture has thickened enough to coat the back of the spoon (do not let it boil or it will curdle).

Put the chocolate in a bowl, pour on the thickened custard and leave for 2–3 minutes to allow the chocolate to melt. Stir it gently, so it doesn't become aerated. Pour into 8 small tea cups or ramekins and leave in the fridge overnight. Serve chilled.

no-nonsense chocolate soufflé

The thought of making a soufflé is a frightening one for many cooks – such a complicated procedure and the worry of a collapsed mess at the end. This recipe is made from just four ingredients, plus a little icing sugar for dusting, and is simple in every sense. Try it!

25g (1oz) unsalted butter, plus extra for greasing
Icing sugar for dusting
150g (5oz) good-quality dark chocolate (at least
  40% cocoa solids)
6 eggs, separated
30g (1¹/₄oz) caster sugar

Preheat the oven to 200°C/400°F/gas mark 6. Generously butter four 200ml (7fl oz) soufflé dishes and lightly dust them with icing sugar. Set aside.

Break up the chocolate and put it in a bowl with the butter. Set the bowl over a pan of gently simmering water and leave to melt. (Alternatively you could melt the chocolate and butter in a microwave.)

Put the egg yolks and 20g (³/₄oz) of the sugar in a large bowl, set this over another pan of hot water, and whisk with an electric hand-held beater until the mixture has thickened and doubled in volume. Remove from the heat. Pour the melted chocolate on to the egg yolks and fold it in.

In a separate bowl, whisk the egg whites with the remaining sugar until they form stiff peaks, then fold them carefully into the chocolate mixture with a large metal spoon. Pour the mixture into the prepared soufflé dishes so they are three-quarters full, then place on a baking sheet. Place in the oven to bake for 10–12 minutes, until well risen and beautifully light. Dust with icing sugar and serve immediately.

PG TIP At the Lanesborough, vanilla ice-cream is a particular favourite with chocolate soufflé and I find raspberry sorbet always complements it a treat, too.

velvet chocolate mousse with mint glass biscuits

A new twist on the After Eight, no less! A rich, creamy mousse, sandwiched between the crispest mint wafers imaginable. Chocolate and mint are a great combination. Serve with vanilla custard, if liked.

375ml (13fl oz) double cream
350ml (12fl oz) full-fat milk
6 egg yolks
125g (4^1/$_2$ oz) caster sugar
2 gelatine leaves
375g (13oz) good-quality dark chocolate (at least 70% cocoa solids), chopped

FOR THE MINT GLASS BISCUITS:
2 tablespoons mint leaves
100g (3^1/$_2$ oz) unsalted butter
100ml (3^1/$_2$ fl oz) golden syrup
50ml (2fl oz) crème de menthe
200g (7oz) caster sugar
100g (3^1/$_2$ oz) plain flour

Bring the cream and milk to the boil in a saucepan. In a separate bowl, whisk together the egg yolks and sugar until light and creamy. Whisking constantly, pour in the cream and milk and stir well. Return to the pan and cook, stirring, over a low heat, until the mixture has thickened enough to coat the back of the spoon (do not let it boil or it will curdle). Remove from the heat.

Cover the gelatine leaves with cold water and leave to soak for 5 minutes. Drain well, squeezing out excess water, and add to the custard mixture. Stir well to dissolve the gelatine.

Place the chocolate pieces in a bowl, pour over the hot custard and leave to melt, stirring occasionally. When all the chocolate has melted, strain the mixture through a fine sieve into a bowl. Leave to cool, then cover with clingfilm and place in the fridge for at least 4 hours, until set.

To make the biscuits, blanch the mint leaves for 10 seconds in a pan of boiling water, then drain well, refresh in iced water and pat dry. Chop finely and set aside. Put the butter, golden syrup and crème de menthe in a saucepan and heat gently until the butter has melted. Mix the sugar and flour together in a bowl, then pour in the syrup mixture, add the chopped mint and stir well to form a paste. Cover with clingfilm and leave in the fridge for about 1 hour, until very cold.

Preheat the oven to 180°C/350°F/gas mark 4. Remove the biscuit mixture from the fridge and, using the palms of your hands, shape into 12 balls, 2.5cm (1in) in diameter. Place them well spaced out on 2 baking sheets lined with baking parchment and press each one out with your fingers to form a small disc; as they cook they will spread out into thin biscuits. Bake for 8–10 minutes, until pale golden, then remove from the oven and leave to cool and crisp up. Store in a sealed container until ready to use.

To serve, place one mint biscuit on each serving plate, top with a scoop of chocolate mousse, then another biscuit and then another scoop of mousse (you will probably find that there is some mousse left over but it won't hang around for long!). Finally, top with the last biscuit.

PG TIP You will probably have some of the biscuit mixture left over. Shape it into balls, as above, and then store in the fridge or freezer, ready to bake.

chocolate and hazelnut polenta
This rich chocolate and cornmeal pudding comes from South America. It has the characteristics of a soufflé but not quite the lightness. It is, however, utterly delicious and very moreish!

SERVES 8

450g (1lb) good-quality dark chocolate (at least 40% cocoa solids)
100g (3¹/₂ oz) Nutella (or other chocolate-hazelnut spread)
100g (3¹/₂ oz) unsalted butter, plus extra for greasing
50g (2oz) quick-cook polenta (cornmeal)
300ml (¹/₂ pint) full-fat milk
6 egg yolks
8 egg whites
100g (3¹/₂ oz) caster sugar, plus extra for dusting

TO SERVE:
Vanilla or hazelnut ice-cream
Chocolate sauce (see page 42)

Preheat the oven to 200°C/400°F/gas mark 6. Break up the chocolate and put it in a bowl set over a pan of gently simmering water. Leave to melt, then stir in the Nutella.

Meanwhile, melt the butter in a saucepan, stir in the polenta and cook for 2–3 minutes. Stir in the milk, reduce the heat and cook, stirring, over a low heat for 5–10 minutes, until thickened. Stir the cooked polenta into the chocolate mixture, then beat in the egg yolks one at a time.

Generously butter eight 7.5cm (3in) ramekins, dust with caster sugar and set aside. With an electric mixer, beat the egg whites until stiff, adding the sugar gradually. Fold the egg whites into the chocolate polenta mixture. Fill the prepared ramekins with the mixture and bake for 20–25 minutes, until the tops begin to split. Serve hot, topped with a good dollop of vanilla or hazelnut ice-cream and some chocolate sauce.

chocolate and ginger cheesecake
For me, chocolate has always had a great affinity with ginger, and I use them in many combinations. Here is one of my particular favourites.

SERVES 6—8

175g (6oz) chocolate chip cookies, crushed finely in a food processor
50g (2oz) unsalted butter, melted
400g (14oz) good-quality dark chocolate (at least 50% cocoa solids)
50g (2oz) icing sugar
3 pieces of preserved ginger, finely chopped
2 tablespoons syrup from the ginger jar
4 tablespoons dark rum
200g (7oz) fromage frais
125ml (4fl oz) double cream, semi-whipped

TO SERVE:
Whipped cream
Cocoa powder

Oil a 20cm (8in) loose-based cake tin, line the base with greaseproof paper and oil again. Mix together the crushed cookies and melted butter, then press the mixture over the base of the tin. Place in the fridge to set firm.

Break up the chocolate, put it in a large bowl and place it over a pan of gently simmering water. Add the icing sugar, ginger, ginger syrup and rum and stir until the chocolate has melted and the mixture is smooth and glossy. Remove from the heat and leave to cool, stirring occasionally.

Beat in the fromage frais, then fold in the semi-whipped cream. Pour into the tin, cover and place in the fridge for about 3 hours, until set firm. To serve, carefully remove the cheesecake from the tin and cut into wedges. Place on serving plates, top with whipped cream and dust with cocoa powder.

chocolate-dipped florentines

MAKES 20

250g (9oz) unsalted butter

100g (3¹/2 oz) caster sugar

100ml (3¹/2 fl oz) chestnut honey (or other honey)

3 tablespoons liquid glucose (available from
    pharmacists)

3 tablespoons double cream

150g (5oz) candied mixed peel, finely chopped

150g (5oz) hazelnuts, finely chopped

150g (5oz) flaked almonds

100g (3¹/2 oz) best-quality dark chocolate (at least
    70% cocoa solids)

Preheat the oven to 180°C/350°F/gas mark 4. Line a shallow baking tin, about 20 x 25cm (8 x 10in) with baking parchment. Melt the butter in a heavy-based saucepan, add the sugar, honey, glucose and cream and bring to the boil. Boil rapidly until the mixture reaches 110°C/230°F on a sugar thermometer. Remove from the heat, stir in the candied peel and nuts and leave to stand for 1 minute.

Using a spatula, spread the mixture into the lined baking tin, then place in the oven and bake for about 25 minutes, until golden and caramelised. Remove from the oven and leave to cool completely. Cut into twenty 5cm (2in) squares.

Break up the chocolate and put it in a bowl set over a pan of gently simmering water. Stir until melted, then remove from the heat. Dip each florentine into the chocolate, coating just half of it. Place on a wire rack and leave to set. Store in an airtight container.

white chocolate and wild blackberry muffins

MAKES 18

400g (14oz) plain flour

175g (6oz) icing sugar

2¹/2 teaspoons baking powder

A pinch of salt

1 egg

100g (3¹/2 oz) unsalted butter, melted

225ml (8fl oz) full-fat milk

100g (3¹/2 oz) wild blackberries (or frozen
    blackberries)

75g (3oz) good-quality white chocolate, coarsely
    chopped

Preheat the oven to 200°C/400°F/gas mark 6. Sift the flour, sugar, baking powder and salt into a large bowl. In another bowl, whisk the egg until aerated, then gradually whisk in the warm melted butter and the milk. Add to the dry ingredients and mix until only just combined (overmixing will make the muffins tougher in texture). Fold in the berries and chocolate pieces, again being careful not to overmix.

Spoon the mixture into 18 well-buttered deep muffin tins, filling them two-thirds full. Bake for about 20 minutes, until well risen and golden brown. To check if they are done, insert a cocktail stick or skewer in the centre; it should come out clean. Cool the muffins in the tin for a few minutes, then turn out on to a wire rack. They are best served warm, although they are good cold, too.

white chocolate and basil profiteroles with hot chocolate sauce

White chocolate and basil make an interesting twist on this much-loved dessert. The beauty of it is that it can be prepared in advance over several days.

SERVES 4—6

FOR THE WHITE CHOCOLATE AND BASIL ICE-CREAM:

10 basil leaves
200ml (7fl oz) double cream
200ml (7fl oz) full-fat milk
200g (7oz) good-quality white chocolate, broken into
**   small pieces**
4 egg yolks
25g (1oz) caster sugar

FOR THE CHOUX PASTRY:

200ml (7fl oz) full-fat milk
65g (2 1/2 oz) unsalted butter, diced
20g (3/4 oz) caster sugar
125g (4 1/2 oz) plain flour
4 eggs
1 egg yolk, beaten with 2 tablespoons milk
2 tablespoons flaked almonds

FOR THE CHOCOLATE SAUCE:

90g (3 1/2 oz) good-quality dark chocolate (at least
**   40% cocoa solids)**
1/2 tablespoon caster sugar
85ml (3fl oz) double cream
A small knob of butter

To make the ice-cream, tear the basil leaves into small pieces, reserving the stalks, and set aside. Put the stalks in a saucepan with the cream and milk, bring gently to the boil and simmer for 1 minute. Add the white chocolate, stir well, then remove from the heat and leave to infuse for 10 minutes.

In a bowl, whisk together the egg yolks and sugar until creamy. Strain the basil-infused cream on to the egg yolks, whisking constantly, then return to the pan and cook, stirring, over a low heat, until the mixture thickens (do not let it boil or it will curdle). Remove from the heat and leave to cool. Stir in the torn basil leaves, pour into an ice-cream machine and freeze according to the manufacturer's instructions.

Next make the choux pastry. Preheat the oven to 200°C/400°F/gas mark 6. Put the milk, butter and sugar in a medium pan and bring to the boil. As soon as it comes to the boil, quickly rain in the flour and beat with a wooden spoon until the mixture leaves the sides of the pan clean. Allow to cool slightly, then beat in the eggs one by one to give a thick, glossy mixture.

Lightly oil a baking sheet and then sprinkle it with a little water so it is slightly damp. Fit a pastry bag with a 2.5cm (1in) plain nozzle and fill it with the choux pastry. Pipe walnut-sized mounds on to the baking sheet at regular intervals, brush with a little of the beaten egg wash and sprinkle over the flaked almonds. Place in the oven and bake for 15 minutes, then open the oven door slightly and leave for a further 10 minutes so that the profiteroles can dry out. Remove from the oven, pierce each profiterole with a skewer so the steam can escape, then leave to cool (if you make them in advance, store in a biscuit tin).

For the chocolate sauce, place all the ingredients in a pan and bring gently to the boil, then whisk until smooth, adding a little boiling water if it is too thick.

To serve, cut each profiterole in half horizontally (allowing about 3 per person), fill with a ball of the ice-cream and top with the lid. Arrange on serving plates and pour over and around the hot chocolate sauce – pure indulgence!

PG TIP If you don't have an ice-cream machine, pour the ice-cream mixture into a bowl and place it in the freezer. After 30 minutes, when it is beginning to set, remove it from the freezer and beat well with an electric beater or hand blender to disperse any ice crystals, then return it to the freezer. Repeat this 2 or 3 times, then leave until set firm.

cinnamon

True cinnamon and its less refined cousin cassia (*Cinnamomum cassia*) are two of the earliest spices to have been traded between ancient civilisations. References to it are found in the Old Testament in early rituals, while the ancient Egyptians used it for embalming their pharaohs. Roman Emperor Nero reportedly burned his pregnant wife on a cinnamon pyre as a gesture of remorse after murdering her.

True cinnamon is indigenous to Sri Lanka, although it is also grown in India, Indonesia and the Seychelles. The Portuguese colonised Sri Lanka (then Ceylon) for its cinnamon until they were driven out by the Dutch in 1636. The Dutch later controlled prices worldwide by limiting its supply.

DESCRIPTION

Cinnamon is an evergreen tree (*Cinnamomum zeylanicum*) of the laurel family. Sri Lanka is the largest and considered to be the best producer of cinnamon in the world, exporting up to 10,000 tons a year. The spice we use in cooking is the dried inner bark from the branches of the cinnamon tree. This tree can grow as tall as 9–12m (30–40ft) high in the wild, but is cropped when cultivated to 2.4m (8ft) to aid harvesting and to keep the bark both thin and tender.

Harvesting is carried out twice a year, following the rainy seasons in late spring/early summer, and then again in late autumn, when the trees' aromatic oils are at their peak. The finest bark comes from the centre of the plant. The outer bark is carefully scraped away, the paper-thin inner bark is peeled off and rolls naturally into quills as it dries. The rolled quills are eventually tied into large bundles for shipping.

Cinnamon and cassia are very similar, but are different in flavour and in form. Whereas the true cinnamon is rolled, cassia comes as a flat bark which is stronger and sometimes bitter — an inferior relative.

BUYING AND STORING

When buying cinnamon, ensure that quills are long and whole, not chipped. Store in a dry, dark place, wrapped in brown paper. Although good-quality ground cinnamon is readily available, it is easy to grind your own in a spice grinder or blender (some cheaper, ready-ground brands can be lacklustre). Only buy a little at a time, when needed, as it quickly loses its fragrance and the colour fades with age.

CULINARY USES

From a culinary standpoint, cinnamon has a special, somewhat seductive, fragrance and a comforting taste. It flavours sweet and savoury dishes worldwide. In the Far East it is regularly used in rice dishes, especially Malaysian; it is an ingredient in Asian curries, and forms an essential part of garam masala along with cloves, coriander, cardamom and black pepper.

Nearer to home, the Persians created wonderful ingredient dishes with cinnamon, dusted it onto soups and used it to flavour salads and stews. Along with raisins and toasted almonds, it is also used to flavour Persian rice dishes, and is an important ingredient in the spice mix, advieh. In Spain, it is a much-loved commodity which can be traced back to the Moorish occupation. The Spanish add it to pork dishes and dust it over custard desserts.

The Moroccans, whose cuisine I adore, use it in slowly braised stews, tagines and salads. It is an important spice in many Moroccan blends of ras el hanout and forms the main flavour in the classic B'stulla, a savoury yet delicate cinnamon-flavoured pie of pigeon with almonds, eggs and saffron.

In Europe and Britain, the spice is enjoyed in baked goods, bread, apple pies, strudels and as a flavouring in fruit compôtes. It is especially good with pears, plums, apples and in the old recipes for mulled wine. In cooking it can be used whole or freshly ground. I particularly like to use it to flavour milk puddings and custards. It also makes a great ice-cream and is wonderful combined with chocolate in a mousse or sauce. Cinnamon is a spice I could certainly not do without in my kitchen. It is delicate yet intense, as homely as it is comforting, and for me conjures up many happy memories of freshly baked apple pies.

OTHER USES

Cinnamon was prized by ancient physicians for its anti-fungal and anti-bacterial properties and was used in religious ceremonies. Nowadays it is thought to soothe rheumatic pains and its oil is used in the perfume industry.

complementary flavours

MEAT (ESPECIALLY LAMB, CHICKEN AND OTHER WHITE MEATS)

DAIRY PRODUCTS (EGGS, CUSTARDS, ICE-CREAM AND YOGHURT)

CHOCOLATE

NUTS

HONEY

SAFFRON

RICE

COUSCOUS

FRUIT (PEARS, PLUMS, APPLES, ORANGES, CHERRIES, AND APRICOTS)

cinnamon quails

The quails are braised in cinnamon-scented stock, then a little sumac is sprinkled on top before serving. Sumac is the crushed dried berries of the sumac bush and has a pleasant sour lemon flavour. It can be found in Middle Eastern food shops.

25g (1oz) unsalted butter
4 tablespoons vegetable oil
450g (1lb) small shallots, peeled but left whole
75g (3oz) raisins
1 tablespoon best-quality ground cinnamon
750ml (1¼ pints) well-flavoured chicken stock
8 oven-ready quails
75g (3oz) pine kernels, toasted
½ teaspoon sumac
Salt and freshly ground black pepper

Heat the butter and 1 tablespoon of the oil in a saucepan, add the shallots and fry for 2–3 minutes, until golden all over. Add the raisins and cinnamon and cook gently for 5 minutes. Pour in the chicken stock, bring to the boil and simmer for 15–20 minutes.

Heat the remaining oil in a large casserole until very hot. Season the quails and brown them all over in the hot oil. Add the chicken stock, shallots and raisins and bring to the boil. Reduce the heat and simmer for 15 minutes, turning the quails occasionally; the sauce should have reduced a little.

Put the quails in a serving dish, pour over the sauce and sprinkle over the pine kernels and sumac. Serve immediately.

lamb tagine with prunes and cinnamon

This recipe uses all the wonderful flavours of Morocco. The lamb is slow-cooked with ginger and saffron and sweetened with cinnamon, one of Morocco's most popular spices.

4 tablespoons vegetable oil
750g (1lb 10oz) boned leg of lamb, cut into 2.5cm (1in) cubes
2 onions, thinly sliced
2 garlic cloves, crushed
1 tablespoon best-quality ground cinnamon
2.5cm (1in) piece of fresh root ginger, finely chopped
¼ teaspoon saffron strands
1 litre (1¾ pints) lamb stock (or water)
4 tablespoons honey
150g (5oz) whole blanched almonds
175g (6oz) prunes, stoned
2 teaspoons sesame seeds, toasted
Salt and freshly ground black pepper

In a tagine or large casserole, heat the oil until smoking. Add the lamb and fry until golden brown all over (do this in batches if necessary). Add the onions and garlic and cook for 10 minutes, until golden. Sprinkle over half the cinnamon and mix well with the meat. Add the ginger and saffron, cover with the lamb stock or water and bring to the boil. Reduce the heat, cover and cook gently for 1 hour or until the lamb is very tender.

Meanwhile, in a separate pan, heat the honey with the remaining cinnamon. Add the almonds and prunes and cook gently for 2 minutes, until they are glazed.

When the meat is cooked, adjust the seasoning, scatter over the cinnamon-glazed prunes and nuts, sprinkle over the sesame seeds and serve.

date and blood orange salad

A fragrant Moroccan-style salad, highly spiced with *ras el hanout*, a North African spice mix. *Ras el hanout* is made up of some 30 different spices, including dried roses, cardamom, turmeric and cloves. Look for it in Middle Eastern shops and some specialist food shops. Serve this salad as a refreshing side dish.

Juice of 1 lime and 2 lemons
Grated zest of $^1/_2$ lime and 1 lemon
About $^3/_4$ teaspoon ground cinnamon
1 teaspoon orange flower water
2 tablespoons caster sugar

4 blood oranges, peeled and thickly sliced
12 fresh dates, halved, stoned and cut into strips
A pinch of *ras el hanout*

Put the lime and lemon juice and zest in a bowl, add a pinch of the cinnamon, plus the orange flower water and sugar and mix well. Leave for 1 hour at room temperature. Place in a pan and boil for 5 minutes to form a light syrup. Remove from the heat and leave to cool, then chill.

Place the orange slices and dates in a bowl and pour over the chilled syrup. Sprinkle over the ras el hanout, sprinkle over the remaining cinnamon to taste, and serve.

caramelised cinnamon cassata

Cassata is an iced Sicilian dessert usually made with sponge cake or amaretti biscuits. Here I serve these with the dessert rather than using it in the recipe.

SERVES 8

125g (4¹/₂ oz) caster sugar
2 tablespoons freshly ground cinnamon
300ml (¹/₂ pint) full-fat milk
300ml (¹/₂ pint) double cream
8 egg yolks
¹/₂ teaspoon vanilla extract
50g (2oz) mixed almonds, walnuts and hazelnuts,
    lightly toasted and roughly chopped
40g (1¹/₂ oz) mixed candied peel, finely chopped
¹/₂ teaspoon grated lemon zest
125ml (4fl oz) sweet marsala

TO SERVE:

Chocolate sauce (see page 42), lightly flavoured
    with marsala
Amaretti biscuits

Put the sugar and cinnamon in a small, heavy-based pan and heat gently until melted. Raise the heat and cook, without stirring, until it becomes a dark amber colour.

Meanwhile, heat the milk and cream almost to boiling point. When the caramel is ready, whisk it into the cream mixture (take great care; it is best to cover both hands with a cloth as the hot caramel will splatter). Set aside.

In a bowl, whisk the egg yolks and vanilla extract together. Carefully pour on the caramel cream mixture, whisking all the time, then return the mixture to a clean pan and cook, stirring, over a low heat until it has thickened enough to coat the back of the spoon (do not let it boil or it will curdle). Remove from the heat and leave to cool completely. When cool, churn in an ice-cream machine for 20 minutes until just beginning to set, adding the toasted nuts, candied peel, lemon zest and marsala just before the end of the churning process. Line the base of a 1.2 litre (2 pint)

pudding basin or 20cm (8in) springform cake tin with greaseproof paper, fill with the cassata mixture and freeze until required.

To serve, dip the basin or cake tin into hot water and then run a hot knife round the edge. Turn out the cassata on to a plate and cut into wedges. Serve with the chocolate sauce and some amaretti biscuits.

slow-baked tamarillos in cinnamon-wine sauce This very easy

dish is an ideal winter dessert, particularly as tamarillos are now available in most large supermarkets and many greengrocer's shops. If you can't find them, however, plums make a good alternative. It's wonderful served with vanilla ice-cream.

750ml (1¹/₄ pints) Cabernet Sauvignon (or other
    full-bodied red wine)
150g (5oz) soft brown sugar
1 vanilla pod, slit open lengthways
2 cinnamon sticks
1 clove
8 ripe tamarillos, halved

Preheat the oven to 150°C/300°F/gas mark 2. Put the wine, sugar, vanilla pod, cinnamon sticks and clove in a saucepan, bring to simmering point and leave on a low heat for 10 minutes to infuse.

Arrange the tamarillo halves in a single layer in a shallow ovenproof dish, about 25cm (10in) long. Pour over the spiced wine syrup, place in the oven and bake for 40–45 minutes, until the tamarillos are tender, spooning the juices over them a couple of times during baking.

Remove the tamarillos from the dish and keep warm. Strain the sauce through a fine sieve. It should be syrupy and thick; if it is not, pour it into a pan and simmer until it has reduced and thickened enough to coat the back of a spoon. Serve the warm taramillos coated with the sauce.

cinnamon snow eggs with chocolate-cinnamon custard

Snow eggs, also called floating islands, are a classic dessert of which there are many variations. This version includes cinnamon, whose delicate flavour is highly compatible with both eggs and chocolate. It's a marriage made in heaven.

SERVES 6

6 egg whites
A tiny pinch of salt
175g (6oz) caster sugar, mixed with 1 teaspoon best-quality ground cinnamon
25g (1oz) unsalted butter, melted

FOR THE CUSTARD:

300ml (^{1}/$_2$ pint) double cream
150ml (^{1}/$_4$ pint) full-fat milk
1 teaspoon best-quality ground cinnamon
50g (2oz) caster sugar
4 egg yolks
50g (2oz) good-quality milk chocolate, grated or broken into pieces
4 tablespoons dark rum

FOR THE CARAMELISED HAZELNUTS:

50g (2oz) caster sugar
50g (2oz) hazelnuts

Preheat the oven to 130°C/250°F/gas mark ^{1}/$_2$. Put the egg whites and salt in a large, clean bowl and whisk until they form peaks (you can use an electric mixer for this). Gradually mix in the cinnamon sugar and continue whisking until the meringue is stiff.

Lightly grease 6 large dariole moulds or ramekins (about 175–225ml (6–8fl oz) in capacity) with the butter, then fill with the meringue and level off the tops. Tap the moulds on a flat surface to ensure there are no air pockets. Place on a baking tray and bake for 10 minutes at 100°C/200°F/gas mark ^{1}/$_4$, or until just set. Remove from the oven and leave to cool.

For the custard, put the cream, milk, ground cinnamon and half the sugar in a saucepan and bring to the boil. Meanwhile, place the egg yolks and remaining sugar in a bowl and whisk together until pale and creamy. Gradually pour the cinnamon cream on to the egg yolks, whisking constantly. Return the mixture to the saucepan and cook, stirring, until it has thickened enough to coat the back of the spoon (do not let it boil or it will curdle). Remove from the heat, stir in the chocolate and leave until it melts. Strain the custard into a bowl and allow to cool, then stir in the rum.

For the caramelised hazelnuts, put the sugar in a small, heavy-based pan and heat gently until melted. Raise the heat and cook, without stirring, until it becomes a golden amber colour. Add the nuts, stir well, then pour out on to an oiled baking tray. Leave to cool and set, then chop into pieces.

To serve, run a knife around the snow eggs and turn them out on to 6 serving plates. Pour around the custard and sprinkle over the caramelised hazelnuts.

cinnamon milk fritters with hot cherries

750ml (1^1/$_4$ pints) full-fat milk
1 teaspoon vanilla extract
1 tablespoon best-quality ground cinnamon
4 egg yolks
250g (9oz) caster sugar
Grated zest of 1 lemon
125g (4^1/$_2$ oz) plain flour
2 egg whites
100g (3^1/$_2$ oz) fresh white breadcrumbs
Vegetable oil for deep-frying
4 tablespoons cinnamon sugar (see Tip opposite)

450g (1lb) morello cherries (or other fresh cherries), stoned
100g (3¹/₂ oz) preserving sugar (with pectin)
85ml (3fl oz) kirsch

Put the milk, vanilla extract and cinnamon in a saucepan and bring gently to the boil. Meanwhile, beat the egg yolks and sugar together in a bowl until blended, then add the lemon zest and sift in the flour, stirring well. Whisk the boiled milk slowly into the egg mixture, then return to the pan and cook over a medium heat until the custard becomes smooth and thick. Raise the heat to bring it to the boil, then pour into a shallow dish in a layer about 2.5cm (1in) thick. Leave to cool, then transfer to the fridge until set firm.

Meanwhile, prepare the cherries. Put them in a bowl with the sugar and kirsch and mix well. Leave to marinate for 2 hours, during which time they will release their juices. Strain off the juice into a saucepan and simmer until it forms a syrup. Add the cherries and keep warm while you cook the fritters.

To finish the fritters, cut the well-chilled mixture into 7.5cm (3in) squares. Lightly beat the egg whites in a bowl and put the breadcrumbs in another bowl. Dip the custard squares in the egg whites, then dredge them in the breadcrumbs, coating them well all over.

Heat the vegetable oil to 170°C/325°F in a deep-fat fryer or large, deep saucepan. If you are using a saucepan test the temperature of the oil by adding a cube of day-old bread, it should brown in 30 seconds. Fry the fritters a few at a time, until golden and crisp. Remove with a slotted spoon and place in a dish lined with kitchen paper. Dust with the cinnamon sugar and serve with the hot cherries.

PG TIP To make cinnamon sugar, mix 100g (3¹/₂oz) caster sugar with 1 teaspoon of best-quality ground cinnamon and store in an airtight jar.

breakfast brûlée At the Lanesborough we have,

I like to think, a breakfast menu capable of brightening the most jaded palate, ready for the day ahead. A popular dish is this breakfast brûlée, prepared like the classic creme brûlée but with porridge. Try it for breakfast or brunch, topped with some seasonal berries or fruit compôte.

300ml (¹/₂ pint) full-fat milk
A pinch of salt
1 cinnamon stick
4 tablespoons caster sugar
50g (2oz) rolled oats
6 egg yolks
300ml (¹/₂ pint) double cream
4 tablespoons demerara sugar

Bring the milk, salt, cinnamon stick and half the sugar to the boil. Remove from the heat and leave to infuse for 2–3 minutes, then take out the cinnamon stick. Return the pan to the heat and rain in the oats, stirring constantly. Reduce the heat and simmer for 2–3 minutes, then leave to cool.

In another bowl, whisk the egg yolks with the remaining sugar until the sugar has dissolved. Add the double cream and the cooked porridge and mix well.

Preheat the oven to 140°C/275°F/gas mark 1. Divide the porridge custard between 4 shallow gratin dishes, each 200ml (7fl oz) in capacity. Place the dishes in a roasting tin, then place the tin in the oven. Pour enough cold water into the tin to come about half way up the sides of the dishes and bake for 30–35 minutes, until set. Allow to cool for 2 minutes, then sprinkle the brown sugar evenly over the surface of each custard. Use a blowtorch to caramelise the tops, holding it at an angle (the flame should barely touch the surface). Alternatively, caramelise the sugar under a very hot grill.

Serve immediately.

coffee

Over the last five years, coffee has undergone something of revival. Specialist coffee shops and delicatessens are popping up in cities worldwide, and coffee is very much in vogue today.

This was not, however, always the case. Both in America and Britain, coffee consumption dropped rapidly and steadily in the 1970s and 80s by 30–40 per cent, mainly because of growing health concerns. Evidence had begun to surface that linked high coffee consumption with cancer and a number of other serious medical conditions.

Now coffee bars are offering better quality and a greater variety of blends than ever before, so for those like me, who could not live without it (especially to wake up morning spirits!), are now drinking a better tasting brew and becoming more sophisticated in our tastes. Familiarity with cappuccinos, espressos, caffe lattes, mochacinos and other speciality coffees is increasing.

Coffee originated over 100 years ago in North Africa and the wild coffee arabica bush is believed to have been cultivated by African tribesman from the sixth century AD. It is likely that the first berries were chewed, and only later crushed to a wet paste and infused with water. Later still, a more sophisticated coffee was made by fermenting the juice from the ripe berries. Following its inception in Africa, coffee-drinking soon spread quickly to the Middle East (even though the practice was prohibited in Iran in the 1920s as, among other things, coffee was thought to loosen men's tongues), then to central Europe and eventually to Martinique in the West Indies. However the modern drink, as we now know it, was not invented until the thirteenth century, when the beans were cleaned and roasted before infusing.

DESCRIPTION

Coffee grows in the tropics on small, evergreen trees (genus *Coffea*) which bear a fruit that looks like a wild cherry. Each berry contains two small green pods or beans that are released from the fruit by being steeped in water or dried in the sun (wet or dry processing). The manufacturing, wet or dry, affects the final flavour. Wet processing is common in Latin America and parts of Africa where there is plenty of water. The flavour tends to be slightly acidic with citrussy overtones. Countries such as Sumatra and Ethiopia employ the dry method which results in beans with a more earthy, spicy flavour. One tree produces enough beans in one year to yield 450g (1lb) of finished product.

All the world's coffee is grown in a wide band between the Tropics of Cancer and Capricorn. As well as liking warmth, coffee needs moderate rainfall, some shade and good drainage, therefore hillsides are considered the best plantation sites. A coffee tree takes five years to crop. Each tree produces only 1kg (2¼lb) beans per annum.

QUALITIES OF COFFEE

Some of the world's best coffee comes from South America, where Brazil and Columbia are the first and second largest producers in the world. Yet there are more than 100 kinds of coffee from 40 different countries. Quality coffee comes from the coffee arabica plant which is grown at high altitude. The beans from the hardy robusta variety are generally higher in caffeine, inferior in taste and flavour, and used for making instant coffees.

Pure arabica coffees have distinctive flavours. Brazilian coffee, for example, is noted for its smooth richness and somewhat chocolatey taste. Costa Rica produces a mild, popular breakfast

coffee. Jamaican coffee is recognised for its quality and flavour, with famous names such as Blue Mountain. African varieties include Ethiopian (long considered amongst the best in the world) and an especially popular Kenyan (noted for its richness and full fresh flavour). Heavier coffees from Java (smoky and rich with spicy overtones) and Sumatra are particularly favoured in France.

ROASTING COFFEE

Roasting coffee beans develops the flavour and body of the coffee, and brings out the aroma. The beans are only roasted for ten minutes, as any longer would make the coffee bitter.

• Light or pale roasted coffee is good with milk.
• Medium roasted produces a stronger, richer coffee.
• Full roasted is often drunk black.
• High roasted is also called Continental coffee.

BUYING AND STORING

Ideally I find it is best to buy coffee from specialist shops that roast their own beans, thus ensuring freshness. Once roasted, coffee beans lose their aroma after 3–4 days. It is undoubtedly best to grind your own coffee just prior to brewing

it as the aroma is lost even quicker once the beans are ground.

Alternatively, I suggest that you purchase vacuum-packed coffee from supermarkets, which has a decent flavour and aroma. Taste by trial and error, as some smell wonderful but can be disappointing in taste. Store the beans and ground coffee in airtight jars. You can also freeze roasted beans for up to a month in polythene bags and grind them while still frozen for immediate use.

CULINARY USES

As a beverage, coffee can be blended with cocoa powder as mocha, which is valued as an after-dinner drink, with mysore (from southern India), or served as café brulot (a spicy, citrussy blend), calypso coffee (with rum) and Irish coffee (with whiskey), both topped with cream. It is flavoured with spices like cardamom in the Middle East, and with cinnamon, cloves and orange in Mexico. Iced coffee is particularly delicious in hot weather.

Apart from coffee's obvious appeal as a drink, it also plays an important role in desserts and confectionery, cakes and biscuits. I confess to being a bit of a coffee lover and, as a flavouring, I think coffee blends beautifully with many ingredients such as chocolate, berries, nuts and with alcohol such as rum and Tia Maria. The Italians and French are especially fond of coffee in desserts such as mousses and ice-cream (mousse aux café and gelatti) and all manner of wonderful preparations. The hugely popular Italian dessert, tiramisu combines coffee and marscapone cheese. The French also use it to flavour custards (petits pots aux café) and parfaits.

Coffee is used less frequently in savoury dishes although I personally believe it has a role to play – try my Veal Fillet with Mocha Porcini Sauce (page 55).

Plenty of people still consider, as I do, a cup of coffee a small taste of heaven, but remember it has more possibilities in cooking than you suspect.

complementary flavours

CHOCOLATE

NUTS

DAIRY PRODUCTS

FENNEL SEEDS

PRESERVED GINGER

ALCOHOL (MARSALA, RUM, TIA MARIA AND CRÈME DE CACAO)

FRESH COCONUT

FRUIT (BANANAS, PEARS, ORANGES AND RASPBERRIES)

coffee risotto
I featured this unusual sweet risotto in my book, *Great Value Gourmet* (Weidenfeld & Nicolson, 1996). It was a little heretical then but sweet risottos are more common now, and it makes regular appearances on my menu — sometimes on its own, or with poached pears or glazed oranges.

2 tablespoons Camp coffee essence, or 1 tablespoon
   freshly brewed black filter coffee
Juice and grated zest of $^1/_2$ orange
100g ($3^1/_2$ oz) vialone nano risotto rice
600ml (1 pint) milk
2 drops of vanilla extract
100g ($3^1/_2$ oz) caster sugar
25g (1oz) unsalted butter
175ml (6fl oz) whipping cream
2 tablespoons rum (optional)

Place the coffee and orange juice in a saucepan with 150ml ($^1/_4$ pint) of water and bring to the boil. Remove from the heat, add the rice and leave to soak for 5 minutes.

   Return the pan to the heat and add the milk and vanilla extract. Bring to the boil, then reduce the heat and cook gently for 15–18 minutes, until the rice is tender but still slightly firm to the bite. Remove from the heat and add the sugar, orange zest, butter, cream and rum, if using. Stir through gently and serve immediately.

coffee-roasted spare ribs
Everyone loves a barbecue and most of us have our favourite marinades and bastes for adding flavour to meat and fish. Here is an unusual glaze for pork ribs using coffee. Its slightly bitter edge, blended with tomato and spices, gives a wonderful flavour that will surprise you. Bring on the summer, I say!

2 teaspoons dried chilli flakes
150ml ($^1/_4$ pint) strong freshly brewed black
   filter coffee
100ml ($3^1/_2$ fl oz) tomato ketchup
3 garlic cloves, crushed
100ml ($3^1/_2$ fl oz) wine vinegar
3 tablespoons brown sugar
100ml ($3^1/_2$ fl oz) rum
100ml ($3^1/_2$ fl oz) vegetable oil
1 teaspoon ground cumin
$^1/_2$ teaspoon ground coriander
$^1/_8$ teaspoon ground allspice
2 racks of pork spare ribs
Salt

Put everything except the racks and salt in a blender and process to a paste. Season with salt. Coat the racks with the paste, ensuring they are well covered all over. Place in a dish, cover and leave to marinate in the fridge overnight or for at least 8 hours.

   Preheat the oven to 200°C/400°F/gas mark 6. Bring the racks to room temperature, then place in a roasting tin and cook in the oven for 1–1$^1/_2$ hours, brushing then regularly with the marinade. Allow to cool slightly before cutting into individual ribs. Take napkin in hand and begin!

PG TIP Cook these for 20–25 minutes on a berbeque remembering to turn regularly, this gives a lovely smokey flavour to the meet.

veal fillet with mocha porcini

sauce
Here, coffee forms the base of a wonderful wild mushroom sauce, enhanced with red wine and sweet marsala. A creamy celeriac or parsnip purée goes particularly well with this dish.

20g ($^3/_4$ oz) dried porcini mushrooms

85ml (3fl oz) freshly brewed black filter coffee (not espresso)

3 tablespoons vegetable oil

4 x 175g (6oz) veal fillet steaks

25g (1oz) unsalted butter, chilled and cut into small pieces

2 shallots, chopped

1 garlic clove, crushed

1 sprig of thyme

250g (9oz) fresh porcini mushrooms (or chestnut mushrooms), thickly sliced

4 tablespoons good-quality red wine

100ml ($3^1/_2$ fl oz) veal stock (or chicken stock)

85ml (3fl oz) sweet marsala

Salt and freshly ground black pepper

Put the dried porcini in a bowl, pour over the coffee and leave to soak for 30 minutes, until softened. Strain off the liquid and reserve. Chop the mushrooms finely and set aside.

Heat the oil in a large frying pan until very hot, season the veal steaks and fry for 2–3 minutes on each side. Remove from the pan and keep warm, draining off any excess oil left in the pan. Melt 10g ($^1/_4$ oz) of the butter in the pan, then add the shallots, garlic, thyme and soaked dried mushrooms and cook over a high heat for 1 minute. Add the fresh mushrooms and cook for 2 minutes longer. Pour in the red wine, mushroom soaking liquid and stock and boil until the sauce has reduced by half its original volume. Stir in the remaining chilled butter and the marsala and season to taste.

Put the veal steaks on serving plates and coat with the mocha porcini sauce.

pear galettes with coffee and hazelnut meringue

1 quantity of Sweet Pastry (see page 107) or 400g (14oz) shortcrust pastry
4 ripe but firm pears
50g (2oz) unsalted butter
2 tablespoons caster sugar
4 tablespoons poire William liqueur
1 egg, beaten

FOR THE MERINGUE:
2 egg whites
125g (4^1/$_2$ oz) caster sugar
1 tablespoon freshly ground coffee beans
125g (4^1/$_2$ oz) hazelnuts, coarsely ground

Roll out the pastry to approximately 3mm (^{1}/$_8$in) thick and cut out four 15cm (6in) rounds. Place on a lightly greased baking sheet and chill while you cook the pears.

Preheat the oven to 200°C/400°F/gas mark 6. Peel and core the pears, cut them in half vertically, then cut each half into 4 wedges. Heat the butter in a large frying pan, add the pears and sugar and cook for 6–8 minutes, until the pear wedges are beautifully golden and caramelised. Pour over the poire William liqueur and remove from the pan. Leave to cool.

Arrange the caramelised pear wedges in the centre of each pastry round. Fold over the edge of the pastry to form a 2.5cm (1in) border and brush the pastry with the beaten egg. Bake for 15 minutes, then remove from the oven and reduce the oven temperature to 180°C/350°F/gas mark 4.

To make the meringue, whisk the egg whites using an electric mixer with half the sugar until they form stiff peaks. Add the remaining sugar and the ground coffee and whisk again. Finally, fold in the ground hazelnuts.

Top the pear galettes with the coffee meringue and return to the oven for 8–10 minutes to glaze until golden. Serve warm.

coffee and fennel seed biscotti

These delicious crisp, fragrant biscuits are great served with morning coffee or with dessert. Surprisingly, instant coffee powder gives a better flavour than freshly ground coffee, although both work well.

100g (3^1/$_2$ oz) vanilla sugar (see page 177)
1 egg
2 tablespoons aniseed liqueur, such as Ricard or Pernod
1 teaspoon vanilla extract
100g (3^1/$_2$ oz) plain flour, sifted
^{1}/$_2$ teaspoon baking powder
A pinch of salt
2 tablespoons instant coffee powder
50g (2oz) raisins
50g (2oz) almonds, toasted
1 teaspoon fennel seeds, toasted

Preheat the oven to 170°C/325°F/gas mark 3. In a bowl, beat together the vanilla sugar, egg, Ricard and vanilla until thick and pale. Mix together the flour, baking powder, salt and coffee powder and add to the bowl. Stir until well combined, then mix in the raisins, almonds and fennel seeds. Turn the mixture out on to a work surface and shape into a flat log, about 25 x 7.5 x 2.5cm (10 x 3 x 1in). Place on a well-greased baking sheet and bake for 25 minutes, until golden brown. Remove and leave to cool for about 15 minutes, until firm. Meanwhile, reduce the oven temperature to 150°C/300°F/gas mark 2.

With a serrated knife, cut the log into slices 5mm (^{1}/$_4$in) thick. Arrange the slices flat on the baking sheet and return to the oven for 10–15 minutes. Allow to cool completely.

caffe latte with espresso granita

FOR THE GRANITA:

75g (3oz) caster sugar

200ml (7fl oz) strong espresso coffee

2 tablespoons Tia Maria or other coffee liqueur

FOR THE CAFFE LATTE:

75g (3oz) espresso coffee beans, finely ground

2 gelatine leaves

2 eggs

1 egg yolk

50g (2oz) caster sugar

1 tablespoon Tia Maria or other coffee liqueur

225ml (8fl oz) double cream, semi-whipped

TO SERVE:

100ml (3^1/$_2$ fl oz) sweetened whipped cream

A few coffee beans

First make the granita. Put the sugar in a pan with 200ml (7fl oz) water and bring slowly to the boil. Simmer for 10 minutes, then add the espresso coffee and leave to cool. Add the coffee liqueur and pour the mixture into a shallow metal tray. Place in the freezer and, as it begins to freeze and ice crystals form, use a fork to scrape up the mixture from the sides and base occasionally, to flake the ice crystals.

For the caffe latte, pour 175ml (6fl oz) of boiling water over the coffee and leave to infuse (ideally do this in a cafetière). Meanwhile, cover the gelatine leaves with cold water and leave to soak for 5 minutes. Drain well, squeezing out excess water. Strain the coffee, add the soaked gelatine and stir until dissolved. Leave to cool.

Put the eggs, egg yolk and sugar in a bowl set over a pan of simmering water, making sure the water is not touching the base of the bowl. Whisk with a hand-held beater until the mixture is creamy, pale and thick enough to leave a ribbon on the surface when trailed from the whisk. Remove the bowl from the pan of hot water, add the Tia Maria and whisk until cool. Whisk in the coffee and gelatine mixture and leave until almost set, stirring occasionally. Finally, fold in the whipped cream and spoon into 4 large coffee cups or glasses. Place in the fridge until set.

To serve, top the caffe latte with a good spoonful of the granita, then with some whipped cream and coffee beans. Coffee and Fennel Seed Biscotti (see page 56) make a good accompaniment.

coriander

Known as Chinese parsley in the East and cilantro in the West, coriander is related to both parsley and carrots, and is now one of the most popular and commonly used herbs worldwide. Today it is prevalent in the most fashionable cuisines in the world, such as North African, Greek, Middle Eastern, Indian, Thai, Malaysian, Chinese, Mexican and American; in fact in most of the 'hotter' food regions of the world.

recipes

The Chinese have been using coriander since 5000 BC, and it is frequently mentioned in the Bible, so its popularity soon spread far and wide. History tells us that coriander (*Coriandrum sativum*) is indigenous to southern Europe, where it was used for medicinal, as well as culinary, purposes for 5,000 years. It was the Romans who first introduced it to Britain in the form of fresh leaves.

DESCRIPTION

Opinions are divided as to the taste: some say it's soapy, others that it has strong elements of cut wet grass, forest humus and wild mushrooms such as chanterelles. For me, the taste is grassy and a bit oily, with an aftertaste that combines bitter and sweet to leave a faint lemon flavour on the tongue. But I do agree that the scent and flavour of coriander are curiously hard to pin down. The name coriander derives from the Greek word *koris*, meaning insect or bug, and it is has been said that the plant smells like a bed-bug, which I find hard to imagine.

Whatever side of the fence you are on, I personally believe it is a wonderful herb that I could not live without. I find it a breath of fresh air, packed with flavour. If you haven't tasted it yet, try it. I assure you it will soon become a passion.

Coriander leads an exciting dual life as both a herb and a spice. It is an annual (and occasionally a perennial) herb, which grows up to 20–25cm (8–10in) high and has many branches. Its fragrant leaves and wispy stems give coriander a delicate look. The plant bears flowers which mature into seeds, which are picked when ripe. If you are ever lucky enough to eat them green and fresh, you are in for a real treat – an experience I had in Spain in one of the world's greatest restaurants, El Raco de Con Farbas (St Celoni), near Barcelona. More commonly, however, the seeds are dried and used in many preparations with other spices, such as sauces and marinades. The seeds are used both whole and ground. I love the herb and the spice (they have very different tastes) but, for me the leaves have the most magical properties.

BUYING AND STORING

Whenever I purchase coriander leaves in supermarkets, I find the small packages are never large enough so I find it is better and infinitely cheaper to buy it in bunches from Asian stores. When bought like this you have an added bonus: the plant's roots are still attached. These not only prolong the life of the herb, but have a wonderful strong flavour and are used in some recipes such as in spicy pastas, sauces and Asian-style breads.

If you need to keep coriander for longer than one day, I find it is better to stand the plant in a pot of water, enclose the whole bunch in a plastic bag and stand it in the fridge. This year I will attempt to grow coriander in my own garden, as I use it so frequently. It is a hardy plant, easy to grow in warmish climates where an early spring sowing is possible.

Good-quality seeds can either be bought whole, or ground. As ground coriander quickly loses its flavour, it is best to grind your own,

which is easily done using a pestle and mortar or a spice grinder. The whole seeds will keep almost indefinitely.

CULINARY USES

Coriander leaves are used extensively in Mexican, Indian and Thai cooking. The herb's peppery, slightly coarse lemon-aniseed flavour, when added to hot dishes especially, provides a cooling balance to other ingredients such as chillies. It also makes a great partner to lemongrass, coconut milk (which, along with chilli, creates the quintessential 'Thai' taste), cumin and tamarind.

Coriander also has a great affinity with tomatoes, garlic, lemons and limes. I love it chopped or whole, added to soups, salads and made into power-packed chilli sauces to go with

fried eggs (see page 61). When cooked it loses some of its harshness, and imparts a deeper flavour rather than a sharp accent. For most effect in cooked dishes it is best thrown in at the very last moment.

In Indian cooking, coriander leaves are usually chopped up and used as a garnish on curries and raitas (yoghurt-based salad dips). In Mexican cooking, the leaves are generally used in soups, salsas and marinades where the flavours are allowed to infuse and develop. Coriander roots, which have a concentrated and intense flavour, are often used in Thai cooking. Gai Yang (grilled chicken with coriander sauce), for example, uses the leaves, stalk and roots. Coriander also plays an important role in Thai salads (such as Gado gado, a vegetable salad with peanut sauce) and is added to curry pastes and breads.

Coriander seeds, which are often lightly roasted first to enhance their flavour, are used in minced meat dishes such as Middle Eastern koftas, Mexican enchiladas, English black puddings, and sausages such as Italian mortadella. They are also added to cakes, gingerbreads and chutneys. Finely ground coriander is a key ingredient in spice mixes such as garam masala (with cloves, cinnamon, cardamon and black pepper), with cumin in chermoula, with garlic in taklia, and with chillies in salsas and zoug.

The French use it in sauces such as antiboise (with olive oil, garlic and tomatoes) which is served with fish.

OTHER USES

Like most herbs, coriander has reputed medical properties and Chinese doctors have long considered it a powerful remedy for flatulence, arthritis, chest infections and for general well-being.

complementary flavours

COCONUT MILK

SPICES (ESPECIALLY GINGER AND CINNAMON)

YOGHURT

FRUIT (FIGS, NECTARINES, LEMONS, LIMES, MANGOES AND GREEN MANGOES)

VEGETABLES (TOMATOES, CUCUMBER, ONIONS AND GARLIC)

CHICKEN

FISH AND SHELLFISH

beetroot, tomato and coriander salad with labna

400g (14oz) new-season baby beetroot

200g (7oz) red cherry tomatoes, halved

100g (3^1/$_2$ oz) yellow cherry tomatoes, halved

Juice of ^{1}/$_2$ lemon

6 tablespoons virgin olive oil

^{1}/$_2$ teaspoon coriander seeds, lightly cracked in a
   pestle and mortar

Cayenne pepper

100g (3^1/$_2$ oz) fresh coriander, leaves only

20 small balls of labna cheese

Salt

Place the beetroot in a pan, cover with cold water and bring
to the boil. Reduce the heat to a simmer and cook until they
are just tender (alternatively, you could steam them). Drain
well and peel. Cut the beetroot into halves or quarters, so
they are approximately the same size as the tomatoes. Place
the beetroot and tomatoes in a large bowl and add the lemon
juice, olive oil and coriander seeds. Season with salt and a
little cayenne and toss the whole lot together. Finally toss in
the fresh coriander leaves, then serve, topped with the balls
of labna cheese.

PG TIP Labna is a strained yoghurt cheese, available from
Middle Eastern food shops and some supermarkets. It is easy
to make at home: simply strain some thick, Greek-style
yoghurt through a piece of muslin over a period of two days
to drain off the whey, leaving you with a firm yoghurt cheese.
Roll into small balls between your hands.

aztec eggs
This hearty dish is served with a green
salsa made from coriander, green chillies and tomatillos. Tomatillos are a
vital ingredient in many Mexican dishes, particularly sauces and salads.
They are related to the cape gooseberry, and are not green tomatoes, as is
often believed. However, if you cannot find fresh tomatillos (tinned ones
aren't suitable for this recipe), green tomatoes make an acceptable
substitute.

Oil for frying

250g (9oz) cooked new potatoes, peeled and sliced
   1cm (^{1}/$_2$ in) thick

75g (3oz) chorizo, cut into 5mm (^{1}/$_4$in) cubes

4 corn tortillas

4 organic or free range eggs

Salt and freshly ground black pepper

FOR THE GREEN SALSA:

175g (6oz) tomatillos (or green tomatoes)

2 green chillies

1 garlic clove, chopped

4 tablespoons chopped coriander leaves

First make the salsa. If using tomatillos, remove the husks
first, then place all the ingredients in a food processor or
blender and blitz to a coarse purée. Season with salt and
pepper, transfer to a bowl and set aside.

Heat some oil in a frying pan, add the potatoes and
cook until golden on both sides. Add the chorizo and cook
for 2 minutes. Season to taste, remove from the pan and
keep warm.

Wipe out the frying pan, add some more oil and fry
each tortilla until lightly golden and slightly puffed. Remove
from the pan and keep warm. Finally fry the eggs, adding
more oil to the pan if necessary, and season them with salt
and pepper.

To serve, put a tortilla on each serving plate and top with
the potato and chorizo mixture. Place a fried egg on each
pile, spoon over the green salsa and serve immediately.

broad beans with pancetta and coriander

Broad beans are a much underrated vegetable, to my mind. In France they are partnered with savory, in Italy with mint, and in Portugal with coriander. If I had to make a choice, I think the coriander just gets it — particularly when combined with salty pancetta, as in this recipe. These beans make a wonderful accompaniment to chicken or fish.

2kg (4¹/₂ lb) broad beans (unshelled weight)
75g (3oz) piece of smoked pancetta, cut into small
   dice
1 onion, finely chopped
1 bunch of coriander, chopped
Salt and freshly ground black pepper

Shell the broad beans and cook them in a pan of boiling salted water for 4–5 minutes, until just tender. Drain well, refresh in cold water, then drain again and peel off the thin skins. Set aside.

Heat a heavy-based frying pan over a high heat. Add the pancetta and fry until it is golden brown and has released its fat. Remove from the pan with a slotted spoon and set aside. Add the onion to the fat in the pan, reduce the heat and cook until it is tender but not coloured. Return the beans and bacon to the pan, season to taste, then toss through the chopped coriander and serve.

coriander-marinated sardines with coconut milk

This is one of my favourite appetisers. It is so simple to prepare, but has an amazing flavour and freshness. Make sure that your sardines are very fresh or the result will not be as good. If you prefer, tuna (sliced very thinly) could replace the sardines in this Asian-inspired dish.

10 very fresh medium-sized sardines, filleted
Leaves from 1 large bunch of coriander
400g (14oz) can of unsweetened coconut cream
Juice of 4 limes
1 small red chilli, deseeded and finely chopped
2 tablespoons virgin olive oil
A pinch of cayenne pepper
150g (5oz) green beans
Salt and freshly ground black pepper
Lime wedges, to serve

Rinse the sardine fillets under cold running water to clean them thoroughly, then pat dry with a cloth. Layer the fillets in a bowl with the coriander leaves in between each layer, reserving some coriander for garnish.

In another bowl, whisk together the coconut cream, lime juice, chilli and olive oil. Season with salt, pepper and cayenne, then pour this mixture over the sardines and leave to marinate in the fridge for 6 hours.

Cook the green beans in boiling salted water until just tender, then drain well and adjust the seasoning. Divide between 4 serving plates. Arrange the sardine fillets on top, pour over some of the marinating juice and garnish with lime wedges and the remaining coriander leaves. Serve chilled.

coriander-lime grilled figs

You may be amazed by this recipe — grilled figs in a vibrant green, spicy syrup that really adds zip to the fruit. A good dollop of ice-cream is all that is needed to complete an unusual dessert that never fails to impress.

1 bunch of coriander
Juice from a 5cm (2in) piece of fresh root ginger (see page 78)
Juice and grated zest of 2 limes
300ml ($^1/_2$ pint) Sauternes (or other sweet wine)
150ml ($^1/_4$ pint) glucose syrup
4 green cardamom pods, split
12 ripe purple figs
1 $^1/_2$ teaspoons vanilla sugar (see page 177)

Separate the coriander leaves from the stalks. Put the stalks in a pan with the ginger juice, lime juice and zest, wine, glucose syrup and cardamom pods and bring gently to the boil. Reduce the heat and simmer for 5 minutes. Add the whole figs and poach gently for 3 minutes, then remove from the heat and leave to cool.

Remove the figs from the syrup and set aside. Return the syrup to the heat and simmer until it begins to thicken. Meanwhile, blanch the coriander leaves in a large pan of boiling water for a few seconds, then drain well and refresh in iced water. Drain again and pat dry. Add the coriander leaves to the hot syrup and leave for 2–3 minutes. Pour the mixture into a blender and blitz until smooth. Strain and leave to cool, then chill.

Cut the figs lengthways in half and place on a baking tray. Sprinkle with the vanilla sugar and place under a hot grill for 2–3 minutes, until caramelised. Arrange the figs on serving plates, drizzle over the syrup and serve.

cumin
Suited to most cuisines of the world, cumin is an essential spice. Native to Egypt, it has been used by the Egyptians for over 5,000 years.

DESCRIPTION

Cumin seeds are the fruit of the annual herb (*Cuminum cyminum*), a close cousin of parsley, coriander, dill and fennel. It is also related to caraway, and their seeds can easily be confused, so take care when labelling your spice jars.

Cumin thrives in warm weather and is now grown extensively in Iran, India, Morocco, China and Indonesia. The seeds are oval-shaped, with deep longitudinal ridges and are between 3–6mm (1/8–1/4in) long. There are three varieties of cumin. While white and brown are interchangeable, black is less common; it has more flavour, is sweeter, and is used only in specific dishes, such as in the flat breads from Turkey, Cyprus and Lebanon. Black seeds are similar in appearance to nigella seeds, which are quite different so, again, don't get them confused.

The smell of cumin has been described as fresh, strong and bitter. Its taste is quite pronounced, pungent and aromatic.

BUYING, STORING AND PREPARATION

As for all spices, buy fresh cumin in small quantities and store in a tightly sealed container in a dark, cool cupboard to retain freshness. Grind as required or buy best-quality ground cumin.

Most of my recipes call for cumin seeds used whole. To bring out their flavour, toast the seeds lightly before adding them to recipes. To toast, simply add the seeds to a heated dry pan on a medium heat and toss them around for between 30–60 seconds until they darken slightly and release their aroma.

For ground cumin tip the seeds into a mortar or spice grinder and crush or grind. The volatile oils don't last long, so if a recipe calls for ground cumin it is best to grind the seeds just before use.

CULINARY USES

From its origin in Egypt, cumin travelled to Asia, Iran and India where its popularity spread quickly, and it became a standard ingredient for panch phora (a Bengali mix of five spices), garam masala, tandoori masala and curry paste. It is also used in India to season many yoghurt-based raitas and is mixed with tamarind water to created the refreshing drink, zeera pani.

In hotter countries such as Egypt, where cumin originated, the spice was used to preserve meat. North African Muslims flavour couscous and tajines with cumin, and mix it in spice blends, including ras el hanout. Cumin is also often sprinkled over rice and lentil dishes, rubbed into meat (especially lamb) before grilling, and used to spice up mince meat dishes. Other Mediterranean recipes call for it to be added to marinades for olives, pickles, relishes, salads (particularly tomato) and sausages such as merguez. It is also sometimes included in hummus (the popular tangy yoghurt-chickpea dip).

The Moors carried the spice to Spain where it was and still is used in stews with saffron and sweet cinnamon. It is also used to great effect in the Spanish dishes, Arroz Con Pollo (chicken with rice) and Gazpacho Andalusian; and in Portuguese fish stews and with salted pork. It is thought to have then travelled to Mexico where it soon became an essential component of their cuisine –

complementary flavours

VEGETABLES (ESPECIALLY ONIONS, FENNEL, GARLIC AND TOMATOES)

FISH

MEAT (ESPECIALLY CHICKEN, PORK AND LAMB)

SPICES (CINNAMON, GINGER AND SAFFRON)

YOGHURT

MINT

ORANGE

just think of chilli con carne, black bean soup, adobos (spicy marinades) and peccadilloes (spicy minced meat wrapped in pastry).

Strangely enough, in the past it was used widely in baking — especially in central Europe. During Victorian times, cumin cakes were frequently served, although the spice was considered, like many others at the time, to be an aphrodisiac. The late Elizabeth David always used to add cumin to her hot cross bun recipe.

OTHER USES

Cumin has long been recommended for its curative properties. Taken in hot water, it is said to relieve the symptoms of colds and flu. Blended with honey, it soothes sore throats. In India it is prescribed as a remedy for flatulence, indigestion and diarrhoea. Cumin is a calmative and is used, for this reason, in veterinarian medicine.

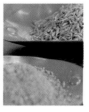

tomato, cumin and pomegranate soup

8 garlic cloves
2 tablespoons olive oil
400g (14oz) can of chopped tomatoes
1 teaspoon cumin seeds
1 onion, chopped
1 carrot, cut into small dice
1 celery stick, cut into small dice
1 red pepper, cut into small dice
1 sprig of thyme
A good pinch of saffron strands
1 bay leaf
1 tablespoon dried pomegranate seeds
750ml (1¼ pints) chicken stock (or vegetable stock)
1 tablespoon pomegranate molasses
Salt and freshly ground black pepper

Preheat the oven to 180°C/350°F/gas mark 4. Place the garlic cloves in a small dish, pour over half the olive oil and roast for 30–40 minutes, until they are soft and caramelised. Leave until cool enough to handle, then pop the garlic flesh out of the skin and place in a blender with the canned tomatoes. Purée until smooth.

Heat a large saucepan until hot, add the cumin seeds and toast for 30 seconds, to release their wonderful fragrance. Remove from the pan and set aside. Heat the remaining oil in the pan, add the onion, carrot, celery, red pepper and thyme and sauté until tender. Stir in the garlic and tomato purée, saffron, bay leaf and pomegranate seeds, then the toasted cumin seeds. Add the stock, bring to the boil, then reduce the heat and simmer for 30 minutes. Stir in the pomegranate molasses, season to taste and serve.

PG TIP Pomegranate molasses (sometimes labelled *dibs rumman* or *dibs rumen*) and dried pomegranate seeds are available from Middle Eastern shops. If necessary, substitute 1½ teaspoons of grenadine for the molasses in this soup.

cumin swordfish souvlaki

If ever a dish was made for a barbecue, this is it: grilled marinated swordfish wrapped in hot flatbread. When I barbecue, I usually consume two or three of these while the guests are waiting for theirs — well, the cook has to have some perks!

750g (1lb 10oz) swordfish fillet, trimmed and cut into
    4cm (1½ in) cubes
2 tablespoons olive oil
2 tablespoons chopped parsley
1 tablespoon chopped oregano
1 teaspoon cumin seeds
A pinch of smoked paprika
2 garlic cloves, crushed
1 lemon
1 red pepper, cut into 2.5cm (1in) dice
1 green pepper, cut into 2.5cm (1in) dice
1 red onion, cut into small wedges

TO SERVE:
8 flatbreads, such as lavash (or even tortillas)
¼ cucumber, deseeded and chopped
150g (5oz) Greek yoghurt
2 tablespoons chopped mint
2 tablespoons chopped coriander
1 garlic clove, crushed
Salt and freshly ground black pepper

Place the swordfish cubes in a bowl, add the olive oil, parsley, oregano, cumin seeds, paprika and garlic and toss well together. Squeeze over the lemon juice and leave to marinate for 30 minutes. Soak the wooden skewers in water to prevent them from burning.

Thread the swordfish on to 8 skewers, alternating it with the peppers and red onion, then brush with the marinade. Cook the souvlaki on a barbecue (or on a preheated ridged grill pan if cooking indoors), turning them frequently and continually basting with the marinade; they will take about 4–5 minutes.

While the swordfish is cooking, wrap the bread in foil and warm it through in a moderate oven. Mix together the

cucumber, Greek yoghurt, herbs and garlic and season to taste. Divide the mixture between the warm flatbreads, spreading it over the surface. Remove the fish from the skewers and place on the yoghurt mixture, then roll up the bread into cones and serve immediately.

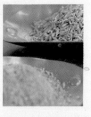

roasted baby carrots
with cumin

2 teaspoons cumin seeds

3 tablespoons olive oil

$1/2$ small garlic clove, crushed

750g (1lb 10oz) baby carrots, lightly scraped

2 tablespoons honey

Juice and grated zest of 1 orange

Chopped mint, to garnish (optional)

Preheat the oven to 200°C/400°F/gas mark 6. Heat a large ovenproof frying pan over a moderate heat, add the cumin seeds and toast for 30 seconds to release their fragrance. Add the olive oil and garlic and mix well. Stir in the carrots and toss until they are sealed and lightly golden all over. Add the honey and orange juice and zest and stir well to combine.

Transfer to the oven and cook for 8–10 minutes, until the carrots are glazed and tender and all the liquid has evaporated. Serve immediately, sprinkled with a little mint, if you like, which goes well with the spiced carrots.

pork adobo

In 1492 the arrival of the Spanish in Cuba introduced a host of new foods to the region, from European spices and vinegar to olive oil and wine. Adobo, made from vinegar, spices and orange juice, has become Cuba's national marinade, used for all manner of dishes. Black beans, spicy salsa, guacamole and warm tortillas make great accompaniments to pork adobo.

750g (1lb 10oz) pork neck end, cut into
  2cm ($^3/_4$ in) pieces
1 teaspoon garlic powder
Groundnut or vegetable oil for frying
300ml ($^1/_2$ pint) dark beer
2 onions, sliced
Salt and freshly ground black pepper

FOR THE MARINADE:
1$^1/_2$ teaspoons achiote seeds or paste (see Tip above
  right)
300ml ($^1/_2$pint) orange juice
175ml (6fl oz) white wine vinegar
2 tablespoons dried oregano
2 tablespoons cumin seeds, toasted in a dry
  frying pan
6 garlic cloves, chopped

To make the marinade, blitz the achiote seeds or paste, orange juice, vinegar, oregano, cumin and garlic together in a blender or food processor and transfer to a large bowl. Season the pork pieces with salt, pepper and the garlic powder, then add them to the marinade and leave for 1 hour.

Preheat the oven to 180°C/350°F/gas mark 4. Heat 2.5cm (1in) of the oil in a large, heavy-based casserole. Remove the pork from the marinade and brown it on all sides in the hot oil, then remove from the pan. Clean the oil from the pan and return the pork, together with the marinade, beer and onions. Season with salt and pepper. Bring to the boil, then cover, transfer to the oven and bake for 1$^1/_2$ hours. Remove from the oven and skim off excess fat from the surface. Take out the meat and keep warm. Put the casserole back on the hob and boil until the liquid has reduced by half. Serve the pork drizzled with the cooking juices.

PG TIP Achiote seeds come from the annatto tree and have a brick-red colour and earthy flavour. Achiote paste is also available. You should find them in some large supermarkets and in shops specialising in South American ingredients.

cumin shortbread

Mention shortbread and you immediately think of Scotland. There are many variations on these crisp, buttery biscuits but this recipe using cumin might come as a surprise. When I found it in a Scottish cookery book dating back to 1840 I had to try it, and was most impressed. The shortbread is particularly good served with an orange mousse.

125g (4$^1/_2$ oz) softened unsalted butter
125g (4$^1/_2$ oz) caster sugar
$^1/_4$ teaspoon salt
250g (9oz) plain flour
2 teaspoons freshly ground cumin
3 tablespoons finely chopped candied orange peel

Beat the butter until it is light and fluffy, then slowly beat in the sugar. Mix in the salt and flour, adding the flour in 4 batches. Add the cumin and orange peel and mix until the dough is smooth and soft.

Turn the dough on to a lightly floured work surface and roll it out into a rectangle 1cm ($^1/_2$in) thick, making sure the top is flat and smooth. Cut into 2.5 x 5cm (1 x 2in) fingers and, with a fork, prick each one 3 times on the diagonal. Chill for up to 2 hours.

Preheat the oven to 150°C/300°F/gas mark 2. Place the shortbread fingers on a greased baking sheet, spacing them about 2.5cm (1in) apart. Bake for 20 minutes, until very pale golden but not browned, then remove from the oven and transfer to a wire rack to cool. They will keep for up to 1 month if stored in an airtight container.

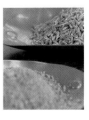

garlic

Originating in central Asia, garlic has been cultivated for over 6,000 years. Garlic was, and still is, prized for its aphrodisiacal and therapeutic properties, in addition to its culinary uses; the ancient Egyptians took it to increase their strength and endurance.

DESCRIPTION

Garlic (*Allium sativum*) is a member of the lily family. It grows underground in bulbs or heads each composed of some eight to twenty smaller inner units called cloves. These are covered in a thin papery skin. Garlic contains a liquid called allecin, which is the compound that gives garlic its aroma, and is also the culprit of smelly garlic breath.

All garlic is harvested and stored for up to one month prior to use to undergo a drying or curing process in which its natural inner moisture evaporates to prevent it from rotting. It is during this time that the flavour of the garlic develops and strengthens. There are over 300 different garlic varieties. All are white inside, but the outer skin can be white, purple, pink and sometimes red. White is the most common and has the strongest flavour. Purple and red varieties are milder and have a shorter shelf life. Elephant garlic is the name given to a very large variety of garlic with an intense flavour. The bulbs of elephant garlic can grow to the size of a small apple and are ideal when you want a lot of garlic in a dish. Use as you would normal garlic. I've tried some amazing picked garlic from Spain. Smoked garlic is also available but I am not a great lover of it.

BUYING AND STORING

Choose garlic that feels firm and heavy for its size and there should be no sign of mould, shrivelling or sprouting. Available all year round, garlic has a long shelf life if stored correctly. It is best kept in a cool, dark, well-ventilated dry place. Do not refrigerate as this promotes rot as well as a smelly fridge. Occasionally garlic will germinate producing green sprouts that will taste bitter. If the cloves are still firm, however, the garlic will be fine, so simply cut away the sprouts.

PREPARATION

Garlic has long had a reputation for being difficult to handle, which is simply not the case if you follow simple guidelines. First you need to break up the bulbs. Simply set the garlic head upside down on a flat surface and use the palm of your hand to press down hard on the root end. All the cloves will break loose, ready to be peeled.

Lots of recipes call for crushed or chopped garlic. To my mind, crushing is a finer, more refined way to use it. I personally always crush it as I find it unpleasant to bite into chunks of chopped garlic. Chunky pieces don't cook well, tend to burn and can entirely ruin a dish with bitterness. Although there are numerous garlic gadgets on the market, all you will need to crush garlic is a large cook's knife — nothing beats the result.

First, chop the garlic as fine as you can on a board, sprinkle over a little salt to aid chopping, and to form a paste. Pull your knife back over the garlic and salt at a 20° angle, crushing and rubbing the garlic into a smooth paste with the inside of your blade. Store in a little oil if not using immediately. For occasions when you need to peel a large amount of garlic, as for my Garlic and Thyme Bisque (page 72), microwave the cloves or blanch in boiling water for 30–40 seconds to loosen the skins. This makes them easier to peel once they have cooled.

CULINARY USES

For me, the scent of fresh garlic, whether raw or cooked, is the aroma and promise of great food to come. It has been used for centuries to invigorate dishes (such as Chicken with 40 Cloves of Garlic, page 74), soups (like Tourin Blanchi) and sauces and is even surprisingly delicious in desserts and ice-cream. Where would the French be without aïoli, North Africans without harissa, or the Americans without their famous Caesar salad dressing? Also take a moment to think of pesto and garlic bread, and the many recipes, too numerous to contemplate, that begin with sautéing a little garlic in oil or butter.... We are talking about a major player on the culinary scene.

The flavour of garlic depends on how you use it, whether raw, smoked, sautéed, roasted or infused into oils or vinegars. Each provides a distinctive taste and range of flavour. Add raw garlic when you want the most bite from the smallest amount, or cook it in fat to sweeten the flavour and make it milder (don't burn it, though: it becomes bitter). As a rule, the smaller you chop it, the more potent the taste and aroma. I love to roast whole cloves in the oven, the roasting caramelises the natural sugars, giving a wonderful almost nutty flavour. In fact, when roasting garlic cloves, I suggest you do extra. They are delicious used in all sorts of things — salads, dressings, marinades or with roasted vegetables.

OTHER PRODUCTS AND THEIR USES

Garlic vinegar: for dressings.
Garlic salt: a blend of dried garlic and salt used as a seasoning.
Garlic powder: dried and crushed into a powder and used as a flavouring.
Garlic flakes: dried and cut into flakes, great with roasted meats.
Garlic oil: for dressings and for dressing.
Garlic purée: manufactured purée. Fine as a substitute when time is short but not as flavourful as fresh crushed garlic.
Garlic leaves: wonderful and fragrant in salads and soups.

OTHER USES

Apart from its culinary versatility, garlic has long been regarded as one of the best all-round healing plants. It is credited with diuretic, antiseptic and cleansing properties and it is an excellent antibiotic, anti-histamine and expectorant. Reputed to give strength and courage in ancient days, it is nowadays widely available as an over-the-counter treatment for high cholesterol.

complementary flavours

TOMATO

MUSTARD

PARMESAN CHEESE

BALSAMIC VINEGAR

BASIL

ONIONS AND SHALLOTS

MUSHROOMS

OLIVE OIL

LEMON

garlic and thyme bisque A wonderful
soup for all garlic lovers who have no qualms about the effect on others!

25g (1oz) unsalted butter
1 onion, chopped
1 small leek, chopped
1 head of garlic, cloves separated and peeled
400ml (14fl oz) full-fat milk
2 teaspoons thyme leaves
450ml ($3/4$ pint) chicken stock (or vegetable stock)
5 slices of baguette, cut 2cm ($3/4$ in) thick
2 tablespoons olive oil
100ml ($3^1/2$ fl oz) double cream
Freshly grated nutmeg
Salt and freshly ground black pepper

Heat the butter in a heavy-based pan, add the onion and leek
and cook gently until soft and tender. Add the garlic cloves
and cook for 10 minutes, until the vegetables and garlic have
become slightly caramelised and very tender. Add the milk,
half the thyme and the stock and bring to the boil.

Lightly toast the bread and rub it with the olive oil. Cut
into smallish pieces, add to the boiling soup and reduce the
heat to a simmer. Cook for about 30 minutes, to allow the
flavours to meld. Pour into a blender and blitz to a creamy
purée, then strain through a fine sieve as well to give an even
smoother finish. Return to the pan, add the double cream and
reheat gently. Season with nutmeg, salt and pepper and
sprinkle over the remaining thyme leaves to garnish.

PG TIP Garlic is great but, jokes aside, the after-effects can
be harsh on others. After eating garlic, chew some parsley,
which helps sweeten the breath.

garlic tartines with grilled scallops and crispy bacon

2 large garlic cloves, peeled
100ml ($3^1/2$ fl oz) full-fat milk
4 tablespoons double cream
Olive oil
8 large, fresh scallops
4 streaky bacon rashers
4 slices of baguette, cut 2cm ($3/4$in) thick
50g (2oz) rocket
50g (2oz) Parmesan cheese, thinly shaved
Salt and freshly ground black pepper

FOR THE DRESSING:
1 tablespoon sherry vinegar (or red wine vinegar)
2 tablespoons walnut oil
2 tablespoons olive oil

Put the garlic cloves in a small pan of boiling water, blanch
for 1 minute, then drain and repeat. Return to the dry pan,
cover with the milk and cook for 12–15 minutes, until tender.
Drain off excess milk, add the cream and return to the boil for
2 minutes. Blitz in a blender to obtain a thick garlic purée.

Make the dressing by whisking all the ingredients
together and seasoning with salt and pepper.

Heat a ridged grill pan, brush it with a little olive oil, then
season the scallops and cook them for 1–2 minutes on each
side, until just done. Set aside and keep warm. Grill the bacon
until crisp.

Toast the baguette slices on the grill. Spoon the garlic
purée liberally over each piece, top with the scallops and
then with the bacon. Toss the rocket with most of the
dressing and serve alongside or on the tartines, drizzling the
remaining dressing over the tartines and scattering over the
Parmesan shavings.

garlic, shallot and portabello mushroom curry

2.5cm (1in) piece of fresh root ginger, chopped

2 onions, chopped

6 garlic cloves, thinly sliced

3 tablespoons Greek yoghurt

100ml (3^1/2 fl oz) vegetable oil

450g (1lb) large portabello mushrooms, thinly sliced

2 teaspoons ground coriander

^{1}/2 teaspoon chilli powder

A pinch of turmeric

1 teaspoon tomato purée

2 tablespoons chopped coriander

Salt and freshly ground black pepper

In a blender or food processor, blitz together the ginger, onions, garlic, yoghurt and 100ml (3^1/2 fl oz) water until smooth.

Heat half the oil in a large frying pan, add the mushrooms and stir-fry until cooked. Remove from the pan and set aside. Heat the remaining oil in the pan, add the spices and cook for 2–3 minutes, until they start to brown. Stir in the yoghurt mixture and tomato purée and cook for a further minute. Then add 300ml (^{1}/2 pint) of water, return the mushrooms to the pan and simmer for 8–10 minutes. Sprinkle over the coriander and serve.

chicken with 40 cloves of garlic

A traditional French dish, perfect for vampires! You may be put off by the thought of so much garlic but in fact the flavour mellows as it cooks.

1 x 1.6–1.8kg (3^1/2–4lb) organic or free range chicken

2 sprigs each of rosemary, thyme and sage

1 small bay leaf

40 garlic cloves, unpeeled

150ml (^{1}/4 pint) olive oil

Salt and freshly ground black pepper

FOR SEALING THE CASSEROLE:

4 tablespoons plain flour

4 tablespoons water mixed with 1 tablespoon oil

Preheat the oven to 180°C/350°F/gas mark 4. Season the chicken liberally with salt and pepper and place it in a large casserole. Tuck the herbs and the garlic cloves in around the bird, then pour over the oil and toss all the ingredients, ensuring the chicken is on top.

Mix together the ingredients for sealing the casserole until you have a smooth paste. Cover the casserole with a lid and seal with the paste, pressing it around the join (this ensures that all the flavour and juices are kept in the casserole). Place in the oven and cook for 1^3/4 hours.

To serve, transfer the casserole to the table and remove the lid to release the wonderful garlicky fragrance inside.

caesar steak sandwich

Olive oil

4 x 150g (5oz) beef minute steaks

2 Little Gem lettuces

25g (1oz) Parmesan cheese, freshly grated

1 focaccia bread, about 25cm (10in) in diameter, cut
   into quarters

4 plum tomatoes, thinly sliced

Salt and freshly ground black pepper

FOR THE DRESSING:

2 organic or free range egg yolks

1 teaspoon Dijon mustard

1/4 teaspoon sugar

1 tablespoon red wine vinegar

3 garlic cloves, crushed

4 tablespoons extra virgin olive oil

2 tablespoons vegetable oil

A drop of Tabasco sauce

Juice of 1/2 lemon

First make the dressing. Put the egg yolks, mustard, sugar
and vinegar in a bowl and mix well. Add the garlic, then slowly
beat in the oils to form a thick sauce. Mix in the Tabasco and
lemon juice and season to taste.

Heat a little olive oil in a ridged grill pan or large frying
pan. Season the steaks, cook until done to your liking, then
remove from the heat and keep warm.

Break up the lettuce leaves, put them in a bowl and toss
with a little of the dressing to bind them. Add the grated
Parmesan and season to taste.

Cut the focaccia quarters horizontally in half and grill on
the ridged grill pan or warm them through briefly in the oven.
Place a little lettuce in each quarter of focaccia, top with
sliced tomato and then with the steak. Drizzle over the
remaining dressing. Finish with lettuce, replace the top half of
the bread and serve immediately.

scampi provençale

32 scampi (fresh or frozen), shelled and de-veined
   (see page 33)

Juice of 1/2 lemon

2 tablespoons olive oil

50g (2oz) unsalted butter

4 garlic cloves, crushed

200g (7oz) sunblush tomatoes

3 tablespoons chopped flat-leaf parsley

Salt and freshly ground black pepper

Defrost the scampi, if frozen and dry thoroughly. Season the
scampi with salt and pepper and squeeze over the lemon
juice. Heat the olive oil in a large frying pan, add the scampi
and fry for 1 minute. Add the butter and garlic and cook for a
further minute. Remove the scampi from the pan and keep
warm. Add the sunblush tomatoes and parsley, cook for a few
minutes, then return the scampi to the pan and toss gently
together so that all the ingredients are spread evenly. Serve
immediately.

spicy garlic and tomato pickle

This makes a delicious summer relish, especially when served with cheese, cold meat or fish.

1kg (2¼lb) tomatoes, skinned and quartered

150ml (¼ pint) white wine vinegar

½ teaspoon ground cloves

1 teaspoon ground cumin

2.5cm (1in) piece of fresh root ginger, chopped

20 plump garlic cloves, peeled but left whole

2 red chillies, finely chopped

150g (5oz) brown sugar

1 teaspoon ground cardamom

2 tablespoons *nam pla* (Thai fish sauce)

Put all the ingredients in a large pan and bring slowly to the boil, stirring occasionally. Reduce the heat and simmer for up to 1 hour or until the mixture is very thick. Leave to cool to room temperature before serving. Leave in the fridge for up to 2 days before using for best results. Or you can put it in sterilised jars (see page 95) and seal if you want to store it for longer.

potatoes with garlic, lemon and walnuts

675g (1½lb) medium-sized waxy new potatoes

2 tablespoons vegetable oil

2 tablespoons walnut oil

25g (1oz) unsalted butter

A pinch of freshly grated nutmeg

4 garlic cloves, crushed

2 tablespoons chopped parsley

Grated zest of ½ lemon

2 tablespoons chopped walnuts

Salt and freshly ground black pepper

Cook the whole, unpeeled potatoes in boiling salted water until almost tender. Drain in a colander and leave until cool enough to handle, then carefully peel off the skins and slice the potatoes 1cm (½in) thick.

Heat the oils together in a large frying pan, add the potatoes and fry quickly to develop the colour. Add the butter and, when it is foaming, gently toss the potatoes in it until beautifully golden in colour. Season with nutmeg, salt and pepper. Add the garlic, parsley, lemon zest and walnuts, toss with the potatoes and serve.

ginger

It is important not to confuse fresh ginger with the powdered form that is widely used throughout the world. While the powder is a ground version of the same plant, the drying significantly reduces the intensity of the flavour.

DESCRIPTION

An aromatic rhizome that is rather ugly in appearance, ginger is thought to have originated in southern Asia. Today most of the world's ginger is cultivated in India and China, although it is also grown in the West Indies, Hawaii, parts of Africa (the best quality coming from Kenya) and northern Australia. Jamaican ginger is regarded as the best.

The ginger plant (*Zingiber officinale*), with its bright green leaves, pretty yellow and purple flowers and creeping rhizome, is a perennial that grows to around 1m (3ft) tall. The roots are tan or pale beige in colour, bulbous and firm. Plants shoot after a couple of weeks and the rhizomes are harvested at 6 months when they are still tender, to use fresh. Ginger that is left for another 3 months becomes very fibrous and needs to be dried or made into ground ginger.

Fresh ginger, when fully mature, can be fibrous with a warm, fresh aroma and a pungent, biting flavour — with a hint of turmeric. The flesh is yellow. Young ginger is milder, less fibrous, has a thinner skin and more delicate flavours. It has a light brown toughish skin with a pale yellow flesh.

BUYING, STORING AND PREPARATION

When buying ginger look for plump, firm, fresh-looking roots with no sign of wrinkles, which are a sign of age. I find it best to store ginger in a dark cupboard or pantry area where it will stay fresh for up to one month. Discard when it begins to wrinkle and soften.

When using fresh ginger, peel it well. Despite its knobbly crevices, I find a potato peeler is ideal for this job as the best flavour lies just below the skin so you want to remove as little flesh as possible. Once peeled and chopped, it will keep well in the fridge, covered with a little lemon juice and topped with clingfilm. For natural ginger juice, I grate it and squeeze through muslin. When grating you will find that the tougher fibres get caught in the grater; these should be discarded.

CULINARY USES

Ginger is a versatile ingredient, and is as happy to act as perfect partner (to chilli and garlic, for example), as it is to dominate.

It is an essential ingredient in the cooking of most Asian countries, and, combined with garlic and chilli (sizzled in hot sesame oil), is used in most Chinese dishes, such as stir-fries, noodles and soups (hot and sour). So diverse are its properties that ginger can be briefly cooked in stir-fries or, in contrast, slow cooked as a base ingredient in many Indian curries and masalas. Ginger is also added to Indian pastes, chutneys and marinades. In Japan, raw, grated ginger is often served as a side dish. It is also added to fish dishes, sauces and marinades. Galangal (see below) is a particularly popular ingredient in Japan.

One of my favourite combinations is ginger added to carrots cooked in butter with lemon.

Although ginger is more generally associated with savoury dishes it has properties that are shown to best advantage in sweet dishes and cakes; in fact a lot of great cakes from the past

Crystallised ginger: Pieces of candied ginger, rolled in a crunchy sugar coating—and sometimes dipped in chocolate. Again, a great store cupboard ingredient that is used extensively in baking.

Galangal and pickled pink ginger: These are used extensively in Asian cooking and are now becoming more readily available. Galangal, known as Laos or Thai ginger, is a camphorised member of the ginger family, sometimes also known as Lesser ginger. It has a pink, knobbly fleshed appearance, a more lemony flavour and a peppery taste. Only use fresh young galangal as it gets tougher as it gets older and more difficult to peel. Otherwise, use and prepare as for root ginger.

Pink ginger is a speciality of the Japanese. It is very thinly sliced ginger that is pickled with vinegar, resulting in a pinkish colour that not only looks magnificent but tastes fantastic. Generally, it is served with raw shashimi and sushi. I like to use it in dressings and in marinades.

OTHER USES

Ginger didn't get the name 'the great medicine', for nothing. Long before it was used in cooking, it was prized for its medicinal properties. The famous Greek physician, Pedanius Dioscorides (around AD 70) recommended ginger for the stomach and as an antidote to poison. An ancient headache remedy was to roast ginger root over an open fire and then to apply slices of it to the temples and forehead. Ginger was also widely prescribed by Indian and Chinese herbalists for a number of ailments from gout to paralysis. Because ginger is a diaphoretic, it was used during the Great Plague in London (1665-6). Fresh and crystallised ginger is said to ease travel sickness.

For a delicious ginger tea that will relieve sore throats and head colds, simply add chunks of peeled ginger to a mug of boiling water, sweeten with a little honey (if desired), and drink. Ginger tea granules are also available from health shops.

include ginger — gingerbread and parkin (see page 85) to name but two. In medieval times, ginger was as common and as expensive as pepper, but was always only used in a sweet form.

Beverages include ginger beer, ginger ale and ginger wine — in fact ginger used to be an essential ingredient in all early wine-making.

OTHER FORMS

Preserved/Stem ginger: Chunks of peeled ginger, cooked in a heavy syrup, known also as glacé ginger or stem ginger. It is exported from China and is traditionally sold in elegant pottery jars around Christmas time. Preserved ginger is a very useful store cupboard ingredient as it can be added to sweet recipes such as ice-cream, steamed pudding, cakes and biscuits. It is also wonderful in orange or apricot marmalade.

complementary flavours

VEGETABLES (ESPECIALLY GARLIC, ONIONS AND CELERY)

FRUIT (RHUBARB, MELON, PINEAPPLE, LIMES, PLUMS AND APPLES)

SPICES (ESPECIALLY CHILLI AND CUMIN)

HERBS (ESPECIALLY CORIANDER AND LEMONGRASS)

DAIRY PRODUCTS (CREAM AND YOGHURT)

HONEY AND TREACLE

SHELLFISH (SCALLOPS, LOBSTER, CRAB AND MUSSELS)

MEAT (CHICKEN, PORK AND BEEF)

chilled avocado and ginger soup

2 large, ripe avocados, stoned and peeled
1 garlic clove, chopped
1 onion, chopped
1 green chilli, finely chopped
Juice of 2 lemons
750ml (1¼ pints) well-flavoured vegetable stock (or chicken stock), chilled
½ teaspoon coriander seeds
Juice from a 5cm (2in) piece of fresh root ginger (see page 78)
2 tablespoons soured cream
4 tablespoons olive oil
Salt and freshly ground black pepper

Place the avocado flesh in a blender with the garlic, onion, chilli, lemon juice and stock and blitz to a smooth purée.

In a small hot frying pan, dry toast the coriander seeds for 20 seconds. Add them to the blender with half the ginger juice and blitz again to give a smooth, silky consistency. Transfer the soup to a bowl and whisk in the soured cream. Season with salt and pepper to taste and chill well.

To serve, pour into chilled soup bowls, mix the remaining ginger juice with the olive oil and drizzle it over the soup.

sashimi salmon with teriyaki ginger dressing
What I love about this dish, apart from its wonderful flavour, is that no cooking is needed. However, that does mean it is vitally important to use the freshest possible salmon.

450g (1lb) very fresh skinless, boneless salmon fillet, well chilled
1 fennel bulb, thinly sliced
¼ cucumber, halved lengthways, deseeded and thinly shaved into ribbons
A handful of coriander leaves
1 bunch of watercress, trimmed
2 oranges, segmented
1 teaspoon black sesame seeds
Salt and freshly ground black pepper

FOR THE DRESSING:
1 garlic clove, crushed
Grated zest of 1 orange
3 tablespoons rice wine vinegar
1 teaspoon cumin seeds, toasted in a dry frying pan
1 tablespoon pickled pink ginger, finely chopped
2 tablespoons teriyaki sauce
1 small red chilli, finely chopped
1 teaspoon sugar
4 tablespoons olive oil
1 tablespoon sesame oil

Using a very thin, sharp knife, cut the salmon into slices 5mm (¼in) thick and set aside.

For the dressing, place the garlic, orange zest, rice wine vinegar and cumin seeds in a bowl and whisk well. Mix in the pink ginger, teriyaki sauce, chilli and sugar, then gradually whisk in both oils to form a light emulsion.

In a large bowl, toss the fennel, cucumber, coriander leaves, watercress and orange segments with a little of the dressing and season to taste. Add the salmon and gently toss again, being carefully not to break the salmon slices.

Arrange on individual plates, pour over the remaining dressing, sprinkle the sesame seeds on top and serve.

steamed mussels with spicy gremolata

The Italian gremolata is traditionally a mixture of finely chopped parsley, garlic, lemon zest and breadcrumbs, sprinkled generously over fish, meat or vegetables to add extra texture and flavour. Here, with a little poetic licence, I include fresh ginger, which makes a perfect topping for the mussels.

1kg (2¼lb) fresh mussels
1 tablespoon olive oil
1 onion, finely chopped
2 garlic cloves, crushed
1 teaspoon ground cumin
4 plum tomatoes, skinned, deseeded and chopped
300ml (½ pint) dry white wine
4 tablespoons ginger wine

FOR THE GREMOLATA:
2.5cm (1in) piece of fresh root ginger, finely chopped
2 tablespoons finely chopped parsley
1 teaspoon finely grated lemon zest
1 garlic clove, crushed

Combine all the ingredients for the gremolata in a bowl and set aside.

Clean the mussels under cold running water and pull out the beards. Discard any open mussels that don't close when tapped on the work surface.

Heat the olive oil in a large, heavy-based saucepan, add the onion and cook over a medium heat until translucent. Add the garlic, cumin and tomatoes, reduce the heat and cook until fragrant. Add the mussels to the pan, then pour in the white wine and ginger wine. Add 100ml (3½ fl oz) water and bring to the boil. Cover the pan and cook over a high heat for 4–5 minutes, until the mussels open. Discard any that remain closed.

Serve the mussels and their cooking liquor in warmed deep bowls, sprinkled with the gremolata.

scallops with ginger, spring onions and sugarsnaps

1 tablespoon light soy sauce
2 teaspoons arrowroot
2 tablespoons vegetable oil
1 tablespoon light sesame oil
10 spring onions, cut into 5cm (2in) lengths
1 teaspoon finely grated fresh root ginger
½ garlic clove, crushed
12 large scallops (ideally diver-caught)
150g (5oz) baby sugarsnap peas, trimmed
150ml (¼ pint) well-flavoured chicken stock
1 teaspoon *nam pla* (Thai fish sauce)
Salt and freshly ground black pepper

Mix together in a small bowl the soy sauce, arrowroot and 4 tablespoons of water to form a paste. Set aside.

In a wok or large, shallow frying pan, heat both the oils until fairly hot. Add the spring onions, ginger and garlic and cook for 1 minute. Add the scallops and fry on a high heat for about 1 minute per side. Add the sugarsnaps and toss for a minute longer, then remove the scallops from the pan and keep warm.

Pour the stock into the pan and bring to the boil. Stir in the arrowroot mixture and cook for about 1 minute, until slightly thickened. Return the scallops to the pan, add the fish sauce and adjust the seasoning.

Put the scallops on serving plates, top with the vegetables, then pour the sauce over and serve immediately.

PG TIP Frozen scallops can be used as a substitute for fresh but they tend to contain loads of water and certainly don't have the same flavour.

pork chops with sage and caramelised ginger apples

4 pork loin chops
2 tablespoons vegetable oil
25g (1oz) unsalted butter
8 sage leaves, shredded, plus a few leaves to garnish
2 tablespoons cider vinegar (or white wine vinegar)
100ml ($3^1/_2$ fl oz) dry cider
150ml ($1/_4$ pint) double cream
100ml ($3^1/_2$ fl oz) well-flavoured chicken stock
1 teaspoon Dijon mustard
Salt and freshly ground black pepper

FOR THE CARAMELISED GINGER APPLES:
2 Granny Smith apples
25g (1oz) unsalted butter
2.5cm (1in) piece of fresh root ginger, finely chopped
1 tablespoon demerara sugar

Season the pork chops on both sides with salt and pepper. Heat the oil in a large frying pan, add the chops and fry for about 3–4 minutes on each side, until golden and cooked through. Remove from the pan and keep warm. Add the butter to the pan, then add the sage and cook for 30 seconds. Stir in the vinegar and cider and boil rapidly, until reduced by about half. Pour in the cream and chicken stock and stir well to scrape up any residue on the base of the pan. Whisk in the mustard, then reduce the heat and simmer until the sauce is thick enough to coat the back of a spoon.

Meanwhile, peel the apples, remove the cores with a corer and slice each apple into 4 rings, about 2cm ($3/_4$in) thick. Heat the butter and ginger in a large frying pan until foaming, add the apple slices and sprinkle over the sugar. Leave them to caramelise before turning them over to caramelise the other side. When beautifully golden and tender, remove from the pan and drain on kitchen paper.

To serve, place the pork chops on 4 serving plates and pour over the sage cream sauce. Top each chop with 2 caramelised ginger apples and garnish with sage leaves.

roasted pears in ginger butter

Serve these wonderful roasted pears with a little mint-flavoured ricotta cheese, or with a scoop of good lemon sorbet.

25g (1oz) caster sugar
2 tablespoons honey
2.5cm (1in) piece of fresh root ginger, finely grated
4 tablespoons white wine
2.5cm (1in) piece of cinnamon stick
4 ripe but firm pears, preferably Williams
50g (2oz) unsalted butter
2 tablespoons rum
1 teaspoon finely chopped preserved ginger

Put the sugar, honey, grated ginger, wine, cinnamon and 150ml ($1/_4$ pint) of water in a pan and bring to the boil, stirring. Simmer until the syrup has reduced by half, then strain and set aside.

Peel and core the pears and cut them in half vertically, but leave the stalks on. Heat a large frying pan (big enough to take the 8 pear halves lying flat), add the butter and heat until it begins to foam. Add the pears, laying them flat around the pan, core-side down. Cook for 2–3 minutes, until golden underneath, then turn and cook the other side. Add the strained syrup and the rum to the pan and cover with a lid. Reduce the heat and leave the pears to caramelise in the buttery syrup, turning occasionally – this will take 4–5 minutes.

Arrange the pears on serving plates, add the preserved ginger to the syrup and pour it over the pears.

parkin

This recipe originates from Yorkshire and is similar to Welsh gingerbread, except it contains oatmeal. It is sometimes served with cheese, particularly Wensleydale, which may sound strange but is surprisingly good. Originally it was made with black treacle but the lighter flavour of golden syrup is more popular now. You could use half treacle and half syrup. Store parkin in an airtight container; the longer you keep it, the stickier it will become.

100g (3^1/$_2$ oz) plain flour
200g (7oz) medium oatmeal
25g (1oz) brown sugar
2.5cm (1in) piece of fresh root ginger, finely grated
A pinch of ground ginger
A pinch of salt
225g (8oz) golden syrup
100g (3^1/$_2$ oz) unsalted butter
1 teaspoon bicarbonate of soda
4 tablespoons full-fat milk, warmed

Preheat the oven to 170°C/325°F/gas mark 3. Mix all the dry ingredients together in a large bowl. Place the syrup and butter in a saucepan and heat gently until the butter has melted. Dissolve the bicarbonate of soda in the warm milk, then pour both liquids into the flour mixture and stir well.

Pour into a greased and lined 20cm (8in) square cake tin and bake for 45–50 minutes; when it is done, a cocktail stick inserted in the centre should come out clean. Leave to cool in the tin, then turn out and cut into squares.

plum, ginger and yoghurt puddings

50g (2oz) unsalted butter
100g (3^1/$_2$oz) plain yoghurt
50g (2oz) caster sugar
50g (2oz) vanilla sugar (see page 177)
5cm (2in) piece of fresh root ginger, finely grated
2 eggs
40g (1^1/$_2$ oz) cornflour
65g (2^1/$_2$ oz) plain flour
1 teaspoon baking powder
150ml (1/$_4$ pint) maple syrup
8 ripe but firm plums, stoned and cut into
    1cm (1/$_2$ in) pieces

In a bowl, beat together the butter, yoghurt, both sugars and ginger until light and fluffy. Beat in the eggs, one by one. Sift together the flours and baking powder and fold into the mixture.

Take 4 large soufflé or ramekin dishes, about 200ml (7fl oz) in capacity, and divide the maple syrup between them. Top with the plums. Spoon the ginger mixture over the plums, then cover the dishes with clingfilm and place in a saucepan. Pour enough boiling water into the pan to come half way up the sides of the dishes, then cover the pan and simmer gently for 25–30 minutes, until a knife inserted in the centre of a pudding comes out clean. Remove the puddings carefully and allow to cool slightly before turning them out on to serving plates. Serve with vanilla ice-cream or crème fraîche.

honey

Honey is a very rich and concentrated food (100g/3¹/₂ oz is equal to 320 calories), a natural sweetener and a great source of energy. Its effect on the body is similar to that of sugar and is, therefore, prohibited in certain medical conditions, such as diabetes. None the less, it is recommended for those who prefer a healthier diet and lifestyle, as it undergoes less processing refinement and contains more complex carbohydrates. Honey was the chief sweet food in medieval times, when cane sugar became too expensive and somewhat of a rarity.

DESCRIPTION

According to a French chef friend of mine, producing honey is easy: you simply take your hives to where the pollen you prefer is abundant, and let the bees loose. They return to the hive, you return home and wait for the bees to begin the process. It sounds simple enough, but like all things in life, I'm sure there is a lot more to it than that — or is there?

The quality, consistency, colour, aroma and flavour of honey all vary according to where it has been gathered, that is to say, according to the nectar-source, or feeding ground of the bees. Honey aficionados will understand how different honey can taste. The flavour can alter from season to season (spring honey is always superior to winter honey), from location to location and from one source of nectar to another. In France, especially in Provence, honey is a serious business, one that requires beekeepers to relocate their hives at different times of the year in order to place the bees close to the lavender fields when the plants are in full bloom.

There are many distinct types of honey, some collected from a single source (such as Scotland's heather honey), and others from mixed nectars. For me, the best honeys are those with a distinctive flavour, such as lavender (delicate and aromatic), pine nut or chestnut (nutty and mild), heather (with its unique, jelly consistency and distinctive full flavour), elderflower and herbs such as thyme and rosemary. Some other favourites are: acacia (a popular, mild honey, delicious on cereals, in ice-cream and yoghurt), clover (sweet, mild and vanilla-flavoured. Usually set) and Greek (a dark, thick honey with a pungent aroma — one of the strongest tasting varieties and superb poured over Greek yoghurt).

Honey can be bought either in the edible wax comb, straight from the hive (honeycomb), or with the comb removed by straining or by centrifugal force, in a machine called a spinner.

Different nectars produce honey that sets (or crystallises) at different rates. Crops such as oil seed rape produce large quantities of nectar that sets very solidly, whereas garden flowers tend to a give a clear, liquid honey. Honey sold as set, creamed, or whipped is honey in its crystallised form.

BUYING AND STORING

When selecting honey, price is generally a good guide to quality. In flavour they vary immensely from mild flavoured cheaper versions to single-flower honeys of intense, sticky rich qualities. The most reputed honeys are those of Hymettus in Greece and the French varieties from Champagne, Savoy and southern France.

Ideally, honey should be stored in a pantry away from direct heat and light, where it retains its natural flavour. All honey will eventually crystallise or solidify. If this happens, and a recipe calls for runny honey, simply heat gently over a low heat until melted.

complementary flavours

HARD FRUITS (LEMONS, PEARS AND BANANAS)

SOFT FRUITS (GOOSEBERRIES, RASPBERRIES AND APRICOTS)

CARROTS AND TURNIPS

DUCK AND CHICKEN (TO GLAZE)

ROSEWATER AND ORANGE FLOWER WATER

NUTS

CHOCOLATE

SPICES (GINGER, CINNAMON AND SAFFRON)

MUSTARD

CULINARY USES

For many people, honey is merely a delicious spread enjoyed on hot, thickly sliced toast, or in tarts and cakes. However, in the Middle East and parts of the Mediterranean, honey is an important and much-loved cooking ingredient. It is poured over pastries and made into biscuits. In Greece it is drizzled over small savoury cheese-filled pastries, and over yoghurt and fruits at breakfast time. In Morocco honey is regularly used in sweet, sticky cakes and pastries, on desserts and added to sweet spicy tagines — a distinctive feature of Moroccan cooking.

The French are fanatical about honey: they use it in many dishes: sweet (like Crème Homère, a crème caramel with honey) and savoury (such as Duck with Lavender Honey). They also bake it in tarts, use it to flavour bread, ice-cream and desserts, and to make their famous white nougats (touvon).

In certain recipes, it may be substituted for sugar, while in others, such as cakes and pastries, it is not a suitable substitute because of its density. Honey makes a great glaze for meats (particularly lamb) and vegetables to be grilled on the barbecue or under the grill, and is a flavoursome sweetening agent for sauces.

Mead, a drink made from honey and water, has been drunk across Europe and Russia for centuries, and is still common today. In Russia, fruit such as black cherries, currants and raspberries are added to the mixture.

OTHER USES

Besides its use in cooking, honey is said to be very good for your health, and in combating ailments. I think we have all in our time had a soothing hot toddy made from honey, brandy and fresh lemon juice to help relieve cold and flu symptoms. It's also said to combat dry skin and aid a good complexion.

Royal jelly, a creamy-white substance that is very rich in protein and fatty acids, is produced by the mouth glands in young bees and fed to the queen bee and larvae. It is very expensive as it is made in such small quantities, and is used in some dietary supplements and cosmetics.

duck steaks with five-spice caramel

1 teaspoon coriander seeds
1 teaspoon cumin seeds
$^1/_2$ teaspoon sesame seeds
100ml (3$^1/_2$ fl oz) honey
$^1/_2$ teaspoon five-spice powder
1 tablespoon red wine vinegar
2 tablespoons soy sauce
2 tablespoons vegetable oil
4 x 175g (6oz) boneless duck breasts, skin on
Salt and freshly ground black pepper

FOR THE ORIENTAL VEGETABLES:
4 tablespoons sesame oil
2 bok choy, halved
6 radishes, sliced
1 carrot, thinly sliced
200g (7oz) Chinese broccoli, cut into florets
2 tablespoons soy sauce

Lightly crack the coriander, cumin and sesame seeds in a pestle and mortar to break them up. Put them in a pan with the honey, five-spice powder, vinegar, soy sauce and some salt and pepper and heat gently until the mixture comes to the boil. Remove from the heat and leave to one side. Preheat the grill to its highest setting.

Heat the vegetable oil in a large frying pan, season the duck breasts and cook them in the hot oil, skin-side down, until golden underneath. Turn and cook the other side for about 4–5 minutes, depending on how well you like it cooked. Remove the duck breasts from the pan and place on the grill pan. Brush them liberally with the honey and spice mixture and place under the hot grill. Reduce the heat and leave until the honey caramelises.

Meanwhile, for the Oriental vegetables, heat the sesame oil in a wok or large frying pan, add all the vegetables and stir-fry until tender but still retaining a little crispness. Season to taste with salt, pepper and the soy sauce. Place the duck breasts on the vegetables and serve.

lavender honey and sauternes lacquered nectarines

The honey and Sauternes syrup is a gorgeous purplish-pink colour, with an intense lavender honey aroma and delicate floral flavour. Melon is another favourite for this perfectly balanced syrup.

100g (3$^1/_2$ oz) caster sugar
1 tablespoon small mint leaves, stalks removed
4 large nectarines
25g (1oz) unsalted butter
85ml (3fl oz) lavender honey
Grated zest of $^1/_4$ lemon
$^1/_2$ teaspoon lavender pollen (see page 93)
100ml (3$^1/_2$ fl oz) Sauternes or other sweet dessert wine
4 tablespoons flaked almonds, lightly toasted

Combine the sugar with 500ml (18fl oz) of water in a saucepan and bring slowly to the boil, stirring to dissolve the sugar. Add the stalks from the mint leaves, then the nectarines and simmer for 5 minutes, turning the nectarines occasionally if the liquid doesn't cover them completely. Remove from the heat and set aside. When the nectarines are cool enough to handle, peel them, cut in half and remove the stones. Return the nectarine halves to the cooked syrup (this may all be done well in advance).

To serve, melt the butter in a large frying pan and stir in the honey, lemon zest and lavender pollen. Drain the nectarines, toss them in the honey mixture and then pour in the Sauternes. Turn the nectarines in the pan until glazed all over. Place the nectarines on serving plates, coat with the lavender honey sauce, scatter over the toasted flaked almonds and mint leaves and serve.

halva

This very sweet confectionery is immensely popular in India and Mediterranean countries. There are many variations on the recipe. My own version is flavoured with honey, cinnamon and saffron. It makes a delicious dessert or petit four and can be eaten warm, although I prefer it at room temperature.

350g (12oz) caster sugar

A pinch of saffron strands

2 cinnamon sticks

1 teaspoon ground cardamom

225ml (8fl oz) olive oil

350g (12oz) semolina

75g (3oz) flaked almonds

125ml (4fl oz) honey

2 tablespoons whole blanched almonds

1 teaspoon ground cinnamon

Place the sugar and saffron in a pan with 600ml (1 pint) of water and bring slowly to the boil, stirring from time to time to dissolve the sugar. Add the cinnamon and cardamom, simmer for 5 minutes, then remove from the heat and leave to infuse.

Meanwhile, in a separate pan, heat the olive oil until quite hot, stir in the semolina, reduce the heat and simmer for 20 minutes, until lightly golden. Add the flaked almonds and cook for 2 minutes. Strain in the saffron syrup and boil together for 5 minutes. Add the honey, remove from the heat and allow to cool slightly. Pour into a greased and lined shallow tin, about 25 x 20cm (10 x 8in), smooth the top and set aside to cool. Cut into small squares, top each one with a blanched almond and dust with the ground cinnamon.

gooseberry omelette with elderflower honey

6 tablespoons elderflower honey
85ml (3fl oz) elderflower cordial
300g (11oz) slightly underripe green gooseberries
Grated zest of $1/2$ lemon
8 eggs, beaten
65g ($2^1/2$oz) caster sugar
25g (1oz) unsalted butter
Icing sugar for dusting
4 tablespoons clotted cream

Put half the honey in a pan with the elderflower cordial and bring to the boil. Reduce the heat to a low simmer, add the green gooseberries and lemon zest and cook gently for 8–10 minutes, until the gooseberries are soft and the liquid is syrupy.

Beat the eggs together in a bowl, add the sugar and 1 tablespoon of water and beat again until light and fluffy.

Heat a quarter of the butter in a 20cm (8in) omelette pan until foaming. Pour in a quarter of the beaten egg mixture and cook for about 30 seconds, lifting the cooked edges of the omelette to allow the uncooked egg to flow underneath. When half set, spoon a quarter of the gooseberries over the top, then fold over the omelette and transfer to a warm serving plate and keep warm. Make the remaining omelettes in the same way. Dust with icing sugar, place the clotted cream on top, drizzle over the remaining honey and serve.

persian-style baked figs

100g ($3^1/2$ oz) mixed dried fruit (such as apricots, prunes, dates and sultanas)
8 large, ripe figs
4 tablespoons honey
Juice and grated zest of 2 oranges
$1/4$ teaspoon ground cinnamon
Pinch of fennel seeds
85ml (3fl oz) anisette or brandy

TO SERVE:
2 teaspoons rosewater
100g ($3^1/2$ oz) crème fraîche
1 tablespoon pine kernels, toasted
A few mint leaves

Soak the dried fruit overnight in water until swollen, then drain and cut into small pieces.

Preheat the oven to 180°C/350°F/gas mark 4. Cut the figs in half, scoop out the centre and fill each fig half with the dried fruit. Place in a shallow baking dish or gratin dish. Combine the honey, orange juice and zest, cinnamon, fennel seeds and anisette or brandy and pour over the figs. Cover and bake for 20 minutes, basting occasionally. Transfer to a serving dish.

Lightly fold the rosewater into the crème fraîche. Serve the figs warm, decorated with the pine kernels and mint leaves and accompanied by the crème fraîche.

lavender

Lavender has been valued for centuries, not just for its sweet-smelling freshness and use as a beauty fragrance, but as a culinary herb with medicinal qualities.

The French have long admired lavender; Provence in spring presents the glorious sight of field after field of mauve lavender and the air is heavy with the scent of the flowers in full bloom. A sensory experience I will never forget.

recipes

OLIVE OIL AND LAVENDER-
SCENTED GUINEA FOWL
(PAGE 94)

TWICE-COOKED DUCK WITH
LAVENDER HONEY (PAGE 95)

APRICOT AND LAVENDER
MARMALADE (PAGE 95)

PEAR BEIGNETS DUSTED
WITH LAVENDER SUGAR
(PAGE 96)

STUFFED APPLES WITH
RHUBARB CRUMBLE AND
LAVENDER (PAGE 96)

SEE ALSO:

LAVENDER HONEY AND
SAUTERNES LACQUERED
NECTARINES (PAGE 88)

DESCRIPTION

Lavender is a perennial plant that may reach between 30–90cm (1–3ft) tall. There are three main varieties, although these in turn have up to thirty other varieties. The colour of the flowers varies depending on the type, with spikes usually appearing in early summer. Only the English (*Lavandula angustifolia*) and French (*L. latifolia*) versions are suitable for cooking. French lavender, which has smaller spikes, is more akin to rosemary and it is without doubt the best one for culinary use. English lavender, or 'true lavender' as it is more commonly known in Britain, is to this day generally used in aromatic bath oils. It is very fragrant and ideal for perfumes. Both English and French lavender are, incidentally, native to the Mediterranean.

BUYING/SELECTING

Nowadays, although lavender is still somewhat hard to obtain, there is a move among chefs to make more use of it. Chefs like myself, in an effort to create new dishes and flavour combinations, source lavender from flower markets and growers, so if you take the trouble, it is available.

When sourcing lavender, however, it is important to buy it untreated with pesticides or fragrance enhancers which not only affect its gentle natural aroma but could upset your digestion. If you are unsure if it has been treated or not, wash it thoroughly.

There is no doubt in my mind that lavender is in for a major comeback over the next few years.

It has a unique flavour, but it must be fresh. On no account be tempted to use sachets or pot-pourri bags with their chemically intensified aroma, making them inedible. Ideally, pick your own lavender in the wild or from the garden.

PREPARATION AND STORING

To prepare lavender, simply pick off the little flowers from the stems and use as directed by the recipe.

When recipes call for dried flowers, simply place the flowers on a baking sheet and dry in a pre-heated oven 50°C (120°F) for 1 hour.

Alternatively, for those in a hurry, you can place the flowers between 2 sheets of greaseproof paper and microwave for 1 minute. The paper will absorb the moisture.

Lavender should be stored in an airtight container, in the fridge.

CULINARY USES

In Provence, lavender is used to make wonderful honey but is also used in sauces, to flavour delicate crème brûlées, to sweeten fruit tarts and as an interesting flavour for a sauce with roast duck (page 95).

Elsewhere in Europe, especially the Mediterranean, lavender also has a place in cookery. The Moroccans, for example, use dried lavender with salt and spices to flavour grilled meats; in fact, I have an old recipe for ras el hanout in my possession which contains lavender.

If you browse through old English recipes, you will discover that lavender was used extensively in

complementary
flavours

SOFT CHEESES (ESPECIALLY
RICOTTA AND MASCARPONE)

ROSEMARY

MEAT (ESPECIALLY LAMB,
CHICKEN AND DUCK)

DRIED FRUIT (IN
PRESERVES)

HONEY

DAIRY PRODUCTS (EGGS,
CUSTARD AND CREAMS)

NUTS (ESPECIALLY WALNUTS)

cooking, its intense yet gentle sweetness valued in puddings and in candied fruits.

Cooking with lavender opens up a great range of interesting uses. I like to use it to flavour milk puddings, custards, butters, mousses, sauces and ice-creams. I have also used lavender successfully in a stuffing for roasted fowl; or added to salads as you would other flowers.

Some of my recipes call for **Lavender pollen**, which is the name given to ground lavender flowers. To make, simply dry the flowers (as described under 'preparation'), then place in a mortar or blender and blitz to a fine powder. Use this to flavour all manner of dishes: for instance add to pasta with chopped parsley and walnuts, or to ricotta with lemon and lime zest and cream to make a wonderful mousse.

For **Lavender sugar**, to sprinkle over fruit tarts, to use in jam-making or to coat crisply fried fruit beignets, simply place the lavender flowers in a jar of caster sugar and leave for 2 weeks before use. Generally, 1 part lavender to 10 parts sugar is a good guide.

Dried lavender flowers make a wonderful garnish for deserts and pastries. Either crystallise them in sugar, or cook them in caramel before crumbling into small pieces as lavender praline.

Lavender praline

100g (3 1/2oz) caster sugar
25g (1oz) fresh lavender flower only
Place the sugar and lavender in a pan and melt over a moderate heat until brown and caramelised. Pour on to a greaseproof tray, allow to cool. Pound to a fine powder or blitz in a blender. Makes a great topping for ice-creams and mousses.

OTHER USES

Lavender has a number of uses, but it has long been recognised for its sedating effect on the nervous system — which is why Queen Elizabeth I drank lavender-infused water daily as a relief for her well-documented migraines and other ailments. She also had her breakfast conserves flavoured with lavender. The Elizabethans considered it an aromatic stimulant and it was used to revive ladies after fainting. The oil is very versatile and is often used in skin care, to ease and treat acne, insect bites and nappy rash.

olive oil and lavender-scented guinea fowl

With lavender's closeness in taste to rosemary, it makes perfect sense to use it as you would rosemary with roast poultry. The people of southern France have long used lavender with chicken and duck. Always look for untreated lavender, free of additives and other harmful properties.

125g (4^1/2oz) unsalted butter
1 lemon
1 tablespoon chopped summer savory
1 tablespoon lavender pollen (see page 93)
1 x 1.6–1.8kg (3^1/2–4lb) guinea fowl
100ml (3^1/2fl oz) olive oil
150ml (^{1}/4 pint) Sauternes (or another sweet white wine)
300ml (^{1}/2 pint) well-flavoured chicken stock
Salt and freshly ground black pepper

FOR THE VEGETABLES:
400g (14oz) baby new potatoes, scrubbed
1 aubergine, cut into 2.5cm (1in) dice
1 red pepper, cut into quarters
1 fennel bulb, cut into wedges
8 garlic cloves, unpeeled

In a bowl, beat the butter to soften it slightly, then grate in the zest from the lemon and add the chopped savory and lavender pollen. Mix well and season with salt and pepper. Season the guinea fowl all over with salt and pepper. Carefully lift the skin of the breast and push the flavoured butter underneath so it sits on top of the breasts. Place in the fridge to firm up for 1 hour.

Preheat the oven to 200°C/400°F/gas mark 6. Place the guinea fowl in a large roasting tin. Cut the lemon in half and rub it all over the fowl, squeezing the juice over. Pour the olive oil over the bird, then place in the oven and roast for 30 minutes. Remove from the oven, add the potatoes and return to the oven until they are tender and golden. Add the remaining vegetables and cook until lightly caramelised.

Transfer the guinea fowl and vegetables to a serving dish and keep warm. Place the roasting tin on the heat, add the sweet white wine and bring to the boil, stirring to scrape up any residue from the base of the tin. Add the stock, return to the boil and simmer until the sauce has reduced enough to coat the back of a spoon. Adjust the seasoning, then pour the sauce over the guinea fowl and serve surrounded by the roasted vegetables.

twice-cooked duck with lavender honey

If you have any reservations about using lavender in cooking, do me one favour and try this roasted duck dish. I promise you it will open your eyes to its possibilities. The sauce has a wonderfully rich flavour that acts as a superb foil for the duck – go on, give it a go!

4 teaspoons fresh lavender flowers

1 tablespoon thyme leaves

1/4 teaspoon black peppercorns

2 teaspoons coarse salt

1 x 2.2kg (5lb) duck, cleaned of all giblets except the liver

85ml (3fl oz) red wine vinegar

600ml (1 pint) duck stock (or chicken stock)

150ml (1/4 pint) red wine

2 tablespoons lavender honey

2 tablespoons vegetable oil

4 slices of baguette, toasted (1cm/1/2in thick)

Salt and freshly ground black pepper

Preheat the oven to 200°C/400°F/gas mark 6. Place half the fresh lavender flowers in a mortar with the thyme, peppercorns and salt (or use a spice grinder) and grind to a powder. With a knife, lightly score the duck breasts in a criss-cross pattern, ensuring you don't cut through them. Rub the surface and outside of the duck with half the spice mixture. Place the duck in a roasting tin and roast for 1 3/4 hours.

Remove from the oven, transfer the duck to a plate and keep warm. Pour off excess fat from the tin and place the tin on the stove over a high heat. Pour in the red wine vinegar and bring to the boil, stirring to scrape up any residue from the base of the tin. Pour in the stock and red wine and bring to the boil. Return the duck to the pan and brush half the lavender honey over it. Return to the oven and cook, basting the duck once or twice with the pan juices, brushing it with the remaining honey and sprinkling over the remaining spice mixture. After about 15 minutes the duck should be beautifully caramelised. Remove it from the roasting tin and keep warm. Put the roasting tin back on the stove and simmer the cooking liquid until it is thick enough to coat the back of a spoon. Strain through a fine sieve, then taste and adjust the seasoning. Keep warm.

Sauté the duck liver in the vegetable oil for 3–4 minutes. Remove and mash in a bowl with a little salt and pepper, then spread it over the 4 toasted baguette slices. Cut the duck into 8 pieces and arrange in a serving dish. Pour over the sauce and garnish with the liver toasts.

apricot and lavender marmalade

This marmalade makes a great breakfast treat, spread thickly on buttered country toast or brioche. If, like me, you don't worry too much about the calories, top it with a dollop of crème fraîche. Close your eyes and you could be in Provence.

MAKES ABOUT 1.3KG (3LB)

1kg (2¹/4lb) apricots

1kg (2¹/4lb) caster sugar

Juice of 1/2 lemon

100ml (3¹/2fl oz) lavender honey

2 tablespoons dried lavender flowers

Halve and stone the apricots. Combine the apricots, sugar and lemon juice in a preserving pan or large, heavy-based saucepan. Leave to macerate for 3–4 hours at room temperature.

Place the pan on the heat, add the honey and dried lavender and bring to the boil over a high heat, stirring often. Reduce the heat and cook for 40–45 minutes, scraping the bottom of the pan with a wooden spoon occasionally so the mixture doesn't catch.

To test if the marmalade has reached setting point (105°C/220°F on a sugar thermometer), put a teaspoonful of it on a cold saucer, leave for a minute or two, then push it with your finger – if it wrinkles, the marmalade is ready. Remove from the heat and leave to stand for 10 minutes. Pour into sterilised jars (see below) and seal.

PG TIP To sterilise jars, wash them thoroughly in hot soapy water, then rinse well and place on a baking tray. Dry in an oven preheated to 140°C/275°F/gas mark 1.

pear beignets dusted with lavender sugar

Lavender sugar has a wonderful perfume that can pervade a room. It is best made in advance, for it just gets better as time goes by. Be sure to make plenty, as it is also good sprinkled on fruit tarts and other sweet confections.

4 ripe pears
Oil for deep-frying

FOR THE LAVENDER SUGAR:
5 tablespoons caster sugar
1¹/₂ teaspoons dried lavender flowers

FOR THE BATTER:
175g (6oz) plain flour
1 egg
2 egg yolks
2 tablespoons olive oil
20g (³/₄oz) caster sugar
A pinch of salt
300ml (¹/₂ pint) full-fat milk

To make the lavender sugar, mix the caster sugar and lavender flowers together, place in a sealed jar and leave for up to 2 weeks, ideally, although it's fine to use it straight away if necessary.

For the batter, whisk all the ingredients together, holding back half the milk. When smooth, whisk in the remainder of the milk. Strain through a fine sieve and leave to rest for 30 minutes before use.

Peel the pears, remove the core and cut them into thick slices or wedges. Heat the oil to 170°C/325°F in a deep-fat fryer or a large, deep saucepan. Dip the pears into the batter and fry them in the hot oil until golden and crisp. Drain on kitchen paper and place in a serving dish. Sprinkle liberally with the lavender sugar and serve immediately.

PG TIP If you don't have a deep-fat fryer, test the oil by adding a cube if day-old bread to the pan; if it browns in 30 seconds the oil is hot enough.

stuffed apples with rhubarb crumble and lavender

Here is a sexy preparation for our much-loved apple crumble, served in a baked apple. The crumble mixture includes dried lavender, which gives it an unusual fragrant taste.

600g (1¹/₄lb) rhubarb, chopped
Juice and grated zest of 1 orange
75g (3oz) demerara sugar
1 teaspoon ground cinnamon
4 Russet or Golden Delicious apples

FOR THE CRUMBLE TOPPING:
150g (5oz) plain flour
1 teaspoon baking powder
75g (3oz) demerara sugar
1 teaspoon lavender pollen (see page 93)
75g (3oz) blanched almonds, chopped (optional)
75g (3oz) unsalted butter, diced
1 teaspoon lavender flowers, to decorate

Put the rhubarb, orange juice and zest, sugar and cinnamon in a saucepan and bring to the boil. Cover and simmer for 8–10 minutes, then cool slightly.

Cut the tops off the apples, about 2cm (³/₄in) from the top, and with a small teaspoon carefully scoop out the core and pips. Fill the apples with the rhubarb mixture.

Preheat the oven to 180°C/350°F/gas mark 4. For the topping, sift the flour and baking powder into a bowl and stir in the sugar, lavender pollen and almonds, if using. Rub the butter into the flour mixture until it resembles breadcrumbs. Sprinkle the crumble mixture over the apples, pressing down lightly to form a crust.

Place the apples in a buttered ovenproof dish and bake for 35–40 minutes, until they are tender and the crumble is golden and crisp. Decorate with the lavender flowers and serve with lashings of cream or good old custard.

lemons and limes

I have always tended to think of lemons as being truly Mediterranean, but they were, in fact, discovered in South-east Asia. Both China and India claim to be their birthplace, although according to history India seems the more logical choice.

The Romans used lemons as an antidote to poison as well as a moth repellent, rather than as a food during the first century AD. From Rome, lemons found their way to Persia, from where they spread to Spain and North Africa.

recipes

DESCRIPTION

Lemon trees (*Citrus limon*) are fairly small with glossy, dark, evergreen leaves and fragrant blossom. The fruit ripens in winter and lemons taste best when left to ripen on the tree then picked and used quickly as their fragrance tends to disappear after a day or two. Limes, fruit of the *Citrus aurantifolia*, are always picked unripe and green; if left on the tree longer, they would turn yellow. While both Lemons and limes are rich in vitamin C, lemons contain almost twice as much as limes.

LEMONS

Lemons must surely be the most versatile and indispensable food item for any cook. They provide a range of effects: sharp juice for a clean, fresh flavour; zest for scented sharpness to a mousse or sauce; they are wonderful in tarts, puddings, refreshing sorbets and long summer drinks. They also add a piquant sour tang to salad dressings, give a lift when squeezed over grilled meat, while fish and seafood could not live without an accompanying wedge of lemon.

As well as adding flavour to a range of foods, lemon juice is also used as a tenderiser for fish and meat. It can be used as a bleach, too, and rubbed on cut surfaces of fruits and vegetables, such as apples, pears, artichokes and salsify to stop them turning brown before cooking, and also during cooking adding a few drops to the water keeps them beautifully white.

There are numerous varieties of lemons grown and used throughout the world. In Spain the Verna lemon is held in great affection, while in Italy chefs have particular regard for the Ferminetto, brought over by the Arabs in the ninth century. Invernali has a soft skin and is a very juicy variety, and the prized Verdelli is much sought after. The Meyer lemon is adored by Americans who love its tart yet sweet flavour in creamy desserts.

LIMES

Limes prefer a hotter, wetter climate than lemons and flourish in the tropics, where they replace lemons. They originated in Malaysia but are also now grown in Mexico, the Caribbean, Florida and tropical Africa.

British sailors consumed copious amounts of lime on long sea voyages during the late nineteenth century to ward off scurvy, a deadly maritime disease. This practice actually became law with the Merchant Shipping Act of 1894 which required each crew member, after ten days at sea to consume 2 tablespoons of lime juice daily. Thankfully for the sailors a little rum was added to it, by way of preservation, and coaxing! Sailors thus acquired the nickname 'Limeys'. Fortunately scurvy is extinct these days and our vitamin C intake is more readily under control.

There are a number of varieties of lime, most notably the American Key Lime, a West Indian variety which grows in the Florida Keys, and is

BUYING AND STORING LEMONS AND LIMES

Always try to buy organic lemons and limes where possible, as they are the two fruit that I think are all the better for it. When buying lemons from supermarkets, do bear in mind that most (commercially grown) lemons are unfortunately picked unripe as their high acid content helps them last longer in storage. They are therefore treated with ethylene oxide, which turns their chlorophyll green into an enticing lemon yellow.

So remember, the juciest lemons and limes will never look good but will undoubtedly have the best flavour. When buying lemons and limes, thin-skinned varieties tend to be juicier whereas thicker-skinned varieties are better for zesting. When purchasing, they should feel weighty – an indication of their juiciness. Keep them in a bowl in the kitchen: they will not only stay at their best, but will brighten up the room no end.

A common practice is to wax lemons to give a wonderful shiny gloss, so if you plan to zest them, first wash them well in boiling water and dry thoroughly before use.

USING LEMONS AND LIMES

Lemon skins contain an oil which is used in confectionery and in perfumery. Twenty drops of lemon oil is equivalent to the juice of an average lemon, so you can see why the finely grated zest is such an effective flavouring.

To extract the most juice from lemons and limes, here's a tip. Simply roll them under the palm of your hand for a while to help release the inner juices. Another trade secret in these modern days is to place the fruit in the microwave for 30 seconds, or some chefs suggest immersing them in warm water for 20 seconds will give a better yield.

As a guide, one medium lemon equals 2–3 tablespoons of juice and approximately 3 teaspoons of freshly grated zest or rind.

complementary flavours

FOR LEMON:

VANILLA

SEAFOOD

MEAT (ESPECIALLY LAMB, CHICKEN, VEAL AND DUCK)

HONEY

NUTS

HERBS (ESPECIALLY THYME AND ROSEMARY)

FRUIT (ESPECIALLY RASPBERRIES, STRAWBERRIES AND BLACKCURRANTS)

FOR LIME:

COCONUT MILK

CHILLIES

LEMONGRASS

CORIANDER

AVOCADO

TOMATO

HONEY

SHELLFISH

adored by Americans in their Key Lime Pie. Another one is the Tahitian (sometimes also called the Persian lime).

The dark green, knobbly skinned kaffir or wild lime (*Citrus hystrix*) is an essential ingredient in many Thai dishes. These limes do not have much juice, but both the skin and the distinctive, 'winged' leaves are frequently used. The leaves are added whole to curries and soups (like Tom Yam) to infuse flavour and should be removed before serving. They are also shredded very finely and added to salads. The leaves are best used fresh. The zest tends to be even more intense than that of limes.

The acid in lemons and limes has a pickling effect on fish and seafood, such as my Tiritas (page 101), where the acid cooks the fish during the marinating process. Keep in mind that limes are more acidic than lemons.

Use lemon juice for a sharper flavour or to counteract oiliness or greasiness. It is more aromatic than vinegar, and is an essential ingredient in mayonnaise, hollandaise and béarnaise sauces.

Lime juice can be used for almost all the same purposes as lemon, although it has a rather sweeter flavour.

CULINARY USES

Lemons and limes are used throughout the world. In the Middle East cooks use lemon as a souring agent. They love to make fresh lemonade using the rind and pulp of freshly picked lemons, with added water and sugar. They add lemon to their dips such as Baba Ghanousch, Moutabel and Hummus. The Greeks add lemon to Skordalia, a highly aromatic garlic sauce that accompanies vegetables.

Limes add a wonderful sweet sharp flavour to Asian dressings such as my Nam Jim (page 102). In India limes are salted like lemons or preserved as a pickle, highly seasoned with chillies.

In Morocco, lemons are preserved in salt (page 106), before being added to their tagines and rice dishes. The juice is added to tea to make a refreshing drink in the hot climate.

The Italians have a great affection for lemons, too, which they add to pasta sauces and dips, and make their wonderful lemoncello drink from zest and pulp of lemon mixed with sugar, water and 30 per cent natural alcohol. (I first experienced this when it was added to an ice-cream by the chef of the Hassler Hotel in Rome during one of our many guest chef promotions. I use it to this day.) Lemons are also a major ingredient in Italian cakes, cocktails and desserts.

In Mexico limes are the god of fruits, added to *mojos* (pronounced *mohos*) a sauce similar to a salsa for grilled meats and fish; they are also squeezed over fruits such as strawberries with a dash of tequila, used in marinades, soups and, well, just about anything.

As a chef, I use lemons daily in one form or another: I add them to sauces to give a discerning sharp flavour, to help balance the concentrated flavours of a reduced sauce, to give a lift to desserts, to soups, to dressings etc. All in all, citrus fruits hold unlimited use in cooking.

LEMON AND LIME TIPS

• When grating lemons and limes, place a sheet of greaseproof paper between the fruit and the grater before grating normally. The zest will stick to the paper and not the grater, and can be just scooped up with a knife.
• Cut lemons and limes in half and wrap in muslin. The muslin stops the pips falling out and prevents the juice from spurting everywhere. Your guests will be impressed when served with fish dishes.
• Excess lime and lemon juice freezes well, so keep in plastic ice cube trays and store in the freezer for use at any time.
• Use lemon and lime leaves to wrap fish and meat prior to grilling.
• 3 tablespoons of lemon or lime juice equals 1 average lemon or lime.

OTHER USES

Lemons and limes have a very high vitamin C content, which explains why they have been used to treat everything from scurvy to the common cold. Aside from medicinal applications, lemons can also be used as a bleaching and cleaning agent. Adding a few slices of lemon to boiling water when cooking eggs, prevents a ring forming in the pan. Rubbing cut lemon over your board after chopping onions, crushing garlic etc, will remove the smell. Lemons are also said to be great for cleaning copper, bleaching blond hair and balancing greasy skin!

tiritas

Tiritas is the first cousin of the Mexican dish, ceviche — white fish 'cooked' in a lime juice marinade. This recipe is from the Yucatán. Tuna, with its vibrant colour, makes a pleasant change from white fish.

400g (14oz) sushi-quality (i.e. extremely fresh) blue
   fin tuna, cut into 1cm (^{1}/$_{2}$in) dice
Juice of 3 limes
2 tablespoons olive oil
2 tablespoons tomato ketchup
A few drops of Tabasco
^{1}/$_{2}$ ripe mango, peeled and cut into 5mm (^{1}/$_{4}$in) dice
^{1}/$_{4}$ red pepper, cut into 5mm (^{1}/$_{4}$in) dice
^{1}/$_{2}$ avocado, peeled and cut into 5mm (^{1}/$_{4}$in) dice
1 red chilli, deseeded and finely chopped
2 spring onions, roughly chopped
2 tablespoons roughly chopped coriander
Salt and freshly ground black pepper

TO SERVE:
Corn tortillas, cut into quarters and fried until crisp
Lime wedges (optional)
Coriander leaves

Place the tuna in a bowl, pour over the lime juice, then add a little salt and leave for 30 minutes, until the tuna becomes opaque. Drain off the juice and combine some of it, according to taste, with the olive oil, tomato ketchup and Tabasco to form a dressing. Add the mango, red pepper, avocado, red chilli, spring onions, coriander and some salt and pepper. Pour this dressing over the tuna, mix well and chill for 1 hour.

Serve in cocktail-style glasses, garnished with the fried corn tortillas, lime wedges and coriander leaves.

roasted skate with lemon and caper sauce

4 x 275–350g (10–12oz) skate wings
4 tablespoons olive oil
25g (1oz) unsalted butter
Salt and freshly ground black pepper

FOR THE SAUCE:
4 tablespoons olive oil
2 shallots, chopped
1 garlic clove, crushed
1 tablespoon chopped preserved lemons
   (see page 106)
2 tablespoons superfine capers, drained and rinsed
A pinch of ground cumin
1 tablespoon chopped coriander
1/2 tablespoon chopped mint
125ml (4fl oz) hot fish stock (or water)
25g (1oz) chilled unsalted butter, diced

Preheat the oven to 200°C/400°F/gas mark 6. Season the skate wings with salt and pepper. Heat the oil in a large ovenproof frying pan, add the butter and, when it begins to foam, add the skate wings. Cook for 2 minutes on each side, until golden, then place in the oven for 5–6 minutes, until cooked through.

Meanwhile, for the sauce, heat the oil in a pan, add the shallots, garlic, preserved lemon, capers and cumin and cook over a gentle heat for 2 minutes. Add the herbs and hot stock, then whisk in the diced butter over a low heat to form a light sauce. Adjust the seasoning and keep warm.

Put the skate on serving plates and spoon over the sauce. Serve with plain potatoes and buttered spinach.

nam jim (lime and green chilli dressing)

This power-packed dressing from Southeast Asia combines sour, sweet, hot and salty flavours to great effect. I love it with crab, prawns, chicken and vegetables. For a spicier dressing still, leave the chilli seeds in.

2 tablespoons palm sugar (or demerara sugar)
2 tablespoons sea salt
3 garlic cloves, chopped
A good handful of coriander leaves
5 hot green chillies, deseeded and finely chopped
1 cm (1/2in) piece of fresh root ginger, finely grated
   (optional)
4 large shallots, chopped
3 tablespoons nam pla (Thai fish sauce)
Juice of 8 limes

Put the palm sugar into a small pan and melt over a low heat, then set aside.

With a pestle and mortar, crush the sea salt, garlic and coriander leaves to a pulp. Add the chopped chillies, sugar and ginger, if using, and pound again. Mix in the shallots, fish sauce and lime juice. Leave for up to 1 hour before use to allow the flavours to develop. It will keep in the fridge for about a week.

sea bream with anchovy, mozzarella and roasted lemons

4 x 175g (6oz) sea bream fillets
2 tablespoons olive oil
2 small lemons, cut into slices 2cm (3/4in) thick
2 plum tomatoes, peeled and sliced
1 buffalo mozzarella, cut into 4 slices
1/2 teaspoon lemon thyme leaves
Salt and freshly ground black pepper

FOR THE ANCHOVY SAUCE:

4 tablespoons extra virgin olive oil

1 shallot, finely chopped

2 anchovy fillets, finely chopped

1 garlic clove, crushed

1 tablespoon lemon juice

1 tablespoon sherry vinegar

8 basil leaves

Preheat the oven to 200°C/400°F/gas mark 6. Season the fish liberally with salt and pepper. Heat the oil in a large frying pan, place the fish in it skin-side down and cook for 2 minutes, without turning. Remove from the pan and set aside, skin-side up. Add the lemon slices to the oil and cook for 3–4 minutes on each side, until coloured. Remove from the pan and set aside.

Place 2 slices of tomato on each fish fillet, top with a slice of mozzarella, then season with salt and pepper and sprinkle with the lemon thyme leaves. Return the fish to the pan and add the lemon slices. Place in the oven for 5–6 minutes, until the fish is cooked and the cheese is melting.

Meanwhile, make the sauce. Heat the oil in a small pan over a low heat, add the shallot, anchovies and garlic and cook gently for 2–3 minutes. Stir in the lemon juice, sherry vinegar and basil and season to taste.

To serve, place the fish on serving plates, pour the anchovy sauce around and top with the roasted lemons. Great served with wilted spinach.

veal chops with lemon sauce and swiss chard

4 x 200g (7oz) thick veal cutlets
2 tablespoons olive oil
50g (2oz) chilled unsalted butter, diced
Juice and grated zest of 1 lemon
1 tablespoon brown sugar
125ml (4fl oz) dry white wine
300ml (1/2 pint) brown veal stock (or other meat stock)
1 lemon, peel and pith removed, cut into slices
Salt and freshly ground black pepper

FOR THE SWISS CHARD:
1 tablespoon olive oil
1 large head of Swiss chard, leaves only, coarsely
   chopped
1 garlic clove, crushed
2 tablespoons raisins, soaked in warm water until
   swollen, then drained
2 tablespoons pine kernels, toasted

Season the veal with salt and pepper. Heat the oil in a frying pan, add half the butter and when it foams add the veal chops. Cook over a moderate heat for about 4–5 minutes on each side, until just tender. Remove from the pan and keep warm.

Remove any excess fat from the pan, add the lemon juice and sugar and cook until lightly caramelised. Pour in the white wine, raise the heat and boil for 2 minutes. Add the stock, return to the boil and stir in the lemon zest. Reduce the heat and simmer until the sauce is reduced by half.

Meanwhile, for the Swiss chard, heat the olive oil in a pan, add the chard, garlic and raisins and cook for 1 minute. Stir in 100ml (3 1/2fl oz) water, cover and cook for 4–5 minutes, until the chard is tender and all the liquid has evaporated. Add the pine kernels and season with salt and pepper.

Finish the lemon sauce by whisking in the remaining butter, a little at a time. Taste and adjust the seasoning.

Put the Swiss chard on 4 serving plates and top with the veal. Put a lemon slice on each veal chop, pour over the lemon sauce and serve.

poached asparagus with avgolemono

Avgolemono, meaning egg and lemon, is a staple of Greek cooking. The name often refers to a soup made from chicken stock and rice and finished with egg and lemon but it can also be a sauce, served with fish and vegetables.

32 asparagus spears

FOR THE AVGOLEMONO:
2 egg yolks
Juice of 2 lemons
2 teaspoons cornflour
2 tablespoons double cream
Salt and freshly ground black pepper

Peel the asparagus spears, reserving the peelings, and snap off the base of each one at its natural breaking point (about 2.5cm/1in from the end). Tie the asparagus into 4 bundles with string and set aside. Bring 1 litre (1 3/4 pints) of water to the boil in a large saucepan, add the asparagus peelings and simmer for 20 minutes to form a light asparagus stock. Strain into a clean pan and return to the boil. Poach the asparagus spears in the stock for 4–5 minutes, until just tender. Remove from the pan with a slotted spoon and keep warm. Boil the stock until it has reduced to 300ml (1/2 pint).

To make the sauce, whisk the egg yolks and lemon juice together in a heavy-based pan, off the heat. Mix the cornflour to a paste with 1 tablespoon of water and add to the egg yolks. Gradually add the hot asparagus stock, whisking constantly. Place on a low heat and cook, stirring, until the mixture has thickened just enough to coat the back of a spoon. It should not boil.

Remove from the heat, add the cream and season to taste. Pour the sauce over the asparagus and serve immediately.

with half the remaining salt. Pack the lemons in tightly, pushing them down well to release their juices. Push the bay leaves in between the lemons. Mix the remaining salt with the sugar, allspice berries, coriander seeds and star anise and sprinkle it over the lemons. Squeeze the juice from the remaining 6 lemons and strain into the jar. Seal and leave in a cool place for at least 1 month, turning the jar on end each day. When using the preserved lemons, cut off the flesh and use only the peel.

lemon chiffon cream If you are searching
for a very light and refreshing dessert, look no further. This is so airy and delicate that it might just float away if left unattended — beware! It's a delicious summer dish served with fresh berries. You could make it with limes instead of lemons.

2 gelatine leaves
Juice and grated zest of 2 lemons
175g (6oz) caster sugar
3 large eggs, separated
300ml (1/2 pint) double cream, semi-whipped

Cover the gelatine leaves with cold water for 5 minutes, then squeeze out excess water with your hands. Place the gelatine in a small pan with half the lemon juice and warm very gently, stirring until dissolved. Remove from the heat and set aside.

In a bowl, whisk the sugar and egg yolks together until thick and creamy. Add the lemon zest and the remaining juice, then stir in the dissolved gelatine.

In a separate bowl, whisk the egg whites until stiff. Fold the semi-whipped cream into the lemon mixture then, with a metal spoon, carefully fold in the egg whites. Pour into a bowl, cover with clingfilm and chill until set.

preserved lemons Some recipes for preserved lemons are
too salty for my taste. Here's a milder version that can be used in all sorts of dishes. They will keep, unopened, for up to 1 year and for up to a month once opened. Try preserving limes in the same way.

12 medium lemons
350g (12oz) coarse sea salt
3 bay leaves
2 tablespoons caster sugar
15 allspice berries
15 coriander seeds
5 star anise

Slit 6 of the lemons into quarters vertically, taking the cuts to within 1cm (1/2 in) of the base. Open them out carefully with your hands. Pack some of the salt into the centre of each lemon and press together to re-form its shape.

Sterilise a 1 litre (1 3/4 pint) preserving jar (see page 95) and fill

lemon and almond butter tart

SERVES 6

2 large eggs
100g (3¹/₂ oz) caster sugar
Juice and grated zest of 2 lemons
125g (4¹/₂oz) unsalted butter, melted
75g (3oz) ground almonds
Icing sugar for dusting

FOR THE SWEET PASTRY:
350g (12oz) plain flour, sifted
225g (8oz) unsalted butter (at room temperature),
    cut into small pieces
A pinch of salt
100g (3¹/₂ oz) icing sugar, sifted
Finely grated zest of ¹/₂ lemon
1 egg

First make the pastry. Put the sifted flour on to a work surface and make a well in the centre. Put the diced butter, salt, sugar and lemon zest in the well and then add the egg. With your fingertips, gradually bring the flour into the centre until all the ingredients come together to form a soft dough. Knead lightly for 1 minute, until completely smooth, then shape the dough into a ball, place in a bowl and cover with clingfilm. Leave to rest in the fridge for 2 hours.

Preheat the oven to 190°C/375°F/gas mark 5. Roll out the sweet pastry to 3mm (¹/₈in) thick and use to line a 25cm (10in) tart tin. Prick the base lightly all over with a fork. Line with greaseproof paper, fill with baking beans and bake blind for 10 minutes or until the pastry is set but not coloured. Remove the beans and paper and return the pastry case to the oven for 5 minutes, then leave to cool. Reduce the oven temperature to 180°C/350°F/gas mark 4.

For the filling, beat the eggs and sugar with an electric, or hand-held beater until light and creamy and thick enough to leave a trail when the whisk is lifted. Fold in the lemon juice and zest and the melted butter, then finally add the ground almonds. Pour the mixture into the tart case, return to the oven and bake for 25–30 minutes, until golden and set. Leave to cool and then dust with icing sugar before serving.

lime posset with champagne red berry jelly

1 tablespoon caster sugar
300ml (¹/₂ pint) double cream
Juice and grated zest of 2 juicy limes, plus a little
    extra grated zest to decorate
2 small egg whites
1¹/₂ teaspoons icing sugar

FOR THE JELLY:
2 gelatine leaves
75g (3oz) caster sugar
250ml (9fl oz) champagne (or sparkling wine)
300g (11oz) mixed red berries (such as raspberries,
    strawberries and blackberries), plus a few extra to
    decorate

First make the jelly. Cover the gelatine leaves with cold water for 5 minutes to soften them. Meanwhile, put the sugar and champagne in a saucepan and bring to the boil, stirring occasionally to dissolve the sugar. Remove from the heat, add the berries and stir well. Squeeze out excess water from the gelatine. Add the gelatine to the hot fruit syrup and stir until dissolved. Allow to cool, then divide the fruit jelly between 4 tall sundae glasses; it should come almost half way up them. Place in the fridge to set.

For the posset, bring the sugar and cream to the boil in a pan and cook over a high heat for 3–4 minutes. Remove from the heat, add the lime juice and zest, then pour into a large bowl and leave to cool. Whisk the egg whites with the icing sugar until stiff, then fold into the chilled cream. To finish, top each jelly-filled glass with the lime posset and decorate with lime zest and a few red berries. Serve chilled.

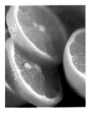

lemongrass

This is grown in tropical Asia, but has spread to Africa and America and can, in fact, be grown successfully anywhere with a temperate climate. It is said that Queen Victoria regularly enjoyed lemongrass tea during her reign

DESCRIPTION

Growing in tall bunches of leaves on a 1m (3ft) perennial, greenish plant, lemongrass (*Cymbopogon citratus*) is a grass-like herb with a refreshing citrus tang and flavour, with gingerish overtones.

Similar to spring onions in appearance, it is generally used as a seasoning and aromatic in southern Asia, although nowadays it is one Asian flavour that crosses over comfortably with Western-style dishes.

BUYING AND STORING

When buying lemongrass, look for firm, smooth stems and green leaves without any brown edges. Lemongrass loses its flavour within a few days of being picked, so buy it as fresh as possible and use it up quickly. Having said this, it will keep for a couple of weeks, if wrapped in paper in the fridge. Ensure, however, that it is securely covered, as its smell can permeate other foods.

PREPARATION

To prepare lemongrass, first discard the tough upper end of the stalk and use only the bottom 12–15cm (5–6in). Lemongrass can be used in a number of ways. Trimmed with a knife, the stems make a flavourful and strong skewer for grilling fish, meat and fruit. When adding to soups and other dishes as a flavouring, the stalk should be coarsely cut into pieces and then bruised (by bashing them with the back of a knife or a pestle, like the Thais do). This helps to release the inner oils and lemony flavour. The pieces, which will be quite tough, should be removed before serving. Another way to use lemongrass is to strip away all the hard outer layers and slice the tender inner core, very finely, into rings. These can be added to all manner of dishes, from salads to stir-fries.

Dried lemongrass is available, as is a variety in a water solution in a jar; I find both rather flavourless so unless you can get the real thing, I suggest you leave it out. Occasionally, I resort to using a little finely grated lemon zest, simply soaked in water for 2 hours before use (1 tablespoon is roughly equal to 1 fresh lemongrass stick) as a substitute. This won't, however, achieve the unique flavour of lemongrass.

CULINARY USES

Lemongrass, with its distinctive citrus and ginger notes, is a key ingredient in Thai cooking and is often used as a flavouring for seafood. In traditional Thai and Vietnamese cookery the stems are used whole and roughly cut to flavour soups, curries and stews, while the tender inner parts are used in Asian spice pastes. I find that, when chopped very finely, they equally give a wonderful twist to Western-style dressings and salads.

As a delicate flavouring in a soup (try my Lemongrass and Crab Broth, page 110), sautéed with wild mushrooms, or used in a set custard with coconut milk, lemongrass always gives an intriguingly different flavour note.

OTHER USES

Lemongrass tea is said to be good for stimulating appetite and, as a mild diruretic, helps to clear the skin. The essential oil is used in aromatherapy to treat stress-related conditions, as it has sedative effect, and can also serve as an insect repellent.

complementary flavours

GARLIC

SHALLOTS

CHILLIES

FRESH CORIANDER

SHELLFISH (ESPECIALLY
PRAWNS, LOBSTER AND
CRAB)

MEAT (ESPECIALLY PORK)

COCONUT MILK

lemongrass and crab broth

750ml (1¹/₄ pints) well-flavoured fish stock (or
    chicken stock)
400g (14oz) can of chopped tomatoes
2 teaspoons grated fresh root ginger (or galangal)
4 lemongrass stalks, white part only, halved
    lengthways
2 kaffir lime leaves
100g (3¹/₂ oz) Chinese vermicelli rice noodles
1 teaspoon brown sugar
1 garlic clove, crushed
1¹/₂ teaspoons *nam pla* (Thai fish sauce)
450g (1lb) fresh white crabmeat
4 spring onions, finely shredded
A handful of baby spinach leaves (optional)
8 Thai basil leaves, torn into small pieces
Salt and freshly ground black pepper

Put the stock in a saucepan with the tomatoes, ginger,
lemongrass and lime leaves and bring to the boil. Reduce
the heat and simmer for 8–10 minutes, then remove and
discard the lemongrass. Add the noodles, sugar and garlic
and simmer for 3–4 minutes.

    Stir in the fish sauce, crabmeat, spring onions and
spinach, if using, and heat through for 2 minutes. Season to
taste, sprinkle over the Thai basil and serve immediately.

wok-fried fungi with lemongrass

2 tablespoons sesame oil
25g (1oz) unsalted butter
1 garlic clove, crushed
2 shallots, finely chopped
600g (1¹/₄ lb) mixed mushrooms (such as oysters,
    shiitake, trompettes and girolles), cut into
    thick pieces
2 lemongrass stalks, outer layers removed, tender
    inner core very finely chopped
A handful of coriander leaves
1 tablespoon soy sauce
Salt and freshly ground black pepper

Heat a wok until almost smoking, add the sesame oil
and butter, then add the garlic and shallots and cook for
30 seconds. Throw in the wild mushrooms and stir-fry for
2 minutes. Add the lemongrass, coriander leaves and soy
sauce and toss well. Season to taste and serve immediately.

lemongrass soy chicken skewers

4 skinless, boneless chicken breasts, cut into
    2.5cm (1in) cubes
8 lemongrass stalks, outer layers removed

FOR THE MARINADE:
1 tablespoon honey or maple syrup
4 garlic cloves, crushed
2.5cm (1in) piece of fresh root ginger, finely chopped
2 green chillies, finely chopped
Juice of 2 limes

Grated zest of 1 lime
4 tablespoons rice wine vinegar
2 tablespoons sweet chilli sauce
4 tablespoons dark soy sauce, plus extra to serve
A pinch of turmeric

Place all the marinade ingredients in a bowl and mix together well. Add the chicken, then cover and leave to marinate in the fridge for at least 8 hours – preferably 2 days for the best flavour.

Remove the chicken cubes from the marinade and thread them on to the 8 lemongrass stalks. Heat a barbecue, ideally, or a ridged grill pan until smoking. Add the skewers and cook for 8–10 minutes, turning them regularly and brushing liberally with the marinade. Serve hot from the grill, with some extra soy sauce for dipping.

lemongrass, coconut and vanilla panna cotta

1 vanilla pod
2 lemongrass stalks, outer layers removed
350ml (12fl oz) double cream
150ml (^{1}/4 pint) unsweetened coconut milk
40g (1^1/2 oz) caster sugar
1^1/2 gelatine leaves
Assortment of exotic fruits (such as mango, papaya,
    lychee and dragonfruit), peeled and diced, to serve

FOR THE PASSIONFRUIT-CHILLI SYRUP:
2 passionfruit, halved
100ml (3^1/2fl oz) Stock Syrup (see page 13)
Juice and grated zest of ^{1}/2 a lime
^{1}/8 teaspoon deseeded and finely diced red chilli

Cut the vanilla pod in half lengthways and scrape out the seeds with the tip of a sharp knife. Bruise the lemongrass (see page 108) and shred it finely. Heat the cream, coconut milk, vanilla seeds, lemongrass and sugar in a pan but do not let it boil. Meanwhile, cover the gelatine leaves with cold water for 5 minutes, then squeeze out excess water. Remove the cream mixture from the heat, add the softened gelatine and stir until dissolved. Leave to cool, stirring occasionally, then strain into individual tumbler-style glasses and place in the fridge overnight.

For the passionfruit-chilli syrup, scrape the juice and seeds from the passionfruit into a small pan, add the stock syrup and heat gently. Leave for 10–15 minutes to infuse, then strain. Add the lime juice and zest and the diced chilli and leave to cool.

Arrange the exotic fruits on top of the panna cotta, pour over a little of the chilli syrup and serve.

lychee and lemongrass sorbet

I think lychees are one of those exotic fruits that were made to be canned. They work much better than fresh in this particular sorbet.

2 tablespoons caster sugar
1 tablespoon finely grated fresh root ginger
4 lemongrass stalks, outer layers removed, tender
    inner core very finely chopped
850g (1lb 14oz) canned lychees in syrup
2 tablespoons white rum

Place the sugar, ginger and lemongrass in a pan with 100ml (3^1/2 fl oz) water. Bring to the boil and simmer for 5 minutes, until the sugar has dissolved. Remove from the heat and leave to cool.

Drain the lychees, reserving 150ml (^{1}/4 pint) of their syrup. Purée the lychees in a blender, then add the reserved lychee syrup and the lemongrass syrup and blitz to a smooth purée. Strain through a fine sieve into a bowl and stir in the rum. Pour into an ice-cream machine and freeze according to the manufacturer's instructions. Or if you don't have an ice-cream machine, refer to the tip on page 42.

mint

If there is an easier herb to grow than mint, I have yet to come across it! So many mint lovers who grow the herb are at pains to control its rapid expansion and prevent it from completely crowding out other plants. A tip I have learned over the years for restricting mint growth is to plant it in a separate garden bed or container, placed above ground.

Few things smell as much like summer as freshly snipped mint from the garden. I know I'm one chef who couldn't live without its freshness in the kitchen.

recipes

DESCRIPTION

There are around thirty species of mint (genus *Mentha*), apart from the common garden mint; among them the widely available spearmint, so commonly confused with the common mint, and peppermint. Nowadays other unusual varieties are propagated, too, hybrids such as apple, lemon, pineapple, bergamot and, if you really have an open mind, varieties of lavender, ginger and even chocolate! As yet I have only seen them in America, but I'm sure they will spread far and wide eventually. All mint varieties are perennials, and all have invasive roots and a tendency to take over. The common, or garden, mint originated in Greece.

BUYING, STORING AND PREPARATION

Although dried mint is available, I never use it. Always choose bright green leaves with no bruising or wilting and a strong aroma. Fresh leaves can be kept for a couple of days in the refrigerator, or in a glass of water with their stems immersed.

Remove the leaves from the stems before use.

CULINARY USES

Mint is primarily used for flavourings and garnishes. Garden mint is used in both sweet and savoury dishes, to decorate desserts or is added (chopped or whole) to salads. With its rounded green and sweet-smelling leaves, it is the one most frequently used in the kitchen. Generally it is also the variety preferred in Mediterranean and Middle Eastern countries, as in the classic Middle Eastern cracked wheat salad, Tabouleh, in which mint is used as a primary ingredient (or why not try my Fruit Tabouleh, see page 120) In Greece, mint is often used to flavour dolmas (stuffed vine leaves) and in stuffed vegetables.

Mint is added to yoghurt-based dips in a number of countries, for example, in the Greek tzatziki, some Indian raitas and the Turkish haydari (it is also added to a abdug, a rejuvenating yoghurt drink). Mint jelly or sauce served with roast lamb is, of course, a British classic. One of my favourite ways of using mint is to flavour boiled, freshly dug potatoes. It also works very well with tender new carrots or peas.

Spearmint, a close relation, is suitable for use in most recipes in place of garden mint. A native of the Mediterranean, it has long light-green narrow leaves with serrated edges and a distinctive fresh flavour.

Peppermint is used in preparing desserts, and forms the basis of crème de menthe liqueur. It is delicious when added to chilled long drinks, sherberts, punches and tea.

Another variety of mint that I very much favour is Vietnamese mint, or 'Hot' mint, which is in fact not a mint at all. It has a hot, slightly spicy, acidic flavour, much admired in the Far East. I use

complementary flavours

GREEN VEGETABLES
(ESPECIALLY PEAS, BROAD
BEANS, FENNEL AND
ARTICHOKES)

FRUIT (ALL HARD FRUITS,
ESPECIALLY WATERMELON)

SOFT FRUITS (PEACHES,
STRAWBERRIES AND
RASPBERRIES)

MILK PRODUCTS (CREAM,
EGGS AND YOGHURT)

MEAT (ESPECIALLY LAMB)

CHEESE (FETA AND RICOTTA)

it in salads, Asian marinades, in Vietnamese spring rolls, and it's great in soup. It is hard to find but well worth shopping around for.

IDEAS WITH MINT
• Use to infuse in olive oil for salad dressings (Substitute mint for the basil in the recipe on page 15).
• Add leaves to sweet syrup to poach fruits.
• Use small mint leaves to decorate desserts.
• Add chopped leaves to Greek yoghurt and serve with grilled lamb and fish.
• Add leaves to infuse in tea, served hot or chilled in summer.

OTHER USES
Apart from mint's superb culinary attributes, it is much favoured for its medicinal qualities, especially peppermint, which is said to aid digestion, cure hiccups, clear the mind and treat the common cold. It is also used to make a soothing and relaxing tea to calm weary travellers, as for example the iced mint tea served in Middle Eastern and Mediterranean countries as a sign of hospitality. All mint contains a volatile oil called menthol which gives it its characteristic cool, clean feeling, but peppermint has the highest concentration of it — which is why it's such a popular flavourant in chewing gums and toothpastes.

roman-style artichokes

For centuries the Italians have had a love and admiration for artichokes. However some of us find their preparation a little too laborious, but with practice it does get easier. Choose firm artichokes for the job; the baby ones are very tender and delicious.

20 baby artichokes
6 tablespoons olive oil
1 garlic clove, crushed
1 teaspoon dried chilli flakes
175ml (6fl oz) dry white wine
1 good bunch of mint, roughly chopped
Grated zest of 1 lemon
Coarse salt and freshly ground black pepper

Preheat the oven to 150°C/300°F/gas mark 2. Trim the leaves from the artichokes and cut 5mm (1/4 in) off the top of each one, but leave the stalks intact. Place in a bowl of water acidulated with a little lemon juice as you go.

Heat the oil in a casserole, add the garlic and chilli flakes and cook for 2 minutes. Add the artichokes, pour over the wine, then cover with a lid or foil and place in the oven to braise for 15–20 minutes, until the artichokes are tender.

Stir in the chopped mint and lemon zest, season to taste and serve. It can be served at room temperature, if you prefer.

minted chicken and aubergine salad

Pick up a cookery magazine almost anywhere in the world and I bet you will find a recipe for an Asian-style salad within. Fish and meat in fragrant Asian dressings really hit the spot. Here is my version, using Vietnamese mint as a prime ingredient. I find it best served at room temperature.

Sesame oil
4 skinless, boneless chicken breasts
1 aubergine, cut into slices 1cm (1/2 in) thick
2 tablespoons brown sugar
1 tablespoon *nam pla* (Thai fish sauce)
1 garlic clove, crushed
2 green chillies, thinly sliced
Juice of 4 limes
1 lemongrass stalk, outer layers removed, tender
  inner core very finely chopped
1 onion, thinly sliced
2 shallots, chopped
50g (2oz) Vietnamese mint leaves
4 tablespoons roasted peanuts, chopped
Salt and freshly ground black pepper

Heat a ridged grill pan, brush it with a little sesame oil, then season the chicken breasts and place on the grill. Cook for 5-6 minutes on each side, until lightly charred and cooked through. Brush the aubergine slices with sesame oil, place on the grill and cook until lightly charred, turning them regularly and brushing with a little more oil if necessary.

Meanwhile, place the sugar in a bowl, add the fish sauce, garlic, chillies and lime juice and mix well. Stir in the lemongrass, onion and shallots.

Remove the chicken and aubergine from the grill and leave to cool, then shred the chicken and cut the aubergine into small dice. Add to the bowl, toss well, cover with clingfilm and leave to marinate at room temperature for 1 hour.

Add the mint leaves and serve in a deep bowl, sprinkled with the peanuts.

linguine with pumpkin seed-mint sauce and feta cheese

Pumpkin seeds are full of flavour and very nutritious. You should certainly find them in health food stores but they are generally becoming more available everywhere. They give a wonderful nuttiness to the sauce in this unusual pasta dish.

250g (9oz) pumpkin flesh, cut into 1cm (^{1}/2 in) dice
4 tablespoons olive oil
450g (1lb) linguine
100g (3^1/2 oz) feta cheese, crumbled
Salt and freshly ground black pepper
Shavings of Parmesan cheese (or freshly grated
    Parmesan), to serve

FOR THE PUMPKIN SEED-MINT SAUCE:
150g (5oz) pumpkin seeds
50g (2oz) mint leaves
3 garlic cloves, chopped
A pinch of ground cumin
^{1}/4 teaspoon dried chilli flakes
About 150ml (^{1}/4 pint) virgin olive oil

Preheat the oven to 180°C/350°F/gas mark 4. or the pumpkin seed-mint sauce, spread the pumpkin seeds out on a baking sheet and roast in the oven for 10 minutes, until fragrant. Leave to cool, then place in a blender or food processor with the mint, garlic, cumin and chilli flakes. Blitz to a fine paste and then, with the motor running, slowly pour in enough olive oil to give a smooth, slightly runny sauce. Season to taste and set aside.

   Place the pumpkin on a baking sheet, toss with the olive oil and some salt and pepper and bake for 10–15 minutes, until tender and lightly browned. Meanwhile, cook the pasta in a large pan of boiling salted water until al dente.

   Drain the pasta, toss it with the sauce and adjust the seasoning. Top with the roasted pumpkin and feta cheese, sprinkle over some Parmesan shavings and serve immediately.

sweet and sour courgettes

Courgettes, to my mind, do not have a great flavour. They can be rather bland and watery and I think they generally need something of a helping hand. This sweet and sour dish is best made with very young, tender courgettes, but if you can't get them, simply replace with thickly sliced larger ones. Serve at room temperature for the best results.

2 tablespoons virgin olive oil
450g (1lb) baby courgettes, trimmed
1 small garlic clove, thinly sliced
1 tablespoon raisins
1 teaspoon caster sugar
8 mint leaves, roughly chopped
3 tablespoons white wine vinegar
2 tablespoons pine kernels, toasted

Heat the oil in a large frying pan, add the courgettes and fry until they are beautifully golden and almost tender. Add the garlic and raisins and cook for 2 minutes. Sprinkle over the sugar and mint and toss together so that the courgettes become lightly caramelised. Pour over the vinegar and toss again for 30 seconds. Remove from the heat and leave to cool before serving, scattered with the pine kernels.

seafood with fennel and mint

Visit any Italian coastal town and you will find a similar dish to this one, comprising fresh local seafood in a dressing of good olive oil and lemon juice. The addition of mint gives an unusual twist and complements the seafood beautifully, especially when you leave it overnight for the flavours to develop. On no account overcook the fish or it will become chewy and inedible.

500g (1lb 2oz) fresh mussels
1 onion, roughly chopped
Stalks from the mint leaves for the marinade
100ml (3^1/2 fl oz) dry white wine
300g (11oz) monkfish fillet, cut into 2.5cm (1in) dice
200g (7oz) squid, cut into rings
16 uncooked tiger prawns, de-veined (see page 33)
8 fresh scallops, cut horizontally in half
**1 fennel bulb, very thinly sliced with a large peeler
   or knife**
Salt and freshly ground black pepper

FOR THE MARINADE:
Juice of 2 lemons
100ml (3^1/2 fl oz) virgin olive oil
2 garlic cloves, crushed
2 tablespoons chopped mint
Fronds from the fennel

Clean the mussels under cold running water and pull out the beards. Discard any open mussels that don't close when tapped on the work surface. Place the mussels in a pan, add the onion and mint stalks, then pour over the white wine and 150ml (^{1}/4 pint) of water. Place on a high heat, cover and steam for 3—4 minutes, until the mussels open. Drain in a colander, reserving the cooking liquor. Strain it through a fine sieve back into the pan.

Season the remaining fish and shellfish and cook in the mussel stock — first cook the monkfish for 3—4 minutes, then add the squid, prawns and scallops and cook for a minute longer. Transfer the fish and shellfish to a bowl and set aside. Remove the mussels from their shells and add them to the bowl.

Make the marinade by whisking all the ingredients together

Mix in the cooking liquor from the seafood. Add the shredded fennel to the seafood, then pour over the dressing and mix well. Cover and leave to marinate in the fridge overnight, turning the mixture occasionally.

Serve with lots of crusty farmhouse bread.

fruit tabouleh
Tabouleh is traditionally a cracked wheat (bulgur) salad from the Middle East, made with lots of garlic and parsley. I sometimes prepare it using couscous instead. This fruit variation is very light and fresh, and makes a simple addition to a barbecue dessert table.

75g (3oz) caster sugar
1 vanilla pod
200g (7oz) couscous
225g (8oz) strawberries, cut in half
125g (4^1/2 oz) raspberries
125g (4^1/2 oz) blackberries
1 ripe pear, peeled, cored and cut into wedges
1 ripe nectarine, stoned and cut into wedges
1 banana, peeled and thickly sliced
Leaves from 1 good bunch of mint

Place the sugar in a pan with 600ml (1 pint) of water and bring slowly to the boil. Meanwhile, slit the vanilla pod open lengthways and scrape out the seeds with the tip of a sharp knife. Add the pod and seeds to the pan and simmer for 5 minutes.

Place the couscous in a bowl. Remove the vanilla pod from the sugar syrup and pour the syrup over the couscous. Cover with a lid or clingfilm and leave to steam for 5 minutes. Uncover and fluff up the couscous with a fork, then cover and leave to steam again for 2—3 minutes. Fluff up with a fork again and leave to cool, uncovered.

Add all the fruit to the couscous and mix together carefully. Stir in the mint leaves and mix again. Chill for 30 minutes before serving.

gin, tonic and mint sorbet with pineapple carpaccio

One of my favourite tipples before dinner (or at any time, if I am truthful!) is a good old G&T. In the summer, I like it with extra lemon and a sprig of mint, which funnily enough led me to think about a sorbet on the same lines. I tried it and here it is, served with thin slices of ripe pineapple.

200g (7oz) caster sugar
1 good bunch of mint
300ml (1/2 pint) tonic water
100ml (31/2 fl oz) dry gin
Juice of 6 lemons
Grated zest of 1 lemon
**1 ripe medium-sized pineapple, peel removed, thinly
  sliced**

Place the sugar in a pan with 250ml (9fl oz) water and bring to the boil slowly, to avoid the sugar crystallising. Remove from the heat and leave to cool, then add the mint (reserving a few leaves for decoration) and blitz in a blender. Strain and chill.

Combine the tonic water, gin, lemon juice and zest with the mint syrup. Pour into an ice-cream machine and freeze according to the manufacturer's instructions. (See page 42 if you don't have a machine).

Arrange the slices of pineapple on 4 serving plates, top with a scoop of the sorbet and decorate with the reserved mint

mint turkish delight

I have always enjoyed Turkish delight, even as a child, especially when it is enveloped in a thin coating of chocolate and highly perfumed with rosewater. Well, this recipe uses mint as the main flavour. It is very simple to prepare and you and your guests will love it.

450g (1lb) caster sugar
1 large bunch of mint
1/2 teaspoon lemon juice
75g (3oz) cornflour
1/2 teaspoon cream of tartar
A drop of green food colouring
Icing sugar for dusting

Lightly oil a 20cm (8in) baking tin, line it with clingfilm, then lightly oil the clingfilm.

Place the sugar in a pan with the mint, lemon juice and 250ml (9fl oz) water and bring to the boil slowly, to avoid the sugar crystallising. Leave over a low heat to infuse for 10 minutes, then remove from the heat and strain out the mint. Return to the pan and cook over a high heat until it reaches 115°C (239°F) on a sugar thermometer (soft-ball stage). Remove from the heat.

In a separate pan, blend the cornflour and cream of tartar with 250ml (9fl oz) water. Bring to the boil, whisking constantly, until thick. Gradually pour the hot mint syrup on to the cornflour mixture, then reduce the heat and simmer for 40 minutes, until translucent. Stir in the green food colouring (taking great care not to add too much), then pour into the oiled tin and leave to cool. Cut into cubes and dust very generously with icing sugar before serving.

mustard

I think I am a little compulsive about mustard. In my kitchen at home one of my shelves is about to collapse under the strain of the weight of jars of my favourite condiment, which I add to roasts, meat pies and fish dishes – even to beans on toast.

On my travels, I always seek out the local market to see what new mustard or condiments can be found. In Germany I have enjoyed a selection of mustards with an enormous range of speciality sausages. In Sweden I discovered a sweeter variety called Savora, served with wonderful meat and fish dishes, and in Britain who hasn't enjoyed a dollop of mustard paste made from ground powder, served with traditional favourites such as bangers, chops or cold meats?

recipes

It is unclear who first had the idea of taking mild mustard seeds and crushing them with vinegar to use as a condiment or remedy. In England, where the name of mustard comes from the Latin meaning 'burning must', the seeds were mixed with 'must' or unfermented grape juice.

The Chinese were already using mustard some 3,000 years ago in its whole form. In the first century AD the Roman writer Pliny the Elder proclaimed in his *Natural History* that mustard's pungent flavour burned like fire. In medieval Europe, mustard was one of the few spices ordinary people could afford to use to flavour their bland monotonous dishes.

DESCRIPTION

Mustard, a member of the Cruciferae family, is a herbaceous annual which can grow to 1m (3ft) in height. The plants bear clusters of bright yellow flowers, which in turn yield the fruit pods that contain the mustard seeds. These pods need to be harvested just before they are fully ripe and the pods burst. There are about forty varieties throughout the world, three of which are grown for their seeds:

White mustard (*Brassica alba*), beige-coloured seeds, mild in flavour. This is the most common variety and is used to make American and English mustard, condiments, and for pickling.

Brown or Chinese mustard (*Brassica juncea*), dark brown seeds, used to make strong mustards and added to curry powders and pastes. The seeds are small and not as pungent as the black variety. The leaves (mustard greens) have a peppery flavour and are widely used in Chinese cooking.

Black mustard (*Brassica nigra*), seeds are smaller and more pungent than the white variety. They are used in strong and aromatic mustards such as Meaux, Djion, Bordeaux and German.

To make mustard, the seeds are slightly crushed to crack the outer husk (for coarse-grain mustard the husks remain untouched), then soaked in brandy vinegar, water and salt for several hours, before being weighed, then mixed with spices and ground. The mustard is then matured for several hours in wooden vats, during which time it loses its initial bitter flavour. Finally, citric acid is added and (sometimes) a little turmeric to produce the strong yellow colour.

Blended mustards fall into two categories: smooth and coarse. They can be flavoured with herbs, chillies, green peppercorns or soft berry fruits, especially blackcurrant, and alcohol (such as Champagne). They can be mild or fiery, aromatic or pungent. Originally, when mustard was prepared at home the seeds would be pounded in a mortar and blended with honey and vinegar.

DIJON MUSTARD By the fourteenth century, Dijon in France was firmly established as a mustard-producing centre. Today, much of the world's mustard emanates from Dijon, the capital of Burgundy. Dijon mustard, made with black and brown seeds, is pale, smooth and clean-tasting. Dijon-style mustard can be made legally anywhere on the globe, as the ingredients are not found locally. In fact, the provinces of Saskatchewan, Alberta and Manitoba in Canada provide most of the seeds for the mustard industry in Dijon, the firm of Caveda supplying 90 per cent of the total.

COARSE-GRAIN MUSTARD Coarse-grain or seed mustard is made by leaving the seed husks on, and can vary in flavour from mild to very hot. It has a lot more texture than the smooth Dijon varieties. The most famous is Moutarde de Meaux, which is stored in small earthenware pots.

CULINARY USES
Taillevent, the celebrity French chef and author, used mustard in his seasonings and sauces and even created a recipe for mustard soup. In dishes calling for a lot of mustard, and a little added punch, I usually use my favourite Dijon variety. Coarse-grain mustard is wonderful in sauces, vinegars or dressings, or as an accompaniment to cold meats. It is also great added to a creamy mash. I rub the grains over the skin of pork before roasting and use them in marinades. Mustard and breadcrumbs make a delicious crust for lamb, pork and chicken; The Italian fruit relish, Mostarda di Frutta, is the most famous 'sweet' use of mustard.

Mustard can be kept in the cupboard in a cool place, and should always be added to dishes at the end of cooking, otherwise it loses character. Never boil a sauce once mustard has been added, or it will taste bitter.

Apart from prepared mustard, the seeds are used in their own right. White seeds are used as a pickling spice, while the brown are an important flavouring in south Indian cuisines where they are ground to form the base of sauces for fish. Seeds are also used to flavour butter (tadka) and are added to the Bengali spice mixes, panch phoron and sambal pods. Indian chefs fry black seeds with other seasonings such as cumin in a hot dry pan until they pop. This 'tempering' brings out their nutty flavour before adding them to dishes.

Mustard sprouts, grown from white and brown seeds, add a spark of flavour to sandwiches and salads and can act as a substitute for alfafa sprouts.

Mustard must be used with care, as its true purpose is not to dominate, but to provide subtle background flavours, to add depth and intensity.

OTHER USES
Pliny noted some forty remedies that mustard could cure, including arthritis and loss of appetite, and that it was used in the treatment of wounds. Black mustard was once used for poultices, and mustard plasters are still in use today. Warmed mustard oil is an excellent treatment for easing arthritic pain, and in India it is rubbed into the scalp to promote hair growth. Pythagoras believed that mustard improved the memory.

complementary flavours

MILK- AND CREAM-BASED SAUCES

PEPPERCORNS

VEGETABLES (ESPECIALLY LEEKS, ONIONS AND POTATOES)

HARD CHEESES (EMMENTAL, GRUYÈRE AND CHEDDAR)

OTHER CONDIMENTS (CAPERS AND GHERKINS)

HONEY

HAM AND PORK

SALMON

mini crab pies with mustard and sorrel velouté

These delicious mini pies are basically a fishcake mix baked in crisp puff pastry. The slightly sour mustard sauce acts as a perfect foil to the sweet crabmeat. They make a great dinner party starter.

25g (1oz) unsalted butter
1 onion, finely chopped
1 small leek, finely chopped
200g (7oz) freshly flaked white crabmeat
Juice and grated zest of $1/2$ lemon
1 tablespoon Dijon mustard
1 egg yolk
1 tablespoon crème fraîche
100g ($3^1/2$ oz) fresh white breadcrumbs
$1/2$ tablespoon chopped tarragon
A dash of Tabasco sauce
250g (9oz) puff pastry
Beaten egg, to glaze
Salt and freshly ground black pepper

FOR THE SAUCE:
200ml (7fl oz) fish stock
100ml ($3^1/2$ fl oz) dry white wine
2 shallots, finely chopped
100ml ($3^1/2$ fl oz) double cream
Juice of $1/4$ lemon
$1/2$ teaspoon Dijon mustard
A handful of sorrel leaves

Heat the butter in a pan, add the onion and leek and cook gently until tender. Leave to cool, then place in a bowl and add the crabmeat, lemon juice and zest, mustard, egg yolk and crème fraîche. Stir in the breadcrumbs and tarragon and season with the Tabasco and some salt and pepper.

Preheat the oven to 200°C/400°F/gas mark 6. Roll out the pastry and cut out rounds with a 7.5cm (3in) cutter to line 8 greased mince pie tins, reserving another 8 pastry rounds for the lids. Divide the crab mixture between the pastry-lined tins, brush the pastry edges with beaten egg and top with the pastry lids. Brush each pie with a little more egg glaze, then make 2 small holes in the lid to let the steam escape. Bake for 10–12 minutes, until puffed and golden.

For the sauce, put the fish stock, wine and shallots in a pan and boil over a high heat until it becomes reduced and syrupy in consistency. Add the cream and boil again until the sauce is thick enough to coat the back of a spoon. Strain through a sieve into a clean pan, add the lemon juice and mustard and then drop the sorrel into the sauce. Cook for 30 seconds more, then adjust the seasoning to taste and serve with the mini crab pies.

emmental, mustard and sage beignets
These crisp little fritters are nice served with a tomato sauce or tomato salad. Smaller ones make great nibbles or canapés.

MAKES 32

450g (1lb) Emmental cheese
1 tablespoon Dijon mustard
8 sheets of brik pastry, cut into 4 sections
50g (2oz) unsalted butter, melted
32 small sage leaves
Vegetable oil for deep-frying

FOR THE BATTER:
10g (^{1}/4 oz) fresh yeast
100ml (3^1/2 fl oz) warm milk
100g (3^1/2 oz) cornflour
Salt and freshly ground black pepper

Cut the Emmental into 32 fingers, about 6 x 2.5cm (2^1/2 x 1in) each, and brush them with the mustard. Lay out the brik pastry and brush liberally with melted butter. Put a piece of cheese on top of each piece of pastry and then roll in the ends of the pastry and roll it up like a spring roll. Brush the outside liberally with butter. Put a sage leaf on top of each one, pressing it down lightly so it sticks. Place in the fridge for 1 hour.

To make the batter, place the yeast in a bowl, pour on 2 tablespoons of the warm milk and leave for 1 minute. Mix in the cornflour and then stir in the remaining milk to give a smooth batter. Season to taste.

Heat the oil to 180°C/350°F in a deep-fat fryer or a large, deep saucepan. (Make sure you test the temperature of the oil with a cube of day-old bread before using; if it is hot enough, the bread will brown in 30 seconds.) Drop the sage-covered cheese rolls into the batter, then into the hot oil and cook for 2 minutes, until golden brown and crisp. Drain on kitchen paper to remove excess oil, then serve immediately.

devilled lobster
If the idea of cooking live lobsters doesn't appeal, ask your fishmonger to get you cooked fresh ones, not frozen; as the freshness of the succulent, sweet lobster meat is paramount for this dish.

4 x 675g (1^1/2 lb) live Scottish or Canadian lobsters
1 tablespoon Dijon mustard
100g (3^1/2 oz) unsalted butter, melted
1 garlic clove, crushed
3 tablespoons chopped flat-leaf parsley
2 tablespoons brandy
1 tablespoon Worcestershire sauce
Juice of 1 lemon
125g (4^1/2 oz) fresh white breadcrumbs (allowed to dry out)
Salt and freshly ground black pepper

In the largest pot you have, plunge the lobsters head first into plenty of boiling water, return quickly to the boil and cook for 5 minutes (it may be necessary to cook them one at a time unless you have a very large pot). Transfer the lobsters to a sink of cold water to refresh them until cold.

Remove the claws and crack them to remove the meat. Place it in a bowl. Halve the lobsters lengthways, reserving the shells, and remove and discard the intestines and the sacs near the head. Take out the meat, cut it into 2cm (^{3}/4 in) pieces and add to the bowl. Add the tomalley (a greenish substance) and any coral to the bowl too. Mix in the mustard, half the melted butter, the garlic, parsley, brandy and Worcestershire sauce. Season with salt and pepper and stir in the lemon juice and breadcrumbs.

Preheat the oven to 190°C/375°F/gas mark 5. Season the 8 lobster halves and place them on a baking tray. Fill them with the lobster mixture, packing it firmly into the cavities. Drizzle the remaining melted butter over the lobsters and place in the oven for 5–6 minutes, until heated through and wonderfully golden and crispy on top.

Serve with more melted butter, if liked, and a great big mixed salad.

glazed barbecue mustard squabs with sweet potatoes and fennel

4 x 450g (1lb) squab pigeons

1 teaspoon ground cumin

4 tablespoons Dijon mustard

4 tablespoons olive oil, plus extra to serve

4 tablespoons Madeira

1 tablespoon roughly chopped rosemary

1 tablespoon thyme leaves

1 tablespoon chopped parsley

1 teaspoon black peppercorns

1/2 teaspoon mustard seeds

2 tablespoons honey

25g (1oz) unsalted butter

Salt

Lemon wedges, to serve

FOR THE SWEET POTATOES AND FENNEL:

600g (1 1/4 lb) orange-fleshed sweet potatoes, peeled
and cut into chunks

1 large fennel bulb, cut into wedges

4 tablespoons olive oil

2 garlic cloves, crushed

1 tablespoon chopped rosemary

To prepare the squabs, cut out the backbone with kitchen scissors. Break down the wishbone using your hand, turn each bird cut-side down and flatten it by pressing down with the heel of your hand. Turn it over and remove all the ribcage bones.

Season the squabs with salt and the cumin, then brush with half the Dijon mustard. Place in a dish, pour over the olive oil and Madeira and sprinkle over the herbs. Cover with foil and leave in the refrigerator to marinate for 24 hours, turning occasionally.

Preheat the oven to 200°C/400°F/gas mark 6. Toss the sweet potatoes and fennel with the oil, garlic and rosemary,

transfer to a roasting tin and roast for about 30 minutes, until golden and tender.

Meanwhile, make the glaze. Roughly crack the peppercorns and mustard seeds in a pestle and mortar, then put them in a pan with the remaining mustard and the honey. Bring to the boil, add the butter and remove from the heat. Heat a barbecue or a ridged grill pan. Remove the squabs from the marinade and place on the barbecue or grill. Cook for 4–5 minutes on each side, basting occasionally with the mustard glaze.

To serve, place the sweet potatoes and fennel on serving plates, top with the squabs, then drizzle over a little olive oil and garnish with lemon wedges.

PG TIP The mustard glaze can be used on other grilled meats and fish, with excellent results.

chicken schnitzels with mustard, capers and lemon

4 boneless, skinless chicken breasts

1 large tablespoon Dijon mustard

3 tablespoons honey

Juice and grated zest of 1 lemon

4 tablespoons plain flour

2 eggs, beaten

150g (5oz) fresh white breadcrumbs

2 tablespoons olive oil

50g (2oz) unsalted butter

2 tablespoons superfine capers, drained and rinsed

1 tablespoon chopped parsley

2 lemons, peel and pith removed, cut into slices

Salt and freshly ground black pepper

Place the chicken breasts between 2 sheets of clingfilm and, with a meat mallet or rolling pin, bash them out into escalopes about 1cm (1/2in) thick.

Mix the mustard, honey and lemon zest together in a bowl and then brush the mixture liberally all over the chicken. Season with salt and pepper. Dip the chicken in the flour to coat it, then in the beaten egg, and finally dredge it in the breadcrumbs.

Heat the oil in a large frying pan, add the schnitzels and fry for about 2–3 minutes per side, until golden and cooked through. Add the butter to the pan and, when it begins to foam, add the capers, parsley and lemon juice. Spoon this mixture over the schnitzels, then transfer to 4 warm serving plates. Garnish with the lemon slices and serve immediately.

nutmeg

Nutmeg was first introduced to Britain in the sixteenth century when the British invaded the Molucca Islands (formerly known as the Spice Islands). Soon after, they carried it to the East Indies and the Caribbean. Up until that time, the spice had (almost exclusively) been grown on two small islands. In fact, the Dutch, who controlled the islands before the British (but after the Arabs and Portuguese!), did everything in their power to restrict the cultivation of nutmeg, in order to control its supply and prices.

recipes

Once out, however, it rapidly became very popular, perhaps due to the fact it was thought to have magical properties, and to be an aphrodisiac; even a small amount combined with alcohol is said to heighten the alcohol's narcotic effect. Nutmeg is now very successfully grown in the West Indies and Granada – which has adopted the name 'the nutmeg island'.

DESCRIPTION

Nutmeg grows like fruit on an evergreen tree (*Myristica fragrans*) that is usually 9–12m (30–40ft) tall with dark leaves, the fruit resembling apricots in appearance. When the fruit is ripe, it bursts open and cracks, revealing a bright red outer husk called mace (which is also edible and used in ground form) enveloping the hard, brown kernel which is the nutmeg.

Nutmeg and mace are similar in aroma and taste, although mace is said to be more refined and cleaner in taste – a matter of opinion in my view. Both have a rich, fresh and warm taste, and are hugely aromatic, sweetish in nutmeg, while mace is a little more bitter. Nutmeg and mace are not interchangeable in recipes, however. It is the myristicin in the nut's oil that is responsible for its narcotic effect, its toxicity in high doses, and probably also for its 'magical' reputation.

BUYING AND STORING

Although ground nutmeg is readily available, the flavour of the freshly grated whole spice is far superior. Pre-ground nutmeg quickly loses its aroma and flavour, so whenever possible use whole nutmeg. Small, handy nutmeg graters are stocked by most kitchen shops and supermarkets. Be sure to refrigerate any surplus grated nutmeg in an airtight container, but as a general rule only grate as much as needed for a particular recipe.

CULINARY USES

Nutmeg has a strong, peculiar but delightfully sweet and nutty fragrance, and adds a slightly bitter, warm aroma to food. There is nothing quite like a little freshly grated nutmeg to liven up a dish. Among its supporters are the Indians who use it especially in Moghul dishes and to spice meats, rice dishes and desserts. In southern Asia it is used to make jellies and jam. The Arabs enjoy it in long, slow-braised lamb stews and the Dutch use it as a standard seasoning in many traditional dishes, from mashed potato to fruit puddings and breads.

In Italy, they have long enjoyed nutmeg in savoury dishes with vegetables, in their mortadella sausages and as a seasoning for pasta. In Britain and France a basic white sauce, or spinach cooked in butter, would not be complete without a fresh grating of nutmeg. Britain's Queen Victoria was reported to have been very partial to its use in a special royal household recipe for sweet mincemeat prepared at Christmas-time. It became popular throughout Britain as a flavouring in pies and cakes, to liven up potted fish and the Scottish haggis, and to make a spiced wine drink.

HARD FRUITS (ESPECIALLY PEARS, APPLES AND ORANGES)

DAIRY PRODUCTS (CHEESE SAUCE, CUSTARD, EGGS, RICOTTA CHEESE)

MEAT (ESPECIALLY LAMB AND CHICKEN)

ROOT VEGETABLES (ESPECIALLY POTATOES AND PARSNIPS)

PASTA

SPINACH

DRIED FRUIT

SHELLFISH (POTTED)

FISH

HONEY

In the rest of Europe, nutmeg is most usually found in sweet dishes such as rice puddings, honey cakes, fruit cakes, pastries and occasionally mulled wine. Nutmeg is also used, along with cloves, to spice up eggnog, a popular wintertime drink, commonly served on holiday such as Christmas and New Year.

NB! Never be tempted to add too much, as excessive nutmeg can be poisonous. A couple of pinches should suffice and is perfectly safe.

OTHER USES

Nutmeg has been used as a component in certain medicines and drinks for convalescents for years. Both nutmeg and mace have been used to treat flatulence and to allay nausea. Grated nutmeg mixed with lard is apparently an excellent treatment for piles. It is also thought to aid digestion and improve appetite.

turbot with fried nutmeg brioche crumbs

Butter for greasing
4 x 175g (6oz) turbot fillets
50ml (2fl oz) dry vermouth
250ml (9fl oz) dry white wine
150ml (1/4 pint) well-flavoured fish stock
4 tablespoons double cream
50g (2oz) chilled unsalted butter, cut into small
    pieces
75g (3oz) sorrel, finely chopped
2 eggs, hard-boiled, shelled and finely diced
Salt and freshly ground black pepper

FOR THE NUTMEG BRIOCHE CRUMBS:
50g (2oz) unsalted butter
50g (2oz) fresh brioche crumbs
1/4 teaspoon freshly grated nutmeg

Lightly butter a large shallow pan, big enough to hold the
turbot fillets in a single layer. Season the fish with salt and
pepper and place it in the pan. Pour over the vermouth,
white wine and fish stock, cover with buttered greaseproof
or foil, then place on a moderate heat and bring to the boil.
Reduce the heat to just below simmering point and poach for
5–6 minutes.

Meanwhile, make the nutmeg brioche crumbs. Heat the
butter in a frying pan until foaming, add the crumbs and cook
until golden and crisp. Stir in the nutmeg, remove from the
heat and set aside.

When the fish is done, remove from the pan with a
slotted spoon and keep warm. Return the pan to the heat, add
the cream and bring to the boil. Remove from the heat and
whisk in the butter, a little at a time, until the sauce thickens.
Add the sorrel and leave to cook for 1 minute. Add the hard-
boiled eggs and adjust the seasoning.

To serve, arrange the fish on serving plates, pour over
the sauce and sprinkle over the nutmeg brioche crumbs. I like
to serve the fish on a bed of buttered asparagus tips.

potted shrimps
This basic recipe can be used for
lobster or crab as well. It is very simple, and 100 per cent better than the
commercial variety, which tends to use frozen shrimps and cheap butter.

200g (7oz) good-quality unsalted butter
1 small bay leaf
1/2 teaspoon freshly grated nutmeg
A good pinch of sea salt
A pinch of cayenne pepper
1 teaspoon brandy (optional)
300g (11oz) peeled fresh shrimps
Juice of 1/2 lemon
1 tablespoon chopped flat-leaf parsley
Freshly ground black pepper

TO SERVE:
Fingers of toast or Melba toast
Lemon wedges

Place the butter in a small saucepan, heat slowly to boiling
point and boil for 2 minutes. Strain through a small sieve
lined with muslin and return to the pan. Add the bay leaf,
nutmeg, salt, cayenne, black pepper to taste, and brandy, if
using. Leave on a low heat for 5 minutes to infuse, then
remove the bay leaf. Add the shrimps and lemon juice and
leave for 4–5 minutes longer, then stir in the parsley.

Fill 4 individual ramekins with the shrimps and top with
the butter, which should just cover the shrimps. Leave to cool
and then place in the fridge.

Serve with toast fingers or Melba toast and lemon
wedges. The shrimps are best served at room temperature in
order to appreciate their flavour at its best.

creamy parsnip and nutmeg gratin

750g (1lb 10oz) baby parsnips
300ml (1/2 pint) full-fat milk
450ml (16fl oz) double cream
2 garlic cloves, crushed
1 egg yolk
Freshly grated nutmeg
Butter
Salt and freshly ground black pepper

Preheat the oven to 230°C/450°F/gas mark 8. Peel the parsnips and cut them into 5cm (2in) lengths. Blanch in a large pan of boiling water for 1 minute, then drain. Return to the dried-out pan, along with the milk, cream, garlic and some salt and pepper. Bring to the boil, reduce the heat to a simmer and cook until the parsnips are just tender and the sauce is well reduced. Stir in the egg yolk and season to taste with nutmeg, salt and pepper.

Well butter a shallow gratin dish and pour in the parsnips and their sauce. Dot with a little more butter and add a sprinkling of nutmeg. Bake for about 15 minutes, until golden and crisp.

nutmeg and cheese custard tart

Soft cheese and nutmeg work extremely well together as long as you don't overdo the spice. Although this is not classically a custard filling, it has all the ingredients and is simply put together in minutes. It's also nice to make small tartlets to serve at teatime.

1 quantity of Sweet Pastry (see page 107)
150g (5oz) ricotta cheese
3 eggs
100g (3 1/2 oz) caster sugar
85ml (3fl oz) double cream
2 tablespoons honey
Fresh grated nutmeg

Preheat the oven to 190°C/375°F/gas mark 5. Roll out the pastry on a lightly floured surface to 3mm (1/8in) thick and use to line a 20cm (8in) tart tin. Prick the base lightly all over with a fork. Line with greaseproof paper, fill with baking beans and bake blind for 10 minutes, or until the pastry is set but not coloured. Remove the paper and beans and return the pastry case to the oven for 5 minutes longer.

Beat all the remaining ingredients except the nutmeg together in a bowl until smooth. Pour into the pastry case, grate enough fresh nutmeg over the surface to cover it lightly, then return to the oven for 40 minutes or until the top is a deep golden brown. Serve warm or at room temperature.

eggnog and orange peel ice-cream

200ml (7fl oz) full-fat milk
400ml (14fl oz) double cream
$^1/4$–$^1/2$ teaspoon freshly grated nutmeg
6 egg yolks
150g (5oz) caster sugar
Grated zest of 1 orange
100ml (3$^1/2$ fl oz) dark rum

Put the milk, cream and grated nutmeg in a pan and bring to the boil. In a bowl, whisk the egg yolks, sugar, orange zest and rum together until light and fluffy. Pour in the cream mixture, whisking all the time. Return to the pan and cook gently, stirring constantly, until the mixture thickens enough to coat the back of the spoon; do not let it boil or it will curdle. Leave to cool, then pour into an ice-cream machine and freeze according to the manufacturer's instructions. If you don't have an ice-cream machine, refer to the tip on page 42.

old-fashioned rice pudding

When I was a child, my favourite dessert was rice pudding, a great British classic, which I loved topped with a dollop of jam. Mum always made plenty; she knew it wouldn't be wasted. Here is the recipe, which must have a nutmeg-crusted skin — what memories!

25g (1oz) unsalted butter
125g (4$^1/2$ oz) pudding rice (or other short grain rice)
1 vanilla pod
600ml (1 pint) full-fat milk
100g (3$^1/2$ oz) caster sugar
$^1/2$ teaspoon grated orange zest
500ml (18fl oz) double cream
2 egg yolks
Freshly grated nutmeg

Preheat the oven to 150°C/300°F/gas mark 2. Use the butter to grease a 1.2 litre (2 pint) baking dish or casserole. Scatter the rice into the dish and set aside.

Slit the vanilla pod open lengthways and scrape out the seeds with the tip of a sharp knife. Put the pod and seeds in a pan with the milk, sugar, orange zest and 500ml (18fl oz) of the cream. Bring to the boil, then pour the mixture over the rice and stir well. Cover with a lid or foil and bake for 1$^1/2$–2 hours, until the rice is just tender. Remove from the oven and cool slightly.

In a bowl, whip the remaining cream with the egg yolks until just beginning to thicken. Stir into the rice pudding and grate fresh nutmeg over the surface (you will need about $^1/4$–$^1/2$ teaspoonful). Return to the oven and bake, uncovered, for 15 minutes, until a skin has formed and the top is golden and slightly crusty. Serve plain, or with milk, fresh fruit or a dollop of jam.

apple and nutmeg croustillant
Apples and nutmeg have a great affinity, which is highlighted in this easily prepared dessert.

4 Granny Smith apples

75g (3oz) demerara sugar

25g (1oz) unsalted butter

1/2 teaspoon freshly grated nutmeg

85ml (3fl oz) Calvados (apple brandy)

10g (1/4 oz) cornflour

150ml (1/4 pint) full-fat milk

100ml (31/2 fl oz) good-quality apple juice (not from concentrate)

2 egg yolks

65g (21/2 oz) caster sugar

150ml (1/4 pint) double cream, semi-whipped

Peel the apples, cut them in half and remove the core, then cut each half into 5 sections. Heat a frying pan over a medium heat, add 15g (1/2oz) of the sugar and heat until lightly caramelised. Add the butter and apples and toss together for 3–4 minutes, until the apples are just cooked and lightly golden. Season with the nutmeg, then pour over half the Calvados and toss with the apples. Turn the apples on to a plate and leave to cool.

Mix the cornflour with 2 tablespoons of the milk and set aside. Put the apple juice in a pan with the remaining milk and bring to the boil. Whisk in the cornflour mixture and cook for 30 seconds, then remove from the heat. In a bowl, beat together the egg yolks and caster sugar. Gradually mix in the hot milk and then return to the pan. Bring to the boil quickly, then pour into a bowl and leave to cool. When cold, fold in the whipped cream and add the remaining Calvados.

Divide the caramelised apples between 4 individual glass dishes, then cover with the cream mixture, spreading it out neatly to cover the apples completely. Sprinkle with the remaining demerara sugar and glaze under a hot grill or with a blowtorch until caramelised and crunchy.

date and nutmeg cake

175g (6oz) dried dates, stoned and diced

20g (3/4oz) preserved ginger, diced

1/2 teaspoon bicarbonate of soda

1 teaspoon baking powder

1/2 teaspoon vanilla extract

65g (21/2 oz) softened unsalted butter

65g (21/2 oz) caster sugar

2 eggs, lightly beaten

175g (6oz) plain flour, sifted

1/2 teaspoon freshly grated nutmeg

Preheat the oven to 190°C/375°F/gas mark 5. Mix together the dates and ginger in a bowl, then stir in 250ml (9fl oz) boiling water. Add the bicarbonate of soda, baking powder and vanilla extract and leave to stand.

Meanwhile, beat the butter and sugar together until pale, then beat in the eggs, one at a time. Fold in the flour and nutmeg. Stir in the date mixture and its liquid and mix well.

Pour into a well-greased 20cm (8in) round cake tin and bake for 45–50 minutes, until risen and firm to the touch. When it is done, a cocktail stick inserted in the centre of the cake should come out clean. Cool slightly, then turn out on to a wire rack to cool completely.

olives

Olives are one of the oldest cultivated fruits known to man. They have been grown and used around the Mediterranean for over 2,500 years, whether picked for eating or as a source of oil for cooking.

recipes

DESCRIPTION

The olive tree (*Olea europaea*) is an evergreen, usually around 7m (15ft) in height. The bark is grey and the trunks tend to be gnarled and twisted. The leaves are long and narrow, grey-green on top and white underneath. The olive fruit do not all ripen at the same time and will ripen earlier or later according to the tree's position, the soil and of course the weather.

Olives come in numerous varieties. Their textures vary from firm to fleshy and their shape and size from tiny ovals and half moons to the large fat, round varieties. Their colour is always a measure of ripeness; green olives being picked younger than black. During the ripening process, as the olives become oilier, they pass through a spectrum of shades from pale green to tan, to violet and finally to reddish brown or black before they start to wrinkle under the rays of the hot sun.

Black olives are picked when they are fully formed and ripe. At this point, they are harvested and then treated. They are either picked by hand (the best method, as it minimises bruising and damage, but very labour intensive) or shaken from the tree and caught in a large net that is placed underneath. Freshly picked olives are bitter and virtually inedible. They are cracked and immersed in cold water for up to fifteen days, with the water changed daily. During this procedure they lose their bitterness, and are then salted and flavoured with, for example, aromatics or spices.

A NOTE ON OLIVE OILS

Of equal importance, if not more so, in cooking is the use of olive oil. I have had the pleasure of seeing French olive oil produced. Once the olives are picked, they are transported to the olive mill with all haste before they start to ferment and their acidity increases, thereby affecting the quality of the oil.

They are then crushed once between huge millstones (without breaking their stones), and pressed with a mat which releases their natural oils. The resulting pulp produces the finest flavoured virgin olive oil. To be labelled extra virgin, the oil needs to have an acidity level of less than 1 per cent. A second pressing produces a liquid, usually cleaner in colour, simply called 'olive oil'. A third pressing, with water added, and further pressings only produce oil suitable for soaps and cosmetics.

The current interest in quality olive oils for health reasons means that they have become an expensive commodity. Connoisseurs are at pains to argue over the best available, and olive oil tastings have become nearly as popular as wine tastings. Greece and Spain are believed to be the world's leading olive oil producers.

BUYING

The practice of tasting before we buy is nowadays much more common, and not before time, I may add! There is such a variety of olives available that I firmly believe in tasting them first. I tend to buy my olives loose rather than bottled, as they are fresher, unadulterated and free from additives. I also find the best are those packed in olive oil and not in brine solution, which does nothing for the flavour.

Generally, green olives tend to be lighter and more delicate in flavour and the flesh clings more to the stones. Black olives are stronger and more complex in flavour, and softer in texture.

Choosing a good olive oil depends, again, on

CULINARY USES

Olives are wonderful not only as a nibble before a meal (often stuffed with red pepper or anchovy or, in Spain, almonds) but also as an ingredient in sauces, soups and salad dressings. The Italians have long partnered olives with pasta and used them to adorn their pizzas. In France, especially in the south, they are used in all manner of dishes and tasty dips like tapenade (black olives, capers, anchovies and garlic blended with olive oil) which is spread on crusty bread. In the Middle East and other parts of the Mediterranean they are an indispensable part of the cuisine. In Morocco, olives are added to tagines and salads, and mixed with various spices (such as cumin) for slow-cook chicken. I find it best to add olives at the end of the cooking, to ensure the retention of their shape and texture but, more importantly, so that their salty flavour does not overpower the dish.

You may be surprised to see olives used in a sweet form (try my Calves' Liver with Candied Olives and Grapefruit, see page 140), but they can even be added to ice-cream, sweet sauces and desserts – with a little imagination!

Olive oil has an underlying flavour which it imparts to a dish. In France it is used as a condiment, as the base of vinaigrette, in sauces such as anchoïade (a piquant dressing with crushed anchovies, garlic and herbs), and drizzled over steamed vegetables or grilled meats and fish. In Italy it is drizzled over all manner of rustic soups and pasta. In the Middle East and eastern Mediterranean, olive oil is used to make pastries, biscuits, cakes and dips such as hummus (with chickpeas and garlic).

Using olive oil in your day-to-day diet, rather than animal fat, is believed to significantly reduce cholesterol levels (thereby lowering the risk of heart disease), and to slow down the signs of aging. Having said this, over-consumption of oils and fats is not good for you so, as in all things, moderation is the key.

individual taste – you might prefer a spicy Tuscan oil, a sweet Spanish with fruity overtones or a pungent power-packed Greek one. Your choice should also be guided by what you intend using it for. For general cooking, an inexpensive, mild-flavoured oil is fine but try to use a quality, extra-virgin oil where it will benefit – in sauces, drizzled over a tomato and basil salad, or on meat that is to be grilled...

STORING AND PREPARATION

Contrary to popular opinion, olives do not have to be refrigerated; just store in an airtight container in a dark place. Olive oil should be kept in a dark, cool place as it can quickly go rancid.

If you are going to use olives in cooking, I'm afraid there is no way of avoiding the chore of stoning them. Ready-stoned ones are available, but they tend to be rejects from the curing process. To stone olives I find the best way is simply to cut a slit lengthways along the olive using a sharp knife and pry out the stone within.

complementary flavours

ANCHOVIES

GARLIC AND ONIONS

LEMON

CAPERS

TOMATOES

PEPPERS

MEAT (ESPECIALLY VEAL)

FISH (ESPECIALLY TUNA)

GOAT'S CHEESE AND FETA CHEESE

cauliflower and olive soup

1 medium cauliflower, cut into florets
3 tablespoons virgin olive oil
10g ($^1/_4$ oz) unsalted butter
1 onion, chopped
1 small leek, white part only, chopped
750ml ($1^1/_4$ pints) well-flavoured chicken stock (or
   vegetable stock)
150ml ($^1/_4$ pint) full-fat milk
85ml (3fl oz) double cream
6 black olives, stoned, rinsed, dried and very
   finely chopped
1 tablespoon chopped chives
Salt and freshly ground black pepper

Blanch the cauliflower florets in a pan of boiling salted water
for 2 minutes, then drain well.

   In a large pan, heat 1 tablespoon of the oil with the
butter, add the onion and leek and sweat until tender. Pour
 in the stock and milk and bring to the boil. Add the
cauliflower, then reduce the heat and simmer for 15–20
minutes, until the cauliflower is almost puréed. Place in a
blender or food processor and blitz until smooth. Return to
the pan, add the double cream and olives and lightly season
to taste – remember the olives are already salty.

   To serve, pour into soup bowls, drizzle over the
remaining olive oil and sprinkle over the chives.

chicken with green olives and saffron

3 garlic cloves, chopped
1 teaspoon cumin seeds
1cm ($^1/_2$ in) piece of fresh root ginger, grated
1 teaspoon smoked paprika
1 x 1.8kg (4lb) organic or free range chicken, cut into
   8 portions
3 tablespoons olive oil
150ml ($^1/_4$ pint) white wine
1 lemon
A good pinch of saffron strands
150g (5oz) green olives, stoned
2 tablespoons chopped coriander
Salt and freshly ground black pepper

Crush the garlic, cumin seeds and ginger to a paste in a
mortar. Add the paprika and some salt and then rub the
chicken pieces with this mixture. Heat the olive oil in a large,
heavy-based saucepan, add the seasoned chicken pieces and
cook until golden brown all over. Pour in the wine and bring
to the boil, then squeeze over the juice of the lemon. Add the
saffron, olives and coriander and mix in with the chicken.

   Pour over 600ml (1 pint) of water, then cover and simmer
for 30–40 minutes, until the chicken is cooked and tender
 and the pieces are coated in the sauce. If the sauce is not
at a coating consistency, remove the chicken pieces and boil
the sauce until it thickens. Adjust the seasoning if necessary
and serve.

calves' liver with candied olives and grapefruit

Candied olives might not appeal to everyone initially but once you taste them you'll be converted. The idea comes from the famous French chef, Jacques Chibois, who serves them at his eponymous restaurant near Nice. I now experiment with them regularly in all sorts of dishes. In this one, their sweetness is balanced with sharp-tasting grapefruit. Between them, they act as a foil for the rich calves' liver.

1 pink grapefruit

3 tablespoons sugar

75g (3oz) unsalted butter

1 tablespoon olive oil

8 x 100g (3^{1}/$_2$ oz) slices of calves' liver

1 tablespoon white wine vinegar

4 tablespoons dry white wine

100ml (3^{1}/$_4$ fl oz) veal stock (or beef stock)

Salt and freshly ground black pepper

FOR THE CANDIED OLIVES:

100g (3^{1}/$_2$ oz) black olives

85ml (3fl oz) clear honey

1 sprig of rosemary

First prepare the candied olives, which have to be done 2 days in advance. Halve and stone the olives, then place them in a pan of boiling water and cook for 2 minutes. Drain well and repeat the process 3 times to de-salt them fully.

Put the honey, rosemary sprig and 100ml (3^{1}/$_2$ fl oz) water in a pan and bring to the boil. Add the olives and simmer for 10 minutes. Remove from the heat and leave to soak for 48 hours in the syrup, ready for use.

Using a zester, pare the zest off the grapefruit, place it in a small pan and cover with water. Bring to the boil, then drain the zest and return to the pan. Add 4 tablespoons of water and 1 tablespoon of the sugar and cook for 2 minutes to glaze the zest in the syrup. Remove from the heat and set aside.

Cut off all the peel and pith from the grapefruit, then cut out the segments from between the membranes — do this over a bowl to catch the juice, squeezing out the membrane after you have taken out all the segments. Set aside the juice and the segments.

Heat 25g (1oz) of the butter in a large frying pan with the olive oil. When it begins to sizzle, season the calves' liver and add it to the pan. Cook over a high heat for 2 minutes on each side, keeping it rosy pink in the centre. Remove the meat from the pan and keep warm. Pour away the fat but do not wash the pan. Add the white wine vinegar and remaining sugar and cook until caramelised. Then add the wine and boil for 2–3 minutes, until reduced. Add the grapefruit juice and stock, bring to the boil and simmer until thick enough to coat the back of a spoon. Dice the remaining butter and whisk it into the sauce, then adjust the seasoning.

Arrange the calves' liver on 4 serving plates, garnish with the grapefruit segments and zest and top with a teaspoon of the candied olives. Pour over the sauce and serve. I like to serve this with Risotto or a selection of baby vegetables.

roasted lamb rib eye with red wine and olive caviar

4 tablespoons olive oil

2 x 6-bone racks of lamb, bones removed (you can ask your butcher to do this)

100ml (3$^{1}/_{2}$ fl oz) red wine

300ml ($^{1}/_{2}$ pint) lamb stock (or other meat stock)

25g (1oz) chilled unsalted butter, diced

Salt and freshly ground black pepper

FOR THE OLIVE CAVIAR:

2 tablespoons olive oil

1 onion, finely chopped

2 garlic cloves, crushed

1 small red pepper, finely chopped

150g (5oz) black olives, stoned and finely chopped

2 anchovy fillets, finely chopped

2 tablespoons chopped basil

2 tablespoons chopped flat-leaf parsley

1 tablespoon honey

TO SERVE:

Mashed potatoes

A bunch of watercress

Preheat the oven to 200°C/400°F/gas mark 6. To make the olive caviar, heat the oil in a frying pan, add the onion and garlic and cook until soft but not coloured. Add the red pepper and cook for 2–3 minutes, then add the olives and anchovies and cook for 2 minutes longer, Stir in the basil, parsley and honey. Adjust the seasoning and keep warm.

Heat the olive oil in a roasting tin until smoking. Season the lamb, add to the tin and seal on both sides, until golden. Transfer to the oven and roast for 10–12 minutes, until pink. Remove from the roasting tin and keep warm.

Wipe out any excess oil from the roasting tin, pour in the red wine and boil on the stove for 2 minutes. Add the stock and boil rapidly until reduced by half. Remove from the heat, whisk in the butter a little at a time and then season to taste.

Slice each rib eye into 4 pieces and arrange on a bed of mashed potatoes. Pour a little sauce around, garnish with the olive caviar on the lamb and a little watercress alongside.

fig tapenade I use this classic variation on tapenade in all manner of ways. Try it with fish or chicken, tossed with pasta, or simply on toasted baguette slices as a canapé.

150g (5oz) dried figs

100g (3$^{1}/_{2}$ oz) black olives, stoned

4 anchovy fillets, drained and rinsed

25g (1oz) superfine capers, drained and rinsed

3 garlic cloves, crushed

Juice of $^{1}/_{2}$ lemon

100ml (3$^{1}/_{2}$ fl oz) virgin olive oil

2 tablespoons chopped parsley

Freshly ground black pepper

Soak the figs in warm water for 1 hour until swollen, then drain them and dry well. Chop finely.

Blitz together the olives, anchovies, capers, garlic, lemon juice and a little black pepper in a blender or food processor. Gradually add the olive oil to form a paste, then add the parsley and chopped figs.

PG TIP You can vary the tapenade by adding chopped sun-dried tomatoes and basil.

pepper

The king of spices, pepper is the oldest known spice. Originally from the Malabar coast of India, it appeared in Sanskrit literature over 3,000 years ago. Although common today, it was so highly valued in ancient times that it served as an offering to the gods, a trading medium and a tax; in fact, Attila the Hun and Alaric I the Visigoth demanded pepper as a major part of Rome's ransom.

Today pepper is grown widely, the most important areas of cultivation being India, Malaysia, Brazil, Sri Lanka, China, Vietnam, Thailand and Madagascar.

recipes

CRUSHED GOAT'S CHEESE
WITH PEPPER AND BLACK
CHERRY JAM (PAGE 145)

AROMATIC THAI QUAILS
(PAGE 145)

RASAM (PAGE 146)

BLACK PEPPER-CURED LAMB
WITH AUBERGINES, PEPPERS
AND FETA (PAGE 146)

ANTON'S STEAK AUX QUATRE
POIVRES (PAGE 147)

PEPPER–WHITE CHOCOLATE
FUDGE (PAGE 147)

BLACK PEPPER YOGHURT
SEMI-FREDDO (PAGE 148)

TWO-PEPPER RED WINE
STRAWBERRIES (PAGE 148)

SEE ALSO:

TWICE-COOKED DUCK WITH
LAVENDER HONEY (PAGE 95)

GLAZED BARBECUE MUSTARD
SQUABS WITH SWEET
POTATOES AND FENNEL
(PAGE 126)

DESCRIPTION

Peppercorns are the fruit of the evergreen vine, *Piper nigrum*. Green, black and white pepper all grow on the same plant but are harvested at different stages of development. The familiar black peppercorn is picked while green and left to dry, when it wrinkles and blackens. Green peppercorns are unripe fresh corns which are preserved by bottling in brine or vinegar, or, more recently, by freeze-drying. White peppercorns are mature berries which have been soaked in water and had their outer shells removed.

The peppery flavour and odour come from the essential oils and peperin (which also gives the heat). Black pepper is the most fiery and pungent, followed by white and then green pepper, which is mild with a clean, fresh taste. Pink peppercorns are not peppercorns at all but aromatic berries from the plant *Schinus terebinthfolius*. This species is native to Brazil, where the locals know it as *aroreira*. Pink peppercorns have a pungent sweetish flavour, followed by a peppery aftertaste, and a brittle, slightly bitter skin.

BUYING, STORING AND PREPARATION

The best black peppercorns are said to be Tellicherry, Lampong and Malabar. White pepper varieties include Munkok and Siam. Pink peppercorns, or berries, are available dried or bottled in vinegar. I find the bottled variety has a better flavour. Green and pink peppercorns are most likely to be found in specialist shops.

Peppercorns can be stored for up to a year in airtight containers away from sunlight. Since pepper quickly loses its freshness, flavour, aroma and heat after it has been ground, it is best to buy whole peppercorns and to grind them yourself when needed. Cracked pepper is simply partially broken up corns, crushed using a pestle and mortar or a rolling pin.

CULINARY USES

Pepper has for centuries been used as a standard spice to flavour sauces, pickles and marinades throughout the world.

In Europe, most dishes are seasoned with salt and pepper — a tradition that dates back to medieval times. In addition to being used as a condiment, however, it is also used as a major ingredient, in dishes like the French Steak au Poivre where the steak is coated in freshly ground black pepper before cooking. A pepper crust on tuna also works very well. While peppercorns (ground, crushed or whole) have traditionally been used in savoury dishes, they are now also increasingly being added to desserts, cakes and biscuits. They marry particularly well with strawberries (drawing out the sweetness of the fruit) and chocolate. White pepper is used in light-coloured dishes (such as white sauces and ice-cream) rather than black, to avoid a speckled appearance.

In India pepper is used extensively. In the north it is added particularly to meat dishes; in

complementary flavours

SALT

HERBS (DILL, THYME AND ROSEMARY)

LEMON AND LIME

SOFT CHEESES

STRAWBERRIES

the south to lentil and pulse recipes; and to fish in the east. Pepper is often fried or roasted to extract the aroma and flavour, and is added to pastes and spice mixes like garam masala. Black peppercorns are an optional ingredient in Masala tea (a spicy hot beverage that includes cardamon, cloves and cinnamon) and is a key player in the soup Rasam (which literally translates as 'pepper water').

Green peppercorns are an important addition to the culinary palette. Less biting than black pepper, their piquancy and strikingly fresh aroma go wonderfully well with seafood and grilled meats. They can also simply be added to a cream sauce to accompany fish, or used whole in patés and terrines and curries. In India green peppercorns are pickled alone in brine or in a wonderful blend of oil,

green mango, chilli and ginger. Green peppercorns can also be mashed with garlic or cinnamon to make a spiced butter. Pink peppercorns are used in the same way as green.

Pepper is best ground directly onto food or added towards the end of cooking, to preserve its heat and aroma.

MEDICINAL USES

Pepper stimulates the appetite and salivation, improving digestion and blood circulation. It also calms nausea and has an anti-inflammatory and fever-reducing effect. Warm milk with pepper and honey is an ancient home remedy for treating colds, and white pepper mixed with butter is said to cure sore throats.

crushed goat's cheese with pepper and black cherry jam

This is a great summer treat. It can be served on its own but is also very good with chargrilled vegetables, hot from the grill. The black cherry jam is an idea I saw in the south of France, and it works really well.

350g (12oz) soft goat's cheese
1 teaspoon cracked black pepper (see page 142)
Juice and grated zest of 1 lemon
1 teaspoon thyme leaves
2 tablespoons virgin olive oil
1 baguette, cut into slices and toasted
125g (4¹/₂ oz) good-quality black cherry jam
Coarse salt

Place the cheese in a bowl, add the pepper, lemon juice and zest and crush together with a fork. Add the thyme and season with a little salt to taste. Leave to stand for up to 1 hour to allow the flavours to meld.

Spoon the cheese into a serving dish, drizzle over the olive oil, then serve with the toasted baguette and the black cherry jam.

aromatic thai quails

Ideally these should be chargrilled on hot coals, but a grill pan does a good job too. This dish is a common Thai street food, and each region has a different version. Coconut gives a succulent flavour.

8 quails
2 garlic cloves, chopped
2 teaspoons black peppercorns, freshly ground
2 tablespoons coriander root (from about 2 bunches of coriander)
1 teaspoon ground coriander
¹/₂ teaspoon ground turmeric
300ml (¹/₂ pint) unsweetened coconut milk
4 tablespoons *nam pla* (Thai fish sauce)
Olive oil for brushing
Salt

Cut the quails in half by cutting along the breastbone and then along the backbone. Meanwhile, soak 4 bamboo skewers in warm water. With a pestle and mortar, pound the garlic with the peppercorns, coriander root and a pinch of salt. Add the ground coriander and turmeric and pound for a further minute. Transfer to a dish, add the coconut milk and fish sauce and mix together well. Add the quail halves and leave to marinate at room temperature for 1 hour.

Thread the quail halves on to the soaked skewers. Prepare a barbecue, or heat a ridged grill pan and brush it with olive oil. Grill the quails, skin-side down, for about 8–10 minutes, until cooked through and lightly charred, brushing occasionally with the marinade. Serve with steamed rice.

rasam

A hot and colourful soup from India, whose name translates as 'black pepper water'. It is highly peppery, with a base of lentils and tamarind.

1 onion, finely chopped
2 garlic cloves, chopped
2.5cm (1in) piece of fresh galangal or ginger, finely chopped
1 heaped teaspoon black peppercorns
$1/4$ teaspoon cumin seeds
$1/4$ teaspoon coriander seeds
1 litre ($1^3/4$ pints) well-flavoured chicken stock
125g ($4^1/2$ oz) yellow lentils
2 plum tomatoes, peeled, deseeded and chopped
50g (2oz) sweetcorn kernels
4 spring onions, shredded
1 red chilli, deseeded and thinly sliced
1 teaspoon tamarind paste
1 teaspoon brown sugar
2 tablespoons chopped coriander
Salt

Crush the onion, garlic, galangal or ginger, black peppercorns, cumin and coriander seeds with a pestle and mortar. Place in a saucepan, pour in the stock and bring to the boil. Reduce the heat, add the lentils and simmer gently for 40–45 minutes, until the lentils are tender. Add the vegetables, red chilli, tamarind paste and sugar and cook for a further 5 minutes. Season with a little salt, add the chopped coriander and serve.

black pepper-cured lamb with aubergines, peppers and feta

4 lamb leg steaks
2 tablespoons black peppercorns, cracked (see page 142)
4 tablespoons olive oil
1 onion, finely chopped
2 garlic cloves, crushed
$1^1/2$ teaspoons tomato purée
100ml ($3^1/4$ fl oz) tomato passata
1 teaspoon sugar
3–4 tablespoons vegetable oil
1 aubergine, halved lengthways and cut into slices 2.5cm (1in) thick
2 red peppers, roughly chopped
2 tablespoons balsamic vinegar
1 teaspoon oregano leaves
Salt

TO GARNISH
75g (3oz) feta cheese, diced
Basil leaves

Season the lamb with salt, then sprinkle with the cracked peppercorns. Using the flat of your hand, push the peppercorns into the meat. Leave at room temperature for up to 2 hours.

Heat half the olive oil in a pan, add the onion and half the garlic and cook gently for 5 minutes. Stir in the tomato purée, passata and sugar and cook for 10 minutes longer.

Meanwhile, heat 2–3 tablespoons of the vegetable oil in a large frying pan, add the aubergine and fry for 3–4 minutes. Add the red peppers and cook for 5 minutes. Add the aubergine and peppers to the tomato sauce, reduce the heat, then cover and cook for 5 minutes or until the vegetables are just tender. Stir in the balsamic vinegar.

Grill or fry the lamb in 1 tablespoon of the vegetable oil until done to your liking. Heat the remaining olive oil and add the remaining garlic and the oregano. Stir into the vegetables. Slice the lamb thickly and serve it on top of the vegetables, garnished with basil leaves and the feta.

anton's steak aux quatre poivres

I have many great memories of my time at The Dorchester, and working with Anton Mosimann was one of the highlights of my career. Here is a dish Anton created, blending four varieties of pepper harmoniously with brandy and cream. A take on the classic pepper steak.

1/2 teaspoon white peppercorns, coarsely ground
1/2 teaspoon black peppercorns, coarsely ground
4 x 175g (6oz) sirloin steaks or fillet steaks
2 tablespoons groundnut or vegetable oil
2 tablespoons cognac
200ml (7fl oz) veal stock (or beef stock)
100ml (3 1/2 fl oz) double cream
15g (1/2 oz) chilled unsalted butter, diced
1 teaspoon green peppercorns
1 teaspoon pink peppercorns
Salt

Mix together the white and black peppercorns. Season the steaks with salt, then roll them liberally in the peppercorns.

Heat the oil in a large frying pan, add the steaks and cook them to your preferred degree. Remove from the pan and keep warm. Remove any excess fat from the pan and pour in the cognac. Set it alight with a match, standing well back, then when the flames have died down pour in the stock. Simmer until reduced by half. Add the cream and simmer again until the sauce is thick enough to coat the back of a spoon. Whisk in the chilled butter and season with salt to taste. Add the green and pink peppercorns to the sauce, pour it over the steaks and serve.

pepper-white chocolate fudge

Ever since I was a child, I've loved fudge — it's soft, sugary and totally irresistible. The inclusion of a little black pepper cuts the sweetness without harming the flavour. Liquid glucose is available from pharmacists.

600g (1 1/4 lb) caster sugar
600ml (1 pint) double cream
50ml (2fl oz) liquid glucose
100g (3 1/2 oz) good-quality white chocolate, cut into small pieces
100g (3 1/2 oz) chilled unsalted butter, cut into small pieces
1 teaspoon black peppercorns, cracked (see page 142)
1/2 teaspoon vanilla extract
A pinch of salt

Mix the sugar, cream and glucose together in a heavy-based pan, place on the heat and stir constantly until it comes to the boil. Continue to cook, without stirring, for about 10—15 minutes, until the mixture reaches the 'soft-ball stage' (115°C/239°F on a sugar thermometer). If the mixture does not reach this stage, the fudge will not set properly.

Remove the pan from the heat, stir in the chocolate and butter pieces, then set aside until the temperature drops to around 70°C (150°F). Finally add the cracked pepper, vanilla extract and salt and beat for 1 minute. Line a 25cm (10in) square shallow dish or baking tin with baking parchment and pour in the fudge. Level the surface.

Leave to cool in the tin, then cut into small squares. The fudge will keep for up to a week in an airtight container. Great served with coffee after dinner.

black pepper yoghurt semifreddo

This black pepper parfait topped with a warm tomato, vodka and pineapple sauce is simple and inspiring. It makes a real dinner-party conversation piece.

SERVES 8

3 organic or free range eggs, separated
25g (1oz) caster sugar
$^1/_2$ teaspoon vanilla extract
Grated zest of 1 orange
150ml ($^1/_4$ pint) double cream
125g (4$^1/_2$ oz) Greek-style yoghurt
75g (3oz) meringues, broken into pieces
1 teaspoon black peppercorns, lightly cracked
   (see page 142)

FOR THE SAUCE:

15g (1$^1/_2$ oz) unsalted butter
1 tablespoon caster sugar
75g (3oz) fresh pineapple, cut into 5mm ($^1/_4$ in) dice
2 firm, ripe tomatoes, peeled, deseeded and cut into
   5mm ($^1/_4$in) dice
1 tablespoon vodka
Juice of 1 orange

Put the egg yolks, sugar, vanilla and orange zest in a large bowl placed over a pan of gently simmering water. Whisk with an electric beater until the mixture doubles in volume and becomes pale and thick. Remove the bowl from the pan of water and leave to cool, whisking frequently to prevent a skin forming.

In 2 separate bowls, whisk the cream and egg whites until stiff. Add the yoghurt to the thickened egg yolk mixture and then fold in the whipped cream, followed by the egg whites. Finally add the meringue pieces and the black pepper. Pour into 8 small ramekins and place in the freezer overnight.

To serve, dip the ramekins briefly in hot water and run a knife round the edge to loosen the semifreddo. Turn them out on to serving plates and defrost for 10 minutes while you prepare the sauce.

Heat the butter in a frying pan, add the sugar and cook until lightly caramelised. Add the pineapple and tomatoes, cook for 1 minute, then pour in the vodka and orange juice and boil for 1 minute. Pour the warm sauce over the semifreddo and serve immediately.

two-pepper red wine strawberries

Black pepper and strawberries are made for each other. Here they are served chilled, with vanilla ice-cream, which makes a refreshing combination.

150ml ($^1/_4$ pint) good-quality red wine, preferably
   Cabernet Sauvignon
4 tablespoons caster sugar
$^1/_2$ teaspoon black peppercorns, coarsely cracked
   (see page 142)
5cm (2in) piece of vanilla pod, slit open lengthways
1 teaspoon cornflour
25g (1oz) unsalted butter
450g (1lb) strawberries
$^1/_2$ teaspoon green peppercorns, drained
Vanilla ice-cream, to serve
Mint leaves, to decorate

Put the wine in a saucepan, holding back 2 tablespoons of it, and add the sugar and half the black pepper. Scrape in the seeds from the vanilla pod, add the pod too, and stir over a moderate heat to dissolve the sugar. Bring to the boil. Mix the 2 tablespoons of wine with the cornflour and add to the pan. Cook gently for 1–2 minutes, until the mixture has thickened slightly. Remove the sauce from the heat and take out the vanilla pod.

Melt the butter in a frying pan over a high heat, add the strawberries and the remaining black pepper and cook together for 1 minute, just to warm the strawberries through. Pour over the wine sauce and return to the boil. Add the green peppercorns, then pour into a bowl and leave to cool. Refrigerate overnight to allow the flavours to develop.

To serve, put the strawberry mixture in cocktail glasses, top with vanilla ice-cream and decorate with mint leaves.

rosemary

'Parsley, sage, rosemary and thyme' goes the song that so many of us remember from our childhood, but it is rosemary that, during my long career as a chef, has given me the most pleasure from a culinary standpoint. It was the herb I was most familiar and comfortable with and I love its needlelike texture and its aromatic and intense flavour.

Originally cultivated in the Mediterranean, where it remains a principal component of *herbes de Provence*, and widely used in dishes of the region. Rosemary (*Rosmarinus officinalis*) was introduced to Britain during the eleventh century, where it was commonly believed to encourage merriment. During medieval times it was associated with love and remembrance. Romans placed branches of it in the hands of the dead, and in many older church graveyards, rosemary can be seen planted next to gravestones.

DESCRIPTION

Rosemary is an evergreen perennial, intensely flavourful and aromatic. The shrub can grow up to 1.5m (5ft) in height and has narrow, spiky hard leaves. Rosemary enjoys sun and, because it is hardy, can withstand the wind and salt of coastal regions. It is easy to grow in containers.

BUYING AND STORING

Only buy fresh, firm-looking rosemary. It will keep well in the fridge (or frozen in the freezer) but I find it best kept in a dry, cool place. Of course it is ideal to grow your own so you can pick and use it fresh. Strip the leaves from their woody sprigs before use.

CULINARY USES

People began cooking with rosemary during the Middle Ages. These days it is a particular favourite in Britain, France and Italy where it is used in all manner of savoury and sweet dishes. In southern France, rosemary is added to the coals of a barbecue to grill fish and meat.

Rosemary can be used whole or finely chopped, which helps to release its aroma. Use it whole to flavour roast meats, marinades and infusions during cooking. Flavour your oils and vinegars with a rosemary branch and blend it, chopped finely, with butter and lemon juice for a lovely herbal butter. A sprig of rosemary can also added to bouquet garni (along with sage, thyme, parsley and a bay leaf).

I like to use it to flavour sauces, stews and soups, and I always use it in one form or another with lamb, especially simply roasted (added to garlic it makes a lovely crusty topping). Use fresh rosemary in conjunction with garlic and anchovy, which really brings out the flavours. It is also, to my mind, surprisingly good in sweet dishes, made into syrup and added chopped into shortbread.

Rosemary flowers are very pretty and fragrant and are wonderful included in summer salads, or as a decoration for desserts.

In the following section you will see just how versatile rosemary is, from forming a base for a rabbit stew to using its fresh stems as ideal skewers for grilling scallops. And whatever you do, try to use it with chocolate (see page 38) — for me an unexpected marriage made in heaven!

OTHER USES

Rosemary has special medicinal properties which aid digestion and liver complaints. In Provence, it is regularly made into a herbal tea to encourage a healthy complexion. This tea is also said to be

complementary flavours

GARLIC

MEAT (CHICKEN, LAMB, PORK AND BEEF)

VEGETABLES (ESPECIALLY MUSHROOMS, BUTTERNUT SQUASH, ONIONS AND POTATOES)

FRUITS (ESPECIALLY APPLES, ORANGES, APRICOTS AND PEARS)

SOFT FRUITS (ESPECIALLY STRAWBERRIES AND APRICOTS)

LAVENDER

CHOCOLATE

good for clearing headaches. The aromatic branches are sometimes thrown into fires to scent rooms — and are added to barbecues to flavour whatever is grilling. In medieval times, rosemary was thought to ward off evil spirits and prevent nightmares. It is a key component in many pot-pourris and the essential oil is used extensively in aromatherapy.

rosemary-skewered scallops
with fennel and orange salsa

4 long, bushy stems of rosemary
16 large, fresh scallops
Olive oil
Salt and freshly ground black pepper

FOR THE FENNEL AND ORANGE SALSA:
6 tablespoons virgin olive oil
1 fennel bulb, fronds removed, cut into small dice
2 oranges
4 plum tomatoes, cut into small dice
1 garlic clove, crushed
1 tablespoon balsamic vinegar

Remove the leaves from two-thirds of each rosemary stem so that the top is still bushy but the rest can be threaded through the scallops. Carefully thread 4 scallops on to each rosemary skewer and place in the fridge until required.

For the salsa, heat half the oil in a pan, add the diced fennel and cook for about 8–10 minutes, until golden and tender. Place in a bowl.

Segment one of the oranges by cutting away all the peel and pith, then cutting between the membranes to release the segments. Cut each segment into pieces. Add the diced segments to the fennel in the bowl, then add the tomatoes, garlic, balsamic vinegar, the remaining oil and the juice from the second orange. Leave for 1 hour for the flavours to blend.

Heat a ridged grill pan until smoking and brush with olive oil. Season the scallops with salt and pepper and cook for 1 minute on each side, until golden and caramelised. Place on serving plates, coat with the salsa and grind over some black pepper. Serve as a first course.

rosemary-braised rabbit with
smoked bacon, tomato and broad beans

1 young rabbit (about 1.6kg/3^1/$_2$lb), jointed
2 tablespoons plain flour
2 tablespoons olive oil
25g (1oz) unsalted butter
75g (3oz) smoked bacon lardons
150ml (^{1}/$_4$ pint) dry white wine
300ml (^{1}/$_2$ pint) well-flavoured meat stock
75g (3oz) sunblush tomatoes
50g (2oz) shelled broad beans, cooked
Salt and freshly ground black pepper

FOR THE MARINADE:
12 garlic cloves, peeled but left whole
1 small bay leaf
6 rosemary sprigs, plus extra to garnish
2 tablespoons olive oil

Put the rabbit joints in a dish with all the marinade ingredients. Cover and leave to marinate for 24 hours.

Preheat the oven to 150°C/300°F/gas mark 2. Remove the rabbit from the marinade and dry well, then coat it in the flour. Heat the olive oil and the butter in a large casserole until very hot, then season the rabbit joints and brown them in the hot fat. Add the garlic cloves from the marinade and the smoked bacon and cook for 3–4 minutes. Drain off any excess fat, then return to the heat, pour in the white wine and tuck in the rosemary sprigs and bay leaf from the marinade. Pour over the meat stock and bring to the boil. Reduce the heat, cover and place in the oven. Cook for 1 hour, then add the sunblush tomatoes and cook for 15 minutes longer.

Remove from the oven and strain off the liquid into a saucepan. Simmer until it is thick enough to coat the back of a spoon, then stir in the broad beans and season to taste. Pour the sauce over the rabbit, garnish with a little rosemary and serve. Creamy mashed potato, lightened with olive oil, makes a good accompaniment.

pan-fried sole with rosemary and hazelnuts

75g (3oz) unsalted butter

125g (4¹/₂ oz) hazelnuts, crushed

1 tablespoon finely chopped rosemary

100g (3¹/₂ oz) fresh white breadcrumbs

2 egg yolks

4 x 350–400g (12–14oz) Dover soles, cleaned

2 lemons, peel and pith removed, cut into slices

FOR THE GARNISH:

2 tablespoons olive oil

100g (3¹/₂ oz) bacon lardons

300g (11oz) baby new potatoes, cooked, peeled and
**   cut into slices 1cm (¹/₂ in) thick**

12 asparagus tips, cooked

FOR THE SAUCE:

50g (2oz) unsalted butter

100ml (3¹/₂ fl oz) veal stock (or chicken stock)

2 tablespoons lemon juice

Heat 25g (1oz) of the butter in a frying pan, add the crushed hazelnuts and cook, stirring constantly, over a moderate heat until they turn a light golden colour. Remove from the pan and leave to cool, then place in a blender or food processor and blitz to fine grains. Transfer to a bowl and mix in the rosemary and breadcrumbs.

Beat the egg yolks until fluffy, then brush both sides of the sole with them. Coat the soles with the rosemary and hazelnut mixture, patting it on to ensure they are well covered.

For the garnish, heat the olive oil in a frying pan, add the bacon lardons and fry until crisp. Remove from the pan and set aside. Add the sliced potatoes to the pan and fry until golden on both sides. Add the asparagus and fry with the potatoes until heated through. Return the lardons to the pan and season to taste. Put the mixture on 4 serving plates and keep warm.

Fry the soles in the remaining butter for about 4–5 minutes on each side, until golden. Place on top of the vegetables.

In a small pan, heat the butter for the sauce until it is foaming and gives off a nutty aroma. Whisk in the stock and lemon juice, bring to the boil, then drizzle the sauce over the soles. Top with a slice of lemon and serve immediately.

slow-roast lamb with rosemary and anchoïade

1 x 2.2kg (5lb) leg of lamb

6 anchovy fillets in oil

6 tablespoons olive oil

4 large garlic cloves, cut into thin slivers

30 rosemary sprigs

150ml (¹/₄ pint) red wine

100ml (3¹/₂ fl oz) lamb stock (or other meat stock)

25g (1oz) chilled unsalted butter, diced

Cayenne pepper

Salt and freshly ground black pepper

Preheat the oven to 200°C/400°F/gas mark 6. With a small, sharp knife, make deep slits approximately 2.5cm (1in) apart all over the lamb. Place the anchovies, half the olive oil and a good pinch of salt in a blender or food processor and blitz to a smooth paste. Rub the paste into the slits and all over the lamb. Insert a sliver of garlic and a small sprig of rosemary into each slit in the meat.

Place the lamb in a roasting tin, pour over the remaining olive oil and season lightly with cayenne, salt and pepper. Place in the oven and roast for 20 minutes. Reduce the heat to 110°C/225°F/gas mark ¹/₄ and cook, basting occasionally with the juices, for up to 5 hours, until very tender.

Transfer the lamb to a serving dish and keep warm. Remove the excess fat from the pan juices, pour in the red wine and add a few more rosemary sprigs. Bring to the boil, then add the stock and simmer for 5 minutes. Gradually whisk in the butter, then strain the sauce, adjust the seasoning and serve alongside the leg of lamb.

rosemary-grilled vegetables with feta

100ml (3¹/₂ fl oz) olive oil
2 garlic cloves, crushed
1 bunch of rosemary, roughly chopped
12 asparagus spears
4 small courgettes, halved lengthways
8 baby aubergines, halved
1 red onion, cut into wedges
1 red pepper, cut into wedges
4 portabello mushrooms, thickly sliced
Salt and freshly ground black pepper

FOR THE DRESSING:

1 tablespoon balsamic vinegar
5 tablespoons olive oil
¹/₂ teaspoon Dijon mustard

TO SERVE:

1 bunch of watercress
150g (5oz) baby spinach leaves
100g (3¹/₂ oz) cooked chickpeas (canned are fine)
150g (5oz) feta cheese

Mix the olive oil, garlic and rosemary together in a dish, add the vegetables and toss well together. Leave to marinate for 1 hour at room temperature.

Heat a ridged grill pan (or, better still, a barbecue), brush with a little oil, then season the vegetables and place them on the grill. Cook, turning regularly, until they are tender and slightly charred. Meanwhile, whisk all the ingredients for the dressing together and season to taste.

Put the watercress and spinach in a large, shallow dish and scatter over the chickpeas. Top with the grilled vegetables and pour over the dressing. Crumble over the feta cheese and serve immediately, with lots of crusty bread.

roast butternut squash with ricotta and rosemary

2 butternut squash, peeled, deseeded and cut into large chunks
150ml (¹/₄ pint) olive oil
3 tablespoons rosemary needles, plus a few sprigs to garnish
2 garlic cloves, chopped
100g (3¹/₂ oz) flat-leaf parsley
100g (3¹/₂ oz) ricotta cheese
50g (2oz) Parmesan cheese, freshly grated
Salt and freshly ground black pepper

Preheat the oven to 180°C/350°F/gas mark 4. Toss the squash with 50ml (2fl oz) of the olive oil and place in a large baking tin. Place in the oven and roast for about 25 minutes, until tender, golden and lightly caramelised.

Meanwhile, place the rosemary, garlic and parsley in a blender or food processor and, with the motor running, slowly add the remaining olive oil. Season to taste.

In a small pan, warm the ricotta with a little hot water to form a paste. Add the rosemary mixture and stir until combined.

Put the roasted squash in an ovenproof serving dish and pour over the ricotta and rosemary sauce. Sprinkle over the Parmesan and return to the oven for 10 minutes, until golden. Garnish with rosemary and serve.

baked onions with rosemary

4 large Spanish onions
600ml (1 pint) chicken stock (or vegetable stock)
4 branches of rosemary, roughly chopped
4 tablespoons virgin olive oil
50g (2oz) chilled unsalted butter, diced
Salt and freshly ground black pepper

Preheat the oven to 200°C/400°F/gas mark 6. Peel the onions, trim the top and bottom so they will sit upright, then cut them in half horizontally. Arrange in a baking dish, pour over the stock, then scatter over the chopped rosemary and season well. Pour over the olive oil, place in the oven and bake for about 50 minutes, basting the onions regularly with the stock.

Remove the onions from the oven and pour off the liquid into a pan. Bring to the boil, then remove from the heat and whisk in the butter, a little at a time. Pour the sauce back over the onions and return them to the oven for 15–20 minutes, until they have a wonderful shiny glaze and are very tender.

apple and apricot tarts with rosemary syrup

100g (3$^{1}/_{2}$ oz) dried apricots
2 tablespoons apricot jam
500g (1lb 2oz) puff pastry
6 Granny Smith apples
50g (2oz) unsalted butter
50g (2oz) demerara sugar
$^{1}/_{2}$ tablespoon finely chopped rosemary, plus 4 small
   sprigs to decorate
4 tablespoons Calvados

Soak the dried apricots in hot water for 2 hours, until they are swollen and very soft. Drain well, then purée in a blender with the jam until smooth. Keep chilled until ready to use.

Preheat the oven to 200°C/400°F/gas mark 6. Roll out the pastry until it is 3mm ($^{1}/_{8}$ in) thick and cut out four 15cm (6in) rounds. Place on a baking sheet in the fridge.

Peel the apples, cut them in half and remove the cores. Cut each half into 4 wedges. Melt the butter in a large frying pan, add the apples and fry for 3 minutes. Sprinkle over the sugar and chopped rosemary and fry for a further 2 minutes, stirring gently. By this stage, the apples should be slightly caramelised. Pour over the Calvados, then remove from the heat and leave to infuse. When the apples are cold, drain them well, reserving any caramelised syrup.

Arrange the apples in 4 tartlet tins or other moulds, 10–12.5cm (4–5in) in diameter, top with a good spoonful of the apricot mixture and then place a pastry round on top. With the back of a knife, gently ease the edge of the pastry down between the apples and the tin. Make a small hole in the centre of each pastry lid to allow steam to escape.

Place the moulds on a baking tray and bake for 8–9 minutes, until the pastry is golden. Allow to cool slightly, then turn out the tarts, upside down, on to hot plates. Spoon over the reserved syrup, warming it first if necessary, decorate with rosemary sprigs and serve. A dollop of yoghurt goes particularly well with these tarts.

saffron

Sources differ greatly as to the number of crocus blossoms (*Crocus sativus*) needed to produce 450g (1lb) of fresh saffron, but estimates range from 400,000 to 750,000 – which undoubtedly explains why it is the world's most expensive spice, if not ingredient. It is even more expensive than silver per gram.

recipes

Saffron originated in Persia. It was carried from there to Kashmir, and has been used in Hindu rituals for centuries. Ancient Greeks and Romans later used it as a cosmetic and to dye and scent their bathing water. Emperor Nero ordered that the streets of Rome be doused with saffron oil before he entered astride his horse (could this be the predecessor of today's red carpet ritual, I wonder?). Saffron was a symbol of power, wealth and refinement across Europe until the fall of the Roman Empire, when its use declined tremendously. Throughout its history, the spice has been used to gild all manner of pastries, meat and seafood dishes.

Arab merchants introduced saffron to Spain in the eighth century and today it is the principal producer, along with India, South America and some smaller producers, such as Italy. The best saffron comes from the La Mancha region of Spain.

DESCRIPTION

Saffron is contained in the stigmas of the saffron crocus, a perennial bulb that flowers for two weeks in late autumn. Harvesting, an emormously painstaking and labour-intensive task, is carried out at dawn, before the flowers wilt in the heat of the sun. The ankle-high purple flowers are collected by hand and from each small flower are picked the three tiny red strands which are then dried in sieves over the embers of a fire – a procedure which greatly enhances the flavour, and gives a slightly toasted taste.

BUYING AND STORING

You can buy saffron in two forms, as threads (or hebras), or as a powder. In good-quality saffron the threads should be a fiery reddish brown, wire-like in appearance. The powder comes in small sachets, generally enough for a single use, and is far cheaper and more generally available. However, as a powder it is much harder to detect its quality or pureness; most is adulterated with marigold or safflower (known as bastard saffron) which, while similar in appearance and lending the same beautiful colour to food, has nowhere near the same flavour.

Do not be fooled or tempted to buy cheaper, easily available varieties – especially when on holiday in Spain or other Mediterranean countries. During a recent holiday in Marrakesh I saw mounds of saffron-coloured spices which, while visually appealing, was in fact turmeric (or Indian saffron). It is not the same thing at all, so beware, and remember that price is the definitive guide to the real thing.

Store saffron in a cool dry place, away from light (which can bleach it to a faded yellow) in an airtight jar to keep its fragrance. It may also be well wrapped in clingfilm and kept in the freezer.

CULINARY USES

Traditionally used in Europe in such dishes as French Bouillabaisse and other fish soups, it is more commonly used to flavour dishes such as the Spanish Paella and Italian Risotto a la Milanese. In Morocco, India and throughout the Middle East (but particularly in Iran), saffron is used to flavour and colour rice dishes. In Iran and India it is also used in puddings, breads and cakes for religious celebrations.

complementary flavours

RICE

FISH (ESPECIALLY SEA BASS, TURBOT AND HALIBUT)

SHELLFISH

MEAT (ESPECIALLY CHICKEN AND VEAL)

TOMATOES

BASIL

CHOCOLATE

VANILLA

DAIRY PRODUCTS (CREAM, CUSTARD, YOGHURT, EGGS)

SPICES (SMOKED PAPRIKA AND CINNAMON)

Saffron not only adds a wonderful magical quality to savoury dishes, but it is also used in desserts, transforming milky custard, brûlées and ice-creams, or in sweet syrup to poach fruits. The northern Indians use it to flavour sweet rice dishes such as Pirni, and add it to drinks. Even the simplest dish is transformed with a little pinch of saffron; it gives a vibrant yellow-gold colour and a honey-like musty flavour. I love adding saffron to creamy mashed potatoes or infusing it into mayonnaise for fish.

When using saffron, I prefer to use fresh saffron stigma every time, rather than the powder. Having said this, the powder does have it uses in dishes where the spice can be added at any stage of the cooking process. I prefer to use it in cakes.

Fresh stigmas must be heat-activated before use, or their impact will be disappointing. As a rule saffron is added to hot liquids such as stocks, syrup and sauces to extract its natural colouring and fragrance. I generally rub the stigmas between my fingers prior to adding them to the liquid and steeping them for 20–30 minutes to really liberate the flavours and aromas. Some purists suggest steeping saffron in water (or stock or wine, depending on the recipe) for 4 hours to get the best from it.

One last word on saffron: follow the recipes carefully. Very little is needed to flavour a dish and too much, although it might give a wonderful colour, can leave an unpleasant taste. Never be tempted to add more than a recipe calls for.

OTHER USES

Rich in carotenoid, a light yellow to deep red pigment, saffron was used in ancient times as a dye for fabrics. Nero had filaments of the spice sown onto his pillows believing it to be a remedy for insomnia. It was also thought to be an aphrodisiac and was prescribed for fevers and urinary disorders.

andalusian fish soup with saffron aïoli

100ml (3½ fl oz) olive oil
1 onion, finely chopped
2 garlic cloves, crushed
½ teaspoon dried chilli flakes
1 small bay leaf
½ teaspoon ground cumin
1 teaspoon grated orange zest
A good pinch of saffron strands
1 litre (1¾ pints) fish stock
300g (11oz) mixed shellfish (such as mussels
    and clams)
3 slices of white bread
1 teaspoon tomato purée
1 teaspoon smoked paprika
450g (1lb) mixed fish fillets (such as monkfish,
    snapper and cod), cut into 2.5cm (1in) pieces
Salt and freshly ground black pepper

FOR THE AÏOLI:
1 garlic clove, chopped
A good pinch of saffron strands
1 tablespoon lemon juice
150ml (¼ pint) good-quality mayonnaise

Heat half the oil in a large pan, add the onion and cook for about 8 minutes, until tender. Add the garlic, chilli flakes, bay leaf, cumin, orange zest and saffron. Pour in the fish stock, bring to the boil and simmer for 10–15 minutes.

Meanwhile, clean the mussels and clams under cold running water and pull out the beards from the mussels. Discard any open mussels or clams that don't close when tapped on the work surface.

Soak the bread in a little water, squeeze it dry, then place in a blender with the tomato purée, smoked paprika and the remaining oil. Process to a paste and add to the soup. Carefully add the fish to the soup and simmer gently for 5 minutes. Add the shellfish and cook for 3–4 minutes, until the shells open. Season to taste and keep warm.

To make the aïoli, crush the garlic and saffron in a mortar with the lemon juice and then stir into the mayonnaise.

Divide the fish and shellfish between 4 serving bowls and pour over the broth. Serve with the aïoli, plus some good crusty bread to mop up the juices.

persian scrambled eggs

¼ teaspoon saffron strands
50g (2oz) unsalted butter
6 tablespoons double cream
¼ teaspoon ground cumin
8 large organic or free range eggs
½ tablespoon chopped coriander
1 tablespoon chopped mint
1 small green chilli, deseeded and finely chopped
Salt and freshly ground black pepper
Grilled pita bread, to serve

Place a saucepan over a moderate heat for 1 minute, then add the saffron strands and toast for 10 seconds to release their delicate fragrance. Add the butter and cream and stir well. Bring slowly to the boil and add the cumin.

Lightly beat the eggs in a bowl with some salt and pepper. Pour them into the saffron cream and cook over a gentle heat until they are very softly scrambled. Fold in the herbs and green chilli. Serve with freshly grilled pita bread.

lobster, saffron and mango salad

1/2 red pepper, cut into long shreds 3mm
     (1/8 in thick)
1/2 green pepper, cut into long shreds 3mm
     (1/8 in thick)
1 mango, peeled, stoned and cut into long shreds
     3mm (1/8 in thick)
2.5cm (1in) piece of fresh root ginger, finely
     shredded
2 x 675g (1½ lb) live Scottish or Canadian lobsters
150g (5oz) mixed exotic salad leaves

FOR THE DRESSING:
2 tablespoons maple syrup
1 tablespoon aged balsamic vinegar
4 tablespoons lime juice
6 tablespoons orange juice
4 tablespoons lemon juice
1/4 teaspoon saffron strands
4 tablespoons mango chutney
1 tablespoon chopped mint
1 drop of Tabasco sauce
3 tablespoons sesame oil

First make the dressing (this can be done well in advance). In a
saucepan, warm together the maple syrup, balsamic vinegar
and the lime, orange and lemon juice. Add the saffron and
heat gently for 2 minutes to infuse. Remove from the heat and
leave to cool. Place in a blender or food processor, add the
mango chutney, mint and Tabasco and blitz until smooth. Pour
into a bowl and whisk in the sesame oil. Place the shredded
peppers, mango and ginger in a bowl, pour over about two-
thirds of the dressing and leave for 1 hour to infuse.

   Cook the lobsters (see page 125) and then leave to cool in
a bowl of cold water.

   To serve, cut the lobster bodies and tails in half down the
back and carefully remove the tail meat. Crack the claws to
remove the meat in one piece. Arrange one half-tail section and
claw on each serving plate. Toss the salad leaves with the
remaining dressing and place a small pile of salad leaves at the
head of each plate. Arrange the shredded vegetables and mango
on top of the lobster and pour over any dressing left in the bowl.

saffron brioches

MAKES 24—30

600g (1¼ lb) strong white flour
1 teaspoon salt
1 tablespoon sugar
75g (3oz) softened unsalted butter, cut into small
     pieces
40g (1½ oz) fresh yeast (or 1½ tablespoons dried
     yeast)
3 large eggs
2 good pinches saffron powder
1 egg yolk mixed with 1 tablespoon milk, to glaze

Sift the flour and salt into a warmed bowl and stir in the
sugar. Make a well in the centre and put the butter in it.

   Blend the yeast with 4 tablespoons of warm water. Put
the eggs and saffron powder in a separate bowl and beat
lightly. Pour into the well in the flour and add the yeast
mixture. Mix to a soft dough, then knead for about 5 minutes,
until smooth and elastic. Cover and leave in a warm place for
about 1½ hours, until doubled in size.

   Knock back the risen dough and knead briefly, then roll
out into a sausage shape. Divide into 24—30 pieces, about
4cm (1½in) long. Roll each piece into a ball and place them on
greased baking sheets, ensuring they are at least 5cm (2in)
apart. Cover the rolls with a cloth and leave in a warm place
for about 30 minutes, until risen and puffy.

   Preheat the oven to 220°C/425°F/gas mark 7. Brush the
rolls with the egg glaze and bake for 10—12 minutes, until
golden. Remove from the oven and transfer to a wire rack
to cool.

saffron pavlova with lime curd

SERVES 6

6 egg whites
200g (7oz) caster sugar
4 pinches saffron powder
1 teaspoon white wine vinegar
1 teaspoon boiling water
1/2 teaspoon vanilla extract
1 tablespoon cornflour
Double cream or plain yoghurt, to serve
A little blanched shredded lime zest, to decorate

FOR THE LIME CURD:
6 egg yolks
175g (6oz) caster sugar
Juice and grated zest 6 large limes (you will need
 175ml (1/6 fl oz juice)
A pinch of salt
125g (41/2 oz) chilled unsalted butter, diced

Preheat the oven to 130°C/250°F/gas mark 1/2. Put the egg whites and sugar in a clean, dry bowl and whisk until they form stiff peaks. Mix the saffron powder with the vinegar and boiling water, then whisk it into the beaten whites with the vanilla extract. Finally fold in the cornflour.

Line 2 baking sheets with baking parchment and spread the meringue mixture on it in 6 mounded circles (alternatively, pipe the mixture into 6 nests, using a piping bag with a plain nozzle). Bake for 50–60 minutes, until they are crisp but still pale on the outside and have a soft marshmallow centre. Store in an airtight container until needed.

For the lime curd, beat the egg yolks and sugar together until thick and creamy, then add the lime juice and zest. Place in a heavy-based pan and cook, stirring, over a low heat until the mixture thickens a little. Add the salt and immediately remove from the heat. Whisk in the chilled diced butter and leave to cool. Cover and keep in the fridge until required.

To serve, top each saffron pavlova with a good dollop of lime curd and then pour over some cream or yoghurt and decorate with a little blanched lime zest.

salt

'Take it with a pinch of salt', 'the salt of the earth', 'he's worth his salt': everyday phrases in these days when salt is commonplace and taken for granted.

But in medieval times salt was so precious that it occupied pride of place in the centre of the table, piled in great silver or gold cellars. Commoners sat below the salt, dignitaries above. During Roman times it was as valuable as gold, and Roman soldiers were given a ration to buy salt, a 'salarium' from which we derive the word salary. Salt has also long been regarded as a symbol of hospitality, and in many countries is offered with bread to welcome people into homes.

recipes

SALT-CURED SALMON
(GRAVAD LAX) (PAGE 166)

SALT-GRIDDLED PRAWNS
WITH LIME AND GARLIC
(PAGE 166)

SALT COD PÂTÉ WITH
BALSAMIC PEPPERS AND
OLIVES (PAGE 168)

BURIED SEA BASS IN LEMON
SALT (PAGE 169)

HERB-BAKED CHICKEN IN A
SALT CRUST (PAGE 169)

SEE ALSO:

TWICE-COOKED DUCK WITH
LAVENDER HONEY (PAGE 95)

One thing is for sure; we all need salt in one form or another in our diet. Salt is in our blood, sweat and tears and is essential for our well-being. It helps to maintain the body's fluid balance, regulates blood pressure, sparks nerve communication and aids muscle contraction. Like most things, however, if taken in excess, it can be harmful. There is evidence that links a high salt intake to high blood pressure and heart disease.

Culinary practices influence the consumption or need for salt. Boiling vegetables in a large pot of water, for example, deprives them of much of their natural mineral salts, which we replace by adding salt to the water or at the table. Vegetables steamed in their own juices need much less salt, as do roasted, rather than boiled, potatoes.

How much salt is a matter of taste; some people like lots, others less, some none at all. But for me, any cook worth his or her salt (excuse the pun!) cannot deny its importance in enhancing the taste of food and drawing out natural flavours. Salt is the only mineral condiment we add to our food, and it should be noted by vegetarians especially, that the higher the vegetable content of the diet, the greater the need for salt.

DESCRIPTION

Salt is a mineral consisting mainly of sodium chloride. There are two main types of salt: sea salt, which is distilled from sea water; and rock salt, found in the earth in a crystallised form. In addition to these, there are numerous specialised varieties.

SEA SALT Sea salt contains tiny amounts of important minerals, such as calcium and magnesium, which occur naturally in the sea. It is odourless, has a more refined flavour than most, and is the costliest of all salts to produce. In Britain, Maldon sea salt, made from boiled sea water, is well loved and comes in flaky and fine grain versions. In France the famous *fleur de sel* from Brittany waters is considered the best and most expensive per gram. Grey salt (or *sel gris de guérande*) is an unrefined sea salt produced by natural evaporation.

ROCK SALT Mined from dried-up underground saline lakes and processed to different degrees of fineness. In its crude state, it is used to de-ice roads and in ice-cream machines. In its refined form it is used for culinary purposes. The flavour cannot, however, be compared with sea salt.

TABLE SALT Basic all-purpose cooking salt. It is refined, finely ground rock salt, with added soda to prevent caking (to keep the crystals free-flowing in humid conditions, add a few grains of rice to the salt cellar). Iodised salt is simply table salt with potassium iodide (an essential trace element that is sometimes missing in our diets).

CURING SALT (sel rosé) A pink refined salt with added nitrates, used in hams, cured meats and terrines to enhance the colour.

BLACK SALT Unusual pink-tan (not black) grains, used in Indian cooking and prized in ayurvedic medicine. It has a slightly smoky flavour.

SPICE SALT (sel épicé) A flavoured salt comprising salt, white pepper and mixed spices.

CANNING OR PICKLING SALT A coarse-grained salt, free of all additives to prevent discolouring and to ensure the liquid doesn't cloud.

VEGETABLE SALTS Fine salt with added vegetable extract, such as celery or onion. If you use vegetable salt, cut down on the amount of salt called for in recipes.

STORING

Salt, unlike herbs and spices, keeps indefinitely without losing its flavour; it is not true that grinding your salt in a mill gives a fresher flavour.

CULINARY USES

Salt is probably the most popular seasoning, is one of the four major components of taste (along with sweet, sour and bitter), and is a versatile culinary performer.

It was the Romans who first invented the process of salting to preserve meat, fish, cheese and fruit such as lemons (see page 106) – a technique we still use today. However, there are many other ways to utilise salt in cooking. For example, it can be used as a casing to enclose meat and fish in order to seal in the flavour and moisture while baking.

In addition to its own 'salty' flavour, salt has the ability to bring out the natural flavour of other ingredients and make them more vibrant. It also has the capacity to cut the sweetness of very rich flavours (like chocolate) and can soften the sharpness of acidic ingredients such as citrus fruit, pineapple and tomatoes. Adding salt to sweet dishes is becoming increasingly popular – although it is best to use mellow salts such as *fleur de sel*. Some cooks use salt crystals for their crunchy texture, as well as the flavour, lightly sprinkled on top of chocolate cakes or fruit such as cantaloupe melon.

Salt slows down fermentation and is used in bread-making to help develop the flavour of the wheat and enhance the texture of the dough. It is also used to disgorge the bitter juices from vegetables such as cucumbers and aubergines. Adding salt to water raises the temperature at which it boils, thereby reducing cooking time.

OTHER USES

Because salt is an effective antiseptic, salt water is an excellent gargle for sore throats. It is also said to boost the immune system and to ease depression. Salt is added to commercially produced sports drinks and is a key ingredient in processed foods – often in alarming quantities. It has also, for years, been used as a cleaning agent to remove stains (rub plenty of salt into red wine stains while they are still fresh) and break down grease. And, of course, you will have heard of superstitious people throwing a pinch of salt over their shoulders to ward off bad luck!

salt-cured salmon (gravad lax)

I could not leave this Scandinavian speciality out of this book. The name *gravad lax* means 'buried salmon', and derives from the original method of salt curing — when the fish was prepared in the same manner but buried in a hole in the ground for several weeks.

SERVES 10-12

1 x 2kg (4¹/₂ lb) salmon, filleted
2 bunches of dill
75g (3oz) coarse salt
50g (2oz) caster sugar
2 teaspoons white peppercorns, crushed

FOR THE DILL MUSTARD SAUCE:
4 egg yolks
1¹/₂ teaspoons cider vinegar
1 tablespoon brown sugar
1 tablespoon Dijon mustard
200ml (7fl oz) olive oil
2 tablespoons chopped dill
Salt and freshly ground black pepper

Place one salmon fillet skin-side down in a shallow dish. Spread the dill on top. Mix together the salt, sugar and peppercorns and sprinkle liberally over the fish. Put the other fillet on top, skin-side up. Cover with foil and then weight down the fish with a plank of wood (or a plate or board), topped with some weights or heavy cans. The pressure applied should be approximately the same weight as the salmon. Place in the fridge and leave for 3 days, turning the salmon and spooning the juices back over the fish every 8 hours or so.

To make the sauce, whisk the egg yolks and vinegar together, then whisk in the sugar until dissolved. Add the mustard, then gradually whisk in the oil, as for making mayonnaise. Stir in the dill and adjust the seasoning.

Take the salmon out of the marinade, clean off the dill and spices and pat the fish dry. Cut into thin slices on the diagonal and serve with the dill mustard sauce. In Scandinavia it is usually garnished with a small salad, lemon wedges and toast fingers.

salt-griddled prawns with lime and garlic

20 extra-large uncooked tiger prawns, shell on
4 tablespoons virgin olive oil
Juice of ¹/₄ lemon
¹/₂ teaspoon chopped thyme
¹/₂ teaspoon chopped oregano
2 tablespoons coarse salt
¹/₄ teaspoon garlic salt
Freshly ground black pepper

FOR THE LIME AND GARLIC SAUCE:
200ml (7fl oz) fish stock
Juice of 3 limes
Grated zest of 1 lime
1 garlic clove, crushed
1 small red onion, finely chopped
2 tablespoons chopped flat-leaf parsley
25g (1oz) chilled unsalted butter, diced

Cut down the back of each prawn shell with a sharp knife or kitchen scissors and lift out the black intestinal vein, leaving the shell on. Coat the prawns in the olive oil and lemon juice and season with black pepper. In a bowl, mix together the herbs and salts. Dredge the prawns in the mixture, ensuring they are well coated. Grill the salt-crusted prawns on a hot barbecue or a ridged grill pan for 3–4 minutes on each side.

Meanwhile, make the sauce. Put all the ingredients except the butter in a pan and bring to the boil. Remove from the heat and whisk in the butter.

Remove the prawns from the grill and arrange on a serving dish. Pour the sauce around them and serve.

PG TIP (left) Once you have perfected the basic recipe, you can experiment. Try flavouring the salmon with orange or lemon zest or spices such as cumin or cardamom. In Norway, I encountered it marinated with dill and grated raw beetroot, which gave the fish a wonderfully sweet flavour and a remarkable ruby-red colour when sliced.

salt cod pâté with balsamic peppers and olives

I have never been fond of Mediterranean-style salt cod. I much prefer this lighter version, using fresh cod. It has a mellower taste, which allows the flavour of the fish to stand out, and is far less salty on the palate.

200g (7oz) fresh cod fillet, skinned
50g (2oz) coarse sea salt
200ml (7fl oz) full-fat milk
3 garlic cloves, crushed
300g (11oz) waxy potatoes, peeled and cut into 5mm (1/4 in) dice
3 tablespoons olive oil
A pinch of cayenne pepper
Salt and freshly ground black pepper
A little paprika, for dusting

FOR THE BALSAMIC PEPPERS:
2 large red peppers
1 tablespoon olive oil, plus extra for brushing
1 garlic clove, crushed
1 tablespoon sugar
4 tablespoons balsamic vinegar
20 small black olives

Place the cod in a dish, cover it liberally with the salt and leave for 2 hours. Wash the salt from the fish by running it under cold water. Place in a pan with the milk, garlic and potatoes and bring to a gentle simmer. Poach until the cod and potatoes are tender. Remove the fish and potatoes from the poaching liquid with a slotted spoon and let them cool slightly. Mash them together in a bowl, then stir in the olive oil and enough of the poaching liquid to give a firm consistency, like stiff mashed potatoes Season with salt, pepper and cayenne, leave to cool and then place in the fridge.

Preheat the oven to 200°C/400°F/gas mark 6. Brush the red peppers with oil, then place on a baking sheet and roast until blackened and blistered. Leave until cool enough to handle, then peel off the skins, remove the seeds and cut the peppers into large chunks.

Heat the olive oil and garlic in a pan, add the roasted peppers and fry for 2 minutes. Sprinkle on the sugar, add the balsamic vinegar, then reduce the heat and cook gently for 2–3 minutes, until the peppers take on a sweet and sour flavour. Stir in the olives, season lightly and leave to cool.

To serve, arrange a small mound of peppers and olives on each serving plate. Top with a large quenelle (see Tip below) of the pâté, dust with a little paprika and spoon some of the balsamic syrup around. Serve with good crusty bread.

PG TIP To shape the pâté into quenelles, you will need 2 wet tablespoons. Scoop up some of the pâté in 1 tablespoon and shape it into an oval by scraping it neatly off 1 spoon on to the other several times.

buried sea bass in lemon salt

You might think that burying such a delicate fish as sea bass in salt would ruin the flavour. Wrong! It actually keeps the fish moist and preserves the delicate texture, without making it taste salty. In France chicken and other fish, such as turbot and mullet, are prepared in a similar fashion.

This is very good served on a bed of roasted vegetables such as peppers, courgettes and fennel, cooked in the oven at the same time as the fish.

1 x 1.8kg (4lb) sea bass, cleaned, scaled and washed clean of all traces of blood
1 lemon, thickly sliced
100ml (3¹/₂ fl oz) olive oil
Leaves from 1 small bunch of thyme
1 small bunch of rosemary, chopped
750g (1lb 10oz) coarse sea salt
Grated zest of 1 lemon
1 egg white, lightly beaten
Freshly ground black pepper
Melted butter or lemon wedges, to serve

Preheat the oven to 220°C/425°F/gas mark 7. Fill the belly cavity of the fish with the lemon slices and season inside with pepper. Heat the olive oil in a large, flameproof baking dish. Carefully add the sea bass and cook for 2–3 minutes on each side, until the skin colours and begins to crisp. Remove from the heat.

In a bowl, mix the herbs with the salt, lemon zest and beaten egg white. Mould this mixture all over the fish to cover it. Place in the oven and bake for 20–25 minutes. Remove from the oven and carefully brush away the salt. Serve on a large dish with a little melted butter or simply with lemon wedges.

herb-baked chicken in a salt crust

An impressive way to serve chicken to your guests. Take it to the table, crack the salt crust open in front anyone and wait for the waft of steamed herbs and garlic to pervade the room. The chicken can be prepared in advance up to the baking stage. Serve with roasted new potatoes and creamed spinach.

4 x 175g (6oz) organic or free range chicken breasts, on the bone
2 garlic cloves, crushed
2 tablespoons chopped mixed herbs (such as rosemary, thyme and sage)
Salt and freshly ground black pepper

FOR THE SALT CRUST:
450g (1lb) plain flour
100g (3¹/₂ oz) coarse sea salt
1 tablespoon chopped mixed herbs (such as rosemary, thyme and sage)
1 large egg
175ml (6fl oz) iced water
Beaten egg, to glaze

For the crust, mix the flour, salt and herbs together in a bowl. Make a well in the centre, add the egg and water and bring together to form a dough. Wrap in clingfilm and leave to rest in the fridge for 30 minutes.

Preheat the oven to 200°C/400°F/gas mark 6. Season the chicken breasts with salt and pepper, then roll them in the herbs and garlic, ensuring they are evenly coated. Roll out the dough to about 5mm (¹/₄ in) thick and cut it into quarters. Wrap a chicken breast in each piece, enclosing everything except the wing bone. Brush lightly all over with beaten egg.

Place on a baking sheet and bake for 15–18 minutes, then remove from the oven and leave to stand for 2–3 minutes before serving.

tamarind

Up to five years ago, you would probably only have heard of tamarind as an ingredient found or used in Asian restaurants. Nowadays, with the growing interest in multicultural food, tamarind is becoming an ingredient chefs and food lovers alike are savouring. It has an endearing quality that cooks are discovering with delight, a subtle sweet and sour pulp that works deliciously well in savoury and sweet dishes.

recipes

DESCRIPTION

Tamarind trees (*Tamarindus indica*) are native to East Africa and are now grown throughout India, across South-east Asia and in the tropics. The pods which grow on the large, evergreen, tropical trees are about 5–16 cm (2–6in) long. They are green when young and dark brown when fully ripe, which is when they are harvested. Within the bean-shaped pods are shiny seeds surrounded by a reddish-brown, sticky, intense sour pulp, somewhat similar to dates.

BUYING AND PREPARING

Tamarind can occasionally be bought fresh in the pod from Indian and Oriental shops but is more readily available as a pulp in pre-packed compressed 450g (1lb) blocks and as a smooth purée in jars.

To make a purée from the fresh pods, break them open and remove the inner flesh. Soak in half the amount of cold water, then bring to a simmer for 5 minutes or a little longer depending on the age and hardness of your particular pods. Strain the mixture through a sieve to remove the seeds and tough fibres. If using tamarind blocks, cut it up in pieces and proceed as for fresh.

Fresh tamarind pods and tamarind water can be kept in the fridge for up to 5 days. Tamarind blocks and paste last indefinitely if stored in a cool dark place. The paste is my preferred version for its ease of use.

CULINARY USES

Tamarind is traditionally found in Indian and Asian cooking where it contributes a gentle sour flavour with undercurrents of tropical fruits. It is used in Indian lentil dishes, curries and rasans (spicy Indian soup, highly flavoured with black pepper, see page 146). It is also added to sweet chutneys and tamarind water is used to flavour rice. In Thailand, tamarind water is more frequently used than the paste, and is added to hot and sour soups and curries. In Jamaica tamarind is added to rice dishes, stews and desserts. The natural pectin extracted from the tamarind fruit is also used in jams and jelly preparations.

In Britain, where it is still a largely unfamiliar ingredient, it has, ironically, long been used as a main ingredient of Worcestershire sauce, one of Britain's favourite condiments.

Today, with the ever-increasing availability of new ingredients, tamarind is used with more creativity. I have successfully made a wonderful tamarind water ice-cream (served with mango tart), and fruit syrups. I also like to add it to dressings with Asian flavours, such as ginger and lime.

If tamarind is not readily available, as a last resort lime or lemon may be substituted, but the taste is really not similar, and will consequently not have the same effect.

OTHER USES

Tamarind is a mild laxative and is used in ayurvedic medicine to treat bowel and bronchial disorders. It is rich in vitamins and is reputed to be good for the liver and kidneys. Tamarind is also said to be an outstanding polish for brass and copper.

complementary flavours

CHILLIES

COCONUT MILK

NAM PLA (THAI FISH SAUCE)

HERBS (THAI BASIL AND MINT)

CHICKEN

FISH (FIRM VARIETIES)

SPICES (GINGER AND STAR ANISE)

tamarind and date chutney

This versatile chutney makes a great accompaniment to all sorts of dishes, especially grilled salmon and chicken, or can be served as a dip for spicy poppadoms.

2 tablespoons palm sugar (or demerara sugar)
1 teaspoon cumin seeds
3 tablespoons tamarind paste
75g (3oz) dates, chopped
¹/₂ teaspoon *nam pla* (Thai fish sauce)
2.5cm (1in) piece of fresh root ginger, finely grated
A pinch of cayenne pepper
Salt

Put the sugar in a small pan and place over a low heat until melted. Heat a small frying pan over a medium heat, add the cumin seeds and toast for 10 seconds to release their fragrance. Grind in a spice grinder or with a pestle and mortar. Place in a blender or food processor with the tamarind, dates, sugar, fish sauce and ginger and blitz until smooth. If using as a dip, add enough boiling water to give a spreadable consistency. Season with the cayenne pepper and some salt and use as required. The chutney will keep for up to 1 month in a sealed sterilised jar (see page 95), or for 3–4 days in the fridge.

chargrilled tuna with green papaya salad

A healthy and beautifully flavoured dish. Green papaya salad (*som tam*) is a staple dish from north-east Thailand, prepared daily by roadside traders.

650g (1lb 7oz) small tuna fillet, trimmed

2 tablespoons tamarind paste

2 tablespoons brown sugar

2 red chillies, deseeded and finely chopped

1 tablespoon *nam pla* (Thai fish sauce)

A little oil for grilling

Salt and freshly ground black pepper

1 lime, cut into wedges, to garnish

FOR THE GREEN PAPAYA SALAD:

1 garlic clove, chopped

2 red chillies, deseeded and chopped

1 teaspoon brown sugar

2 green papayas, peeled, deseeded and shredded

Juice of 2 limes

2 tablespoons *nam pla* (Thai fish sauce)

100g (3^1/$_2$ oz) French beans, cooked

2 tablespoons roasted peanuts

10 red cherry tomatoes, halved

10 yellow cherry tomatoes, halved

Cut the tuna into 4 steaks across the fillet. In a bowl, combine the tamarind with the sugar, chillies, fish sauce and some salt and pepper. Pour this mixture over the tuna and set aside for 1 hour to allow the flavours to meld.

For the salad, roughly crush the garlic, chillies, sugar and a quarter of the shredded papaya in a mortar. Transfer to a bowl, add the lime juice and fish sauce and stir well. Add all the remaining ingredients, including the rest of the papaya, toss well and season to taste.

Heat a ridged grill pan until very hot and brush with a little oil. Season the tuna steaks again with salt and pepper and chargrill for 2 minutes on each side, keeping them rare. Remove from the grill and cut each steak into 4 slices.

Arrange a pile of salad on each serving plate, top with the seared tuna, then garnish with the lime wedges and serve.

stir-fried noodles, thai style

225g (8oz) dried rice noodles

2 red chillies, deseeded and finely chopped

2 shallots, sliced

3 tablespoons *nam pla* (Thai fish sauce)

2 tablespoons brown sugar

2 tablespoons tamarind paste

1 teaspoon lime juice

4 tablespoons vegetable oil

125g (4^1/$_2$ oz) pork fillet, cut into small, thin strips

150g (5oz) fresh shrimps, peeled

50g (2oz) shiitake mushrooms, sliced

75g (3oz) beansprouts

2 tablespoons *ketjap manis* (Indonesian soy sauce)

Salt and freshly ground black pepper

Soak the noodles in a bowl of warm water for about 10 minutes, until softened, then drain in a colander.

Place the chillies, shallots, fish sauce and sugar in a mortar and crush to a paste. Add the tamarind and lime juice and pound until smooth. Mix in 2 tablespoons of water and set aside.

Heat the oil in a wok until very hot, add the spice paste and stir-fry for 1 minute. Add the pork and shrimps, mix well with the paste and cook for 2–3 minutes. Add the noodles, mushrooms, beansprouts and *ketjap manis* and season with salt and pepper. Stir-fry for 2 minutes and then serve immediately.

wok-fried monkfish in sour sauce

650g (1lb 7oz) monkfish fillet
4 tablespoons vegetable oil
2 shallots, thinly sliced
3 garlic cloves, crushed
100g (3^1/$_2$ oz) cooked salted black beans (see page 33), washed and drained
2.5cm (1in) piece of fresh root ginger, finely chopped
2 tablespoons soy sauce
2 teaspoons *nam pla* (Thai fish sauce)
4 tablespoons tamarind paste
2 red chillies, deseeded and thinly sliced
2 tablespoons brown sugar
Salt and freshly ground black pepper

TO GARNISH:
2 tablespoons coarsely chopped coriander
3 spring onions, shredded

Cut the monkfish into 1cm (^{1}/$_2$ in) slices along the fillet, season with salt and pepper and set aside.

Heat a wok until almost smoking, add the oil, then add the shallots, garlic, black beans and ginger. Cook for 1 minute, until lightly golden. Add the monkfish pieces and cook over a moderate heat for 5 minutes. Remove the fish from the wok and keep warm. Add the soy sauce, fish sauce, tamarind paste, chillies and sugar to the wok and mix well. Add 100ml (3^1/$_2$ fl oz) of water and boil for 2 minutes, then return the monkfish to the wok and toss well with the sauce.

Serve in bowls with white rice, garnished with the coriander and spring onions.

tamarind-baked winter fruits with star anise

1 vanilla pod, split open lengthways
150g (5oz) palm sugar (or demerara sugar)
2 lemongrass stalks, outer layers removed, tender inner core finely shredded
1^1/$_2$ teaspoons finely grated fresh root ginger
4 star anise
2 tablespoons tamarind paste
50g (2oz) unsalted butter
2 ripe pears, peeled, cored and quartered
6 ripe plums, halved and stoned
8 prunes, stoned
8 dried figs
12 dried apricots
100ml (3^1/$_2$ fl oz) sweet white wine
Juice of 1 lime

Preheat the oven to 190°C/375°F/gas mark 5. Combine the vanilla pod, sugar, lemongrass, ginger, star anise and tamarind in a pan with 150ml (1^1/$_4$ pint) of water, bring to the boil and simmer for 10 minutes. Remove from the heat and set aside.

Heat a casserole or deep, flameproof baking dish on the stove, add the butter, then add all the fruit and fry for 1–2 minutes, until lightly caramelised. Pour over the wine, lime juice and tamarind mixture and stir to coat the fruit. Place in the oven for 10–12 minutes, until the fruit is tender and lightly glazed. Serve warm.

vanilla

Fresh natural vanilla, despite its reputation as one of the world's most expensive ingredients is one that is certainly well worth buying. Since it is always used in small amounts, it is really not too pricey to pay for top quality.

Europeans first tasted vanilla in the sixteenth century when Mexico was invaded by the Spanish, where the Aztec Indians had used it as a flavouring for centuries.

recipes

The Spanish explorers of the New World returned home with the fruit and gave it its name. They loved its aroma and flavour and soon it was being consumed in vast quantities. Today it is perhaps the most popular flavouring, the world over, with the French and Germans the biggest importers. Many countries, including Mexico, Puerto Rico and Tahiti, now produce vanilla, and the island of Madagascar, off Africa's east coast, is the world's largest commercial exporter.

DESCRIPTION

The vanilla plant (*Vanilla planifola*) is a type of orchid (and the only edible one) that must be pollinated and harvested. The orchids are only pollinated unaided in Mexico — on the one day in the year when the flowers bloom. Elsewhere, they have to be pollinated by hand, which highlights why real vanilla is such an expensive commodity. The pods are picked unripe when green, and there follows a lengthy and complicated curing process to extract the vanillin, the primary flavour of vanilla. The oxidisation of the pods causes browning which helps to develop their tobacco-like flavour.

Vanilla has a fabulous tropical scent and a wonderful aroma, sweet smelling and utterly alluring. I once visited the market at Marigot on the island of St Martin in the Caribbean to look at the local produce. The sight, scent and aroma of the vanilla, sold in bunches by market traders that day, will stay with me for the rest of my life.

BUYING, STORING AND PREPARATION

When buying fresh vanilla, look for pods that are dark in colour, plump and pliable. Store them away from heat and light. I suggest also wrapping them in greaseproof paper and placing in an airtight container, which will ensure they keep their flavour indefinitely.

Vanilla can be best utilised in two ways; whole to flavour creamy puddings, custards, crème brûlée etc; or by extracting the seeds. The latter is the best way to extract the vanilla's intense flavour: split the pods lengthways with a small knife and scrape out the thick paste-like inner seeds that hold the vanilla's intense flavour, then use the seeds as directed in the recipe.

OTHER PRODUCTS

As real vanilla is so expensive, cheap imitations such as extracts and essences are commonplace, but have limited use in real cooking, to my mind. However, such commercial products now satisfy 78 per cent of the word's demand for a real vanilla flavour. I recommend you use fresh vanilla (there are some pleasures you just can't put a price on!) or, if this is not possible, the next best thing is vanilla extract.

VANILLA EXTRACT This is the extracted flavour and aroma of the vanilla bean. Pure vanilla extract has a rich perfume and a deep amber colour and contains at least 35 per cent alcohol.

to all manner of desserts, confectionery, syrups and jams. Vanilla is also an essential ingredient in much baking.

Although vanilla's primary use is in sweet recipes, it can also successfully become an unusual flavouring in savoury dishes — particularly in conjunction with fish, chicken and pork.

Only a few drops of vanilla extract are needed to transform a recipe. Try a little in pancake batters, fruit salads, mayonnaise, béarnaise sauce and meat glazes. The pods can be used to flavour jars of sugar (see below) and coffee.

Vanilla is an ingredient in many beverages from the intoxicant (vanilla schnapps, Mexican vanilla liqueur, Galliano, sangria…) to the non-alcoholic (coca cola, for example, is packed with vanilla). One of the earliest beverages to use vanilla was the Aztec cocoa drink, *xocolat*.

Vanilla sugar

Throughout this book you will see recipes that include vanilla sugar, which is simply sugar perfumed with vanilla beans. This has two advantages; first, the sugar helps keep the vanilla at its best, dry and in good condition. Second, the resulting perfume of the sugar is indispensable in baking or as a mild flavouring. Leave the pods in the sugar for 1 week before use on breakfast cereals, in coffee and to flavour desserts and soufflés. One pod can scent a jar of sugar for year.

Vanilla yoghurt

Blend 150g (5oz) Greek yoghurt with the seeds of one fresh vanilla pod, and 1 tablespoon of honey. Great for pies, tarts and fruit.

OTHER USES

Vanilla has long been regarded an aphrodisiac. It is also an effective calmative and for this reason, it has (and still is) used to treat nervous disorders and to settle stomachs.

complementary flavours

DAIRY PRODUCTS (ESPECIALLY CUSTARD AND ICE-CREAMS)

SOFT CHEESES (RICOTTA AND MASCARPONE)

FRUIT (LEMON, APRICOTS, STRAWBERRIES, PEACHES AND NECTARINES)

TEA AND COFFEE

CHOCOLATE

CARDAMOM

MEAT (PORK, CHICKEN)

Mexican vanilla extract is the best. As a guide, I suggest 1 teaspoon of extract could replace one vanilla bean in a recipe. For a wonderful, rich home-made extract, simply place 6 split vanilla pods in a jar (with a lid). Top with a solution of 2 tablespoons sugar, dissolved in 600ml (1 pint) warmed, dark rum. Cover and store in a cool dark place. Leave for up to one month before use.

VANILLA ESSENCE A much inferior product, chemically produced, which has no relevance to the real thing; use only in desperate circumstances.

CULINARY USES

This sweet, perfumed spice with its tobacco-like aroma and its wonderfully mellow fragrance, is ideally suited to enhance sweet flavours. For this reason, it is added

pork loin cooked in vanilla milk

2 plump, soft vanilla pods
1.5kg (3lb 5oz) boneless loin of pork, skin and most
   of the fat removed
A pinch of ground cinnamon
A pinch of freshly grated nutmeg
2 tablespoons olive oil
3 garlic cloves, unpeeled
850ml (1^1/$_2$ pints) full-fat milk
125ml (4fl oz) double cream
1 bay leaf
3 sprigs of thyme
2 large carrots, peeled and cut into segments
1 teaspoon Dijon mustard
Salt and freshly ground black pepper

Cut the vanilla pods in half lengthways. Season the pork loin with the cinnamon and nutmeg and some salt and pepper. Place the pods on the pork and tie down with string, around the pork.

Heat the olive oil in a large casserole, add the pork and cook until sealed and golden all over. Add the garlic cloves and cook for 2 minutes, until coloured. Bring the milk and cream to the boil in a pan, pour them over the pork, then tuck in the bay leaf and thyme and cover with a lid. Cook for 30 minutes, either in an oven preheated to 180°C/350°F/gas mark 4 or on top of the stove on a low heat.

Add the carrots to the casserole and cook for 1 hour, until the pork and carrots are very tender. Remove the pork and carrots from the pan and keep warm.

Press the garlic cloves free from their skin and add to the cooking liquid with the mustard. Pour into a saucepan and simmer for 2 minutes. Strain the sauce through a sieve and adjust the seasoning.

Carve the pork into thin slices, garnish with the carrots, pour over the vanilla sauce and serve.

curried turbot with vanilla and ginger

4 x 175g (6oz) turbot fillets, skinned
1 teaspoon mild curry powder
100ml (3^1/$_2$ fl oz) double cream
200ml (7fl oz) fish stock
4 tablespoons dry white wine
5cm (2in) piece of fresh root ginger, finely chopped
1 vanilla pod, chopped
50g (2oz) unsalted butter
4 tablespoons vegetable oil
200g (7oz) baby courgettes, sliced
200g (7oz) spinach, well washed and dried
12 cherry tomatoes, halved
Salt and freshly ground black pepper

Season the turbot fillets, rub the curry powder over both sides, then set aside.

Put the cream, fish stock, wine and ginger in a pan, bring to the boil and simmer until reduced by half. Pour into a blender or food processor, add the vanilla pod and blitz to a smooth purée. Strain through a fine sieve into a clean pan, whisk in 25g (1oz) of the butter, then season to taste and keep warm.

Heat 2 tablespoons of the oil in a frying pan and add another 15g (^{1}/$_2$ oz) of the butter. When it starts to foam, add the turbot fillets, curried-side down, and cook for 2–3 minutes. Turn the fillets over and cook for a further 2–3 minutes, then remove from the pan and keep warm.

Heat the remaining oil and butter in a separate pan, add the courgettes and fry until golden. Add the spinach and cook together for 2–3 minutes. Finally add the halved cherry tomatoes and season to taste.

Place a pile of the spinach, courgette and tomato mixture in the centre of 4 plates, top with the turbot fillets and pour the sauce around.

strawberry and vanilla custard tart

SERVES 6-8

1 quantity of Sweet Pastry (see page 107)
450g (1lb) strawberries, hulled and halved
4 tablespoons strawberry jam

FOR THE VANILLA CUSTARD:
2 vanilla pods
150ml (^{1}/4 pint) full-fat milk
150ml (^{1}/4 pint) single cream
1 egg
2 egg yolks
100g (3^1/2 oz) vanilla sugar (see page 177)
20g (^{3}/4 oz) plain flour, sifted

Preheat the oven to 190°C/375°F/gas mark 5. Roll out the pastry on a lightly floured surface to 3mm (^{1}/8in) thick and use to line a 23cm (9in) tart tin. Prick the base lightly all over with a fork. Line with greaseproof paper, fill with baking beans and bake blind for 10–15 minutes, until the pastry is set but not coloured. Remove the paper and beans, reduce the oven temperature to 150°C/300°F/gas mark 2 and return the pastry case to the oven for 10 minutes. Remove from the oven and leave to cool.

For the vanilla custard, split the vanilla pods open lengthways and scrape out the seeds with a small teaspoon or the point of a sharp knife. Put the pods and seeds in a pan, add the milk and cream and bring to the boil. Remove from the heat and leave for 15 minutes to infuse.

In a bowl, beat the egg and egg yolks with 75g (3oz) of the vanilla sugar until pale and fluffy. Add the flour and mix well. Strain the vanilla cream on to the egg mixture, stirring constantly. Return to the pan and bring back to the boil, stirring all the time. Simmer for 1–2 minutes, until thickened, then pour into a bowl and leave to cool.

Fill the pastry case with the vanilla custard and arrange the halved strawberries on top, cut-side down. Put the strawberry jam in a pan with 4 tablespoons of water, bring to the boil and strain through a fine sieve. Brush the jam over the strawberries and leave to cool. Sprinkle over the extra vanilla sugar before serving.

real vanilla ice-cream There is only
one ice-cream I would die for and this is it. Fragrant, rich and creamy. Always use good, plump vanilla pods; it really does make such a difference.

250ml (9fl oz) full-fat milk
350ml (12fl oz) double cream
2 plump, soft vanilla pods
6 egg yolks
100g (3^1/2 oz) caster sugar
A pinch of salt

Heat the milk and cream in a pan until almost at boiling point, then remove from the heat. Split the vanilla pods open lengthways and scrape out the seeds with a small teaspoon or the point of a sharp knife. Add the seeds and pods to the milk and leave to infuse for 20 minutes on the lowest possible heat.

Beat the egg yolks and sugar together in a bowl until light and fluffy. Remove the vanilla pods from the milk and gradually whisk the milk into the egg yolk mixture. Return to the pan, add the salt and cook, stirring constantly, over a low heat until the mixture has thickened enough to coat the back of the spoon (do not let it boil or it will curdle).

Remove the mixture from the heat immediately and strain through a fine sieve into a bowl. When cool, chill in the fridge, then freeze in an ice-cream machine according to the manufacturer's instructions. (If you don't have a machine, refer to the PG TIP on page 42.)

vanilla and orange marmalade pudding

SERVES 8

150g (5oz) caster sugar
150g (5oz) unsalted butter
1 teaspoon vanilla extract
3 eggs, separated
100g (3¹/₂ oz) self-raising flour, sifted
4 tablespoons golden syrup
4 tablespoons good-quality orange marmalade
2 vanilla pods

Preheat the oven to 190°C/375°F/gas mark 5. In a bowl, beat 100g (3 ¹/₂oz) of the sugar with the butter until pale and creamy. Add the vanilla extract, then beat in the egg yolks one at a time. Fold in the flour. In a separate bowl, whisk the egg whites with the remaining sugar until they form stiff peaks. Stir a quarter of the whites into the egg yolk mixture to loosen it, then carefully fold in the rest.

Gently heat the golden syrup and marmalade together in a pan. Slit the vanilla pods open lengthways and scrape out the seeds with a small teaspoon or the point of a sharp knife. Add to the marmalade and syrup and mix well.

Grease 8 ramekins and place 2 tablespoons of the vanilla marmalade in the base of each one. Top with the pudding mixture, filling them three-quarters full, and tap the ramekins to release any air pockets. Cover with foil and place in a roasting tin of hot water (the water should come half way up the side of the remekins). Place in the oven and bake for 40–45 minutes.

Run a knife around the edge of each pudding and turn out on to a serving plate. Serve with copious amounts of clotted cream or other cream.

index